AF791730

500/-

$ 25/-

5/2017

~~H/2007~~

Stock

CONTESTING INTERPRETATIONS OF THE SIKH TRADITION

CONTESTING INTERPRETATIONS OF THE SIKH TRADITION

J.S. GREWAL

MANOHAR
1998

First published 1998

© J.S. Grewal 1998

All rights reserved. No part of this publication may be reproduced or transmitted, in any form or by any means, without prior permission of the author and the publisher

ISBN 81-7304-255-1

Published by
Ajay Kumar Jain for
Manohar Publishers & Distributors
2/6 Ansari Road, Daryaganj
New Delhi 110 002

Lasertypeset by
Printech Graphics
S.A.S. Nagar, Punjab

Printed at
Rajkamal Electric Press
B-35/9, G.T. Karnal Road Indl. Area
Delhi 110 033

Contents

Preface

Sikh studies began to emerge in the late eighteenth century to be fairly well launched by the nineteenth-century administrators and 'orientalists'. The early Sikh response to European interpretations of the Sikh tradition transformed an 'orientalist' dialogue into a European-Sikh dialogue. The scope of Sikh studies began to expand in terms of content. The establishment of new universities in the Punjab and the celebration of centenaries from 1966 to 1980 added much to the increasing interest in Sikh studies.

Interest in Sikh studies increased further in the recent decades, partly due to the presence of the Sikhs in UK and North America and partly due to the political crisis in the Punjab. The past decade has witnessed the emergence of a controversy which reflects a wide gulf between the concerns and assumptions of the critics and the authors whom they criticize. In some ways surely, an unprecedented situation has arisen in the history of Sikh studies. The controversy by now has embraced nearly all aspects of the Sikh tradition. My long interest in Sikh studies induced me to take notice of the development of this controversy, to grasp its meaning, and to see the significance of 'contesting interpretations' for my own understanding of the Sikh tradition.

I feel happy to acknowledge that the Indian Council of Historical Research enabled me to study the issues involved in this controversy by inviting me to be its National Fellow from April 1994 to March 1997. I am indebted to a number of scholars for discussion on various aspects of the Sikh tradition. I feel thankful to them. An invitation from the Nehru Memorial Museum and Library first and then from the Punjabi University, Paiala to lecture on Sikh identity resulted in the publication of *Historical Perspectives on Sikh Identity* by the Punjabi University. It is essentially a part of the 'contesting interpretations of the Sikh tradition'.

I feel happy to mention that my wife, Harjinder, has given great support to sustain me in my work over all these years. The historians who have helped me in the preparation of this book at all stages are Professor Indu Banga, Dr Reeta Grewal, and Dr Veena Sachdeva. I am grateful to them.

I am thankful to S. Inderpreet Singh of the Printech Graphics for preparing the master prints with great diligence and care. And I thank Mr. Ramesh Jain most warmly for taking personal interest in this publication.

Lastly, the picture on the dust jacket symbolizes the agony which came to have direct and indirect bearing on the debate.

Sahibzada Ajit Singh Nagar J.S. GREWAL
4 October 1997

Introduction

This book may be introduced in the first person. I was invited by David N. Lorenzen to participate in a seminar on 'Religious Change and Domination' held in Mexico City in August 1976 as part of the 30th International Congress of Human Sciences in Asia and North Africa (formerly the World Orientalist Conference). Lorenzen edited the papers presented at the seminar and published them in 1981 as *Religious Change and Cultural Domination*.

This volume reflects the interest of Western scholars in the history of religion in medieval India. Two papers relate directly to Sikh studies. In one, Lorenzen argues that Kabir could not be regarded as a 'Hindu' reformer because of the extent to which 'he parts company with Hinduism altogether'. In fact he tried to 'separate his religious message from both Islam and Hinduism'. It was only towards the end of the sixteenth century that 'Hinduisation' of the Kabir Panth started and transformed it eventually into a Hindu sect.[1] W.H. McLeod argues at length in his paper that the term 'syncretism' is applicable neither to the religion of Guru Nanak nor to the early Sikh Panth. In his view, the concept of 'syncretism' is better dropped altogether for the study of Sikhism.[2]

In August 1976 itself a conference was held at Berkeley with the deliberate objective of discussing 'the future of Sikh studies'. This was seen by its sponsors as 'the first attempt' in North America to bring together scholars concerned with 'Sikh studies'. The conference was co-sponsored by the Sikh Foundation. Its President, Dr. Narinder Singh Kapany, expressed the view that the Sikhs formed a 'fascinating source' of sociological study. They had demonstrated 'an uncanny capability to retain their identity, beliefs and traditions' and yet to participate 'most actively' in the North American life.[3] Indeed, a considerable number of papers discussed at the conference relate to the 'Sikhs abroad'.[4] We may be sure that an important reason for organizing the conference of Sikh studies at Berkeley was a conspicuous presence of the Sikhs in North America.

Mark Juergensmeyer, one of the editors of the *Sikh Studies: Comparative Perspectives on a Changing Tradition*, published in 1979 on the basis of papers written for the conference, underlines the need of encouraging Sikh studies. He points out that Sikhism has been either ignored, misrepresented, or presented as a syncretism in literature on world religions and in Indian studies. In his view, Sikh studies are relevant for comparative studies: textual, methodological, social and political. Furthermore, the study of Sikhism can enrich general understanding of the Indian religious tradition. Above all, the study of the Sikh tradition, valuable in itself, can provide better understanding of 'a rich and interesting religious tradition'.[5]

With their interest in the history of religion in medieval India, two scholars presented papers carrying implications for Sikh studies. Kenneth E. Bryant refers to a wide academic struggle between Hindus and certain Western scholars on the one hand and Sikhs and certain Western scholars on the other. The former eagerly extend to Sikhism the status of a sect under the all-embracing mantle of Hinduism and the latter vigorously reject the embrace. Yet another arena of conflict is that of poetics, specifically the canons of literary criticism applicable to the works of Guru Nanak and Kabir. In their poetry it is possible to subordinate the medium to the message. In Vaishnava poetry, the medium is the message. The Vaishnava versus the Sant was a dichotomy between form and the name. The Vaishnava Bhakti poetry was 'dramatic'; that of the Sants, dialectical. The Vaishnava poet's task was not to impart new information but to embellish a known episode with new elegance. He did not have to persuade his audience of anything in the realm of doctrine. Unlike the Vaishnava poet, it was not enough for Kabir's audience to say, 'I enjoyed that'; they must also be persuaded to say, 'I believed that'. Language was Kabir's only tool of persuasion.

Bryant tends to assume that Kabir and Guru Nanak stand bracketed in the realm of poetics.[6]

Karine Schomer makes a distinction between *saguṇa bhakti* and *nirguṇa bhakti*, postulating further distinctions in each. In *nirguṇa bhakti* she makes a distinction between 'the religious vision and utterances of the solitary individuals' and 'the doctrinal and other literature of the various organised sects or *panths* developed by their followers'. On the basis of the hymns of Kabir included in Guru Granth Sahib, she discerns some important differences between Kabir the mystic and the organized Sikh Panth, revealing 'the unique features of Sikhism'. The mere inclusion of some of Kabir's hymns in Guru Granth Sahib is no proof for Schomer of an absolute identity of 'moods and motivations' between him and the compilers of the Granth.[7]

Schomer makes a few other perceptive observations on 'traditions and texts'. The date 1604 was late enough to allow for a broad diffusion of Kabir's hymns throughout northern India. The Kabir corpus in Guru Granth Sahib could not possibly represent the sum total of what was accessible to Guru Arjan. 'A selection must have been made, and made on the basis of conformity to the "moods and motivations" of the Sikh religious community at that particular stage in its development'. Schomer points out that the number of hymns common to the Kabir corpus of Guru Granth Sahib and the *Kabir Granthavalī* is much larger than the number of common hymns in Guru Granth Sahib and the *Bījak*. Concentrating on the *dohās* common to Guru Granth Sahib and the *Kabir Granthavalī*, Schomer finds references to God's omnipotence, love of God to the exclusion of all else, the importance of prayer and remembering the Lord's name, the worthiness of saintly people, the meaninglessness of a life empty of devotion to God, and the distinction between hypocritical display and genuine devotion. Nevertheless, there are differences of emphasis between the two traditions relating to relationship between the deity and the devotee, the divine Guru, the way of devotion, concepts of Tantric Yoga, asceticism, ethics, and attitude towards women. Schomer comes to the conclusion that the *dohās* included in Guru Granth Sahib encourage 'moods and motivations' appropriate to 'a solid, moral, God-fearing religious community of house-holders'. Guru Arjan seems to have 'edited out' Kabir the mystic and included only Kabir the teacher.[8]

John C.B. Webster noticed an undercurrent of tension between historical scholarship and received beliefs. Professor Fauja Singh had to give way to 'orthodoxy' when his article on Guru Tegh Bahadur was criticized. The centre of Sikh studies was in the Punjab, where by far the greatest volume of work in Sikh studies was being produced, but historical methodology was not a strong point of these studies. Western scholarship represented the periphery but historical methodology was its strong point. Therefore, the relationship between the periphery and the centre was 'somewhat problematic'. Webster knew that W.H. McLeod's *Gurū Nānak and the Sikh Religion*, published in 1968, had been severely criticized in some quarters. Therefore he observed that Western scholars had to face the charge that, being foreign to the Sikh tradition, they 'don't understand', or that they 'attack' the tradition, or that they apply inappropriate methods for the study of Sikh religion.[9]

Aware of 'sensitivities to foreign interference', W.H. McLeod enunciated nevertheless that 'all sacred texts', irrespective of the tradition to which they belonged, should be subjected to searching academic scrutiny and analysis. A text recorded or transmitted by human hands must always be open to 'textual analysis' to be corrected, understood, and interpreted. The *Ādi Granth* could be textually analysed for at least two reasons. Firstly, there was a phase of obscurity in its history. Secondly, there were numerous deletions in the Kartarpur manuscript, claimed to be the recension prepared by Guru Arjan. Its descriptions by a few scholars raised questions which could be settled by 'a sustained campaign of textual analysis' to get 'a sure and certain text'. Then there was uncertainty as to when the status of the Guru came to be accorded to the *Ādi Granth*. Its cohesive role in the past and its use in the present were two other important issues. There was also the need to collect and preserve all manuscript copies of the *Ādi Granth*. In this connection, McLeod suggested that the Goindwal Pothis 'may still be in existence'. A search for them could be mounted.[10]

C.H. Loehlin, who had taken interest in Sikh studies for over three decades, made a plea for textual study of the Kartarpur Granth. He referred to the claim made by Bhai Ardaman Singh in the *Sikh Review* of August 1975 that Guru Granth Sahib was the only scripture in the world to have been 'written, prepared, and sealed by the Founder who directly received the Word'. This could be true but 'such a forthrightly statement requires further study and proof to put the issue beyond any doubt'.[11] It may be of interest to note that Professor Surjit Singh, Professor of Christian Philosophy, underlined the necessity of preserving original manuscripts, and recommended their photographic reproduction for research purposes. For him too 'the question of originality' was not quite settled. A single authentic text of the Sikh scripture was needed. Piety alone was not enough for this purpose. Technical scholarship would have to play an active role in giving the rightful place to the *Ādi Granth* among the sacred scriptures of the world.[12]

The scope of the conference at Berkeley was not confined to the early Sikh tradition. N. Gerald Barrier made a plea for 'a more accurate assessment of the emergence of modern Sikhism'. He had published a bibliographical study, *The Sikhs and their Literature*, in 1970. In his view, many of the ideas and institutions in contemporary Sikhism had their origin in the historical experience of the Sikh Community between 1870 and 1930. For the Singh Sabha and the Akali eras, therefore, a fresh assessment was required, which in turn demanded research grounded on documents and actual events. Barrier felt convinced that the vitality of the Sikh faith and the strength of the Sikh community were 'more than adequate for such introspection'. He put it rather strongly that the history of modern Sikhism would remain clouded in 'uncertainty and myth' without new questions and thorough investigation.[13]

I have dwelt rather long on the Berkeley conference to suggest that a new interest in Sikh studies was growing in North America. The themes discussed in Berkeley as well as Mexico were serious: the nature of Kabir's message, its relationship with Guru Nanak's teachings, and the nature of the faith of Guru Nanak. The need of textual study and its importance in Sikh studies was underlined. An undercurrent of tension between historical scholarship and belief in the received tradition was also noticed. It may be added that interest in 'Punjab studies' was already there in North America. Apart from N. Gerald Barrier, we can think of the work of scholars like Kenneth Jones, Paul Wallace, Barbara Ramusack, Spencer Lavan and Tom Kessinger. The crystallization of interest in Sikh studies in the late 1970s can be attributed to the presence of Sikhs in North America. A better understanding of the Sikh tradition was expected to lead to a better understanding of the 'American Sikhs'. The enlightened individuals among them were inclined to promote Sikh studies in 'self-interest'.

A similar situation was developing in the United Kingdom. British universities had sponsored individual research on Sikh religion and Sikh history during the colonial period. However, the histories of India coming out from Cambridge and Oxford had taken little notice of the Sikhs. Joyce Pettigrew's *Robber Noblemen*, published in 1975 with its focus on the contemporary Sikh politics, indicated the beginning of a new kind of interest. In 1980, the Cambridge University Press invited me to write a whole volume on the Sikhs of the Punjab for the *New Cambridge History of India* series. Presumably, the presence of a considerable number of Sikhs in the United Kingdom by this time had some relevance for this decision. If anything, the political events of the 1980s made the Sikhs a more important subject. Christopher Shackle published *An Introduction to the Sacred Language of the Sikhs* and also *The Sikhs* before *The Sikhs of the Punjab* was published in 1990. The CUP agreed to add about fifty pages to the volume. The 'Punjab crisis' had been added to Sikh immigration as a factor in the development of Sikh studies.

In February 1987 I participated in conferences on 'Sikh studies' held at Berkeley and the University of Toronto. The Berkeley conference assessed the current status of scholorship in all fields of Sikh studies. For the conference at Toronto, the 'concentration of Canadian Sikhs' in the province of Ontario provided one reason. Another reason for this 'first gathering of its kind in Canada' was 'the current crisis in Sikh life'. The presence of W.H. McLeod as a Visiting Commonwealth Fellow in Toronto served as a kind of 'catalyst'. The mandate of the University to teach and advance research in all aspects of the history and plural cultures of South

Asia provided the theoretical framework for the event. Over a score of papers written for this conference were published in 1988 as *Sikh History and Religion in the Twentieth Century.*

Early in 1988 I was invited to give courses in Sikh history and Sikh religion as a Visiting Professor at the University of Toronto. The students numbered over a score and they showed keen interest in themes related to Sikh studies. The Sikh community in Toronto showed a lively concern for the development of Sikh studies, and I was able to organize a seminar on 'religious identity and political articulation in the Punjab' in April 1988. The overall impression I carried back from Canada was that of a good beginning made in pursuit of Sikh studies. From 1988 to 1992, W.H. McLeod worked at Toronto as a Visiting Professor for five terms. One of his research students, Pashaura Singh, completed a doctoral work in 1991 on 'The Text and Meaning of the Adi Granth'. He was appointed Assistant Professor at Ann Arbor where a few conferences were held subsequently on themes related to Sikh studies.

Before returning to India in May 1988, I participated in a small conference at the University of British Columbia on 'Sikh Literature and Language: Text and Transmission' organized by Harjot Oberoi. He had been appointed to a Chair of Punjabi and Sikh Studies at the UBC in its Department of Asian Studies, and had participated in the conferences at Berkeley and Toronto in 1987 and 1988. Apart from papers on the Singh Sabha Movement and 'Sikh Fundamentalism', he published a revised version of his doctoral work in 1994 as *The Construction of Religious Boundaries: Culture, Identity and Diversity in the Sikh Tradition.*

A conference on 'Sikh Studies' was held at the Columbia University in 1989, the year in which the University published W.H. McLeod's *The Sikhs: History, Religion and Society.* This conference was sponsored by Columbia's Southern Asian Institute and the Sikh Cultural Society of Richmond Hill. Gurinder Singh Mann, who thought of organizing the conference in New York, was giving courses in Sikh religion and Punjabi language at this time. He completed his doctoral work in 1993 on 'The Making of the Sikh Scripture'. This was also the year in which the papers written for the 1989 conference were published as *Studying the*

Sikhs: Issues for North America, edited jointly by John Stratton Hawley and Gurinder Singh Mann. The aim of this publication was 'to open up the major issues involved in pursing Sikh studies in the context of higher education in North America'.[14]

Among other things, some of the contributors to *Studying the Sikhs* noticed that Western scholarship was being criticized by a network of Sikh scholars in India and North America. They appeared to be troubled by the thrust of 'rigorous critical scholarship' in its bearing upon the history of Sikhism. They had access to community publications and influence in Sikh associations. Some of them were quite strident in their criticism. In the *Advanced Studies in Sikhism*, dissatisfaction was expressed with the whole of 'modern critical scholarship'. Some of the contributors to this volume failed to make any distinction between 'criticizing views and imputing motives'. They attacked the personal integrity of those with whom they disagreed or whom they did not understand.[15] In this connection, another publication may also be mentioned: *Perspectives on the Sikh Tradition*. It was highly critical of Western scholarship on Sikhism. It was also noticed that in a 'panthic conference' held at New York in 1990 resolutions were passed to ratify the creation of Khalistan and to denounce McLeod's research.[16]

On invitation from the editors of *Studying the Sikhs*, I contributed a revised version of a lecture I had given in 1972 on the 'present state of Sikh studies'. I pointed out that the interest of foreign scholars in Sikh studies had greatly increased since the early 1970s. This increasing interest in Sikh studies was marked by 'a measure of controversy' also. I was inclined to attribute it to 'an understandable tension between critical scholarship and faith in what is perceived to be the Sikh tradition'. The crisis through which the Sikh community was passing had 'much to do' with this controversy. Its scope was remarkably wide. I expressed the hope that this controversy could turn out to be fruitful if the critical scholars realize the implications of their work for the Sikh community and if their critics 'from within the faith' realize the significance of 'methodological atheism' which characterizes all rational-empirical research in the modern world.[17] By this time, I had begun to reflect seriously on the recent controversy in Sikh studies.

In 1988 I had received an invitation to participate in a Sikh studies conference at Los Angeles. I could not go but I remember the invitation because of its peculiarity: the participants were expected to defend their earlier publications as well. The eristic character of the conference was reflected in the papers published in 1989 as *Advanced Studies in Sikhism*. I discovered that the idea of the Los Angeles conference had come essentially from a book entitled *Perspectives on the Sikh Tradition*, published in 1986. It was meant to demolish W.H. McLeod. I know in retrospect that the scholar who spearheaded the attack was Sardar Daljeet Singh. He had felt unhappy about the publication of McLeod's books: *Gurū Nānak and the Sikh Religion* (1968), *The Evolution of the Sikh Community* (1975), and *The Early Sikh Tradition* (1980). The frankly polemical purpose of the *Perspectives on the Sikh Tradition* is not surprising any more.

I was familiar with W.H. McLeod's work, and I could see that his position was not always fully or fairly presented. I thought of understanding the significance of this controversy. It appeared to relate to some of the most important themes of Sikh religion and Sikh history: the nature of the message of Guru Nanak and its status in the history of religion; Guru Nanak of 'faith' versus Guru Nanak of 'history', raising the issue of the relevance of the *Janamsākhīs* for a historical biography of Guru Nanak; the role of Sikh ideology in Sikh history, especially in relation to the rise of militancy in the Sikh Panth, the institution of the Khalsa, the Khalsa *rahit*, the doctrines of Guru-Granth and Guru-Panth; and caste in the Sikh Panth. The *Perspectives on the Sikh Tradition* was meant to present alternative interpretations of all these vital issues.

I was trying to grapple with these 'contesting interpretations' of the Sikh tradition when more books began to appear in succession, extending the scope of debate in Sikh studies. A number of conferences were held in UK and North America after the publication of the Toronto volume. The papers written for these conferences were published in 1992 as *Recent Researches in Sikhism* and as *Fundamental Issues in Sikh Studies*. The difference in these two books lies more in their titles than in their contents. Before the end of 1992 appeared Professor Piar Singh's *Gāthā Sri Ādi Granth* which immediately started a fierce controversy. Pashaura Singh's doctoral thesis was also being denounced at this time. In 1993 Trilochan Singh published a lengthy critique of W.H. McLeod as *Ernest Trumpp and W.H. McLeod as Scholars of Sikh History, Religion and Culture*. The criticism of Pashaura Singh's doctoral thesis by a large number of scholars was published in 1994 as *Planned Attack on Adi Sri Guru Granth Sahib: Academics or Blasphemy*. A critique of Harjot Oberoi's *Construction of Religious Boundaries* appeared in 1995 as *Invasion of Religious Boundaries*. Piar Singh's *Gatha Sri Adi Granth and the Controversy* appeared in 1996. Gurinder Singh Mann published a book on the Goindwal Pothis. The debate is going on.

From April 1994 to March 1997, as National Fellow of the Indian Council of Historical Research, I devoted most of my time to the study of the recent controversy in the larger context of the development of Sikh studies. The first part of this book deals with the development of Sikh studies from the last quarter of the eighteenth century to the third quarter of the twentieth. The issues raised in the *Perspectives on the Sikh Tradition* are discussed in the second part and the issues raised by the extended controversy are discussed in the third part of this book. Its primary objective is to understand the Sikh tradition through an understanding of the current debate. My own views become a part of the 'contesting interpretations'. Hopefully, this dispassionate discussion may lead to mutual understanding between the contestants for a more fruitful dialogue in Sikh studies.

Finally, I would like to refer to a phrase I use at several places in this book, the 'critics of critical scholarship'. W.H. McLeod is seen by his critics as too critical of the Sikh tradition. For me, he simply represents historical methodology with all its strengths and limitations. 'Critical scholarship' for me, therefore, is merely a description of historical scholarship. Similarly, the 'critics' is a descriptive category for those writers who stand on the other side in the debate. There is no suggestion that their approach is not historical. Some of them do assert, however, that historical approach is not valid for the study of religion.

NOTES

1. *Religious Change and Cultural Domination*, pp. 151-71.
2. Ibid., pp. 173-91.
3. *Sikh Studies*, pp. 207-08.
4. Ibid., pp. 127-206.
5. Ibid., pp. 13-23.
6. Ibid., pp. 65-74.
7. Ibid., pp. 75-76.
8. Ibid., pp. 77-86.
9. Ibid., pp. 25-32.
10. Ibid., pp. 97-105.
11. Ibid., pp. 113-18.
12. Ibid., pp. 119-20.
13. Ibid., pp. 41-51.
14. *Studying the Sikhs*, p. 2.
15. Ibid., pp. 123-24 and 125.
16. Ibid., pp. 42 n 2 and 45 n 35.
17. Ibid., p. 172.

Part One

DEVELOPMENT OF SIKH STUDIES

1. The Emergence of Sikh Studies

In the earliest European references to the Sikhs there is no interest in the Sikh past. Writing from Lahore in 1606, Father Jerome Xavier mentions the execution of Guru Arjan without saying anything about his antecedents. Writing from Delhi in 1716, John Surman and Edward Stephenson inform the Governor of Fort William about what was happening to Banda Bahadur and his fellow prisoners without showing any interest in the history of the Sikhs.[1] However, European writers began to show interest in the Sikh past before the end of the eighteenth century. Two new developments had taken place by then. The East India Company had become a political power in competition with other powers in India. Historical writing in Western Europe had become far more important now than ever before. It was vaguely but generally assumed that knowledge was power and that the present could be understood better in the light of the past.[2]

I

Not surprisingly, individuals connected with the East India Company began to collect information on the Sikhs who had come into power and presented a threat to the dominions of the Mughal emperor in whose fortunes the Company was deeply interested. Colonel A.L.H. Polier was the first to collect information on the striking power of the Sikhs. He talks of their polity and their tenets and manners. His Sikhs stand equated with the Singhs, or the Khalsa. Different from other Indians in some significant ways, they showed taint of the Hindu religion.[3] For another writer, George Thomas, the Sikhs had emerged as a new 'nation' only in the past thirty years. This evidently refers to their emergence as a political power with which Thomas was primarily concerned. There were great many similarities between the Sikhs and the Jats. Thomas tends to equate the Sikh not only with the Singh but also with the Jat Sikh.[4] Both Polier and Thomas made observations on the contemporary Sikhs. Their observations now serve as a source of our information on the late-eighteenth-century Sikhs.

Charles Wilkins, with his interest in Sikh beliefs and practices, wanted to know something of their past when he passed through Patna in 1781 and visited the Sikh shrine associated with the birth of Guru Gobind Singh. He comments on the Sikh congregational worship and system of voluntary contributions. He was told how the initiation rite was performed by five Sikhs. He noticed that two books were held in veneration by the Sikhs. He learnt on verbal inquiry that the founder of the Sikh faith was Nanak Shah who had left behind a book in the Punjabi language and in a script of his own invention; it was called Gurmukhi. He believed in one omnipotent and omnipresent God, and he taught universal philanthropy and tolerance. The epithet 'Sikh' was meant to distinguish his 'sect' from others. Wilkins looked upon the Sikhs as a people distinct from the worshippers of Brahma and the followers of Muhammad.[5]

The first writer to attempt a connected account of 'the origin and progress' of the Sikhs was Major James Browne. His work was made possible by a Persian manuscript in which an account of the Sikhs was given from the time of Guru Nanak to the late eighteenth century. This manuscript, *Risāla-i Nānak Shāh*, was actually commissioned by Browne himself. It had little merit in terms of authentic information, but Browne had no way of knowing this. Later historians also used it for writing about the Sikhs. Historiographically, Browne's *History of the Origin and Progress of the Sikhs* marked the beginning of modern historical writing on the Sikhs.[6]

On the basis of the *Risāla-i Nānak Shāh*, Browne surmised that the doctrine on which Guru Nanak founded his 'sect' bore 'that kind of relation to the Hindu religion, which the Protestant does to the Romish'. He retained all its 'essential principles' but discarded 'most of its ceremonies' and 'subordinate objects of veneration'. The Sikhs became a militant people due to the bigoted measures of persecution adopted by Aurangzeb. The distinction of their sect was based on 'a political as much as a religious principle', and they began to levy contributions from 'all their neighbours who refused to come into their fraternity'.[7]

A more meaningful account of the Sikhs was written by George Forster who claims that no 'favourite system' could induce him to sacrifice 'the principles of truth and reason'. In his account of 'this new and extraordinary people' he refers to Sikh records as well as to European sources. He was not inclined to give credence to 'legends'. In other words, he proposed to give what he thought was strictly a historical account. His account of the Sikhs was neither detailed nor wholly accurate but the broad outline of the early Sikh tradition begins to emerge from his work. Forster presents the life of Guru Nanak and the work of his successors through a factual narrative, noticing in the process that Guru Hargobind was a 'militant priest' and that Guru Gobind Singh came into armed conflict with the hill chiefs and the Mughal *faujdārs* before Banda Bahadur established 'an independent dominion'.[8]

Forster points out that Guru Gobind Singh founded the 'modern order' of the Sikhs, called the Khalsa. By imparting a strong military spirit to his adherents, he deviated from the ordinances of his predecessors. He instructed the Khalsa to grow beards and to keep the hair of the head uncut; he also forbade the use of tobacco. The Sikhs of this military order bore the epithet Singh. They fixed an iron bracelet on the left hand. The regulations instituted by Guru Gobind Singh 'to distinguish them from other nations' came to form 'the essence of their creed'. They observed a distinct ceremony of initiation, which symbolized equality and was meant to destroy the 'fabric of ceremony and form' regarded by the Hindus as the essential principle of their religion. The Khalsa were quite distinct from the non-Khalsa Sikhs, known as 'Khulasa' Sikhs, who adhered to the institutions of Guru Nanak and his eight successors. Forster goes on to describe the contemporary non-Khalsa Sikhs.[9]

After his observations on the Khalsa and the non-Khalsa Sikhs, Forster takes up the political narrative after Banda's execution. In his view, the Sikhs were wholly suppressed through ruthless persecution under Farrukh Siyar. But they re-appeared in arms at the time of Nadir Shah's invasion in 1739 and plundered his baggage on his return from Delhi. Mir Mannu persecuted them with great vigour but Kauṛa Mal, who was a non-Khalsa Sikh, diverted him from reaping the fruit of the advantage he had gained. After the death of both Kauṛa Mal and Mir Mannu, Ahmad Shah Abdali and the Marathas fought over the possession of the Punjab. After the battle of Panipat in 1761, Ahmad Shah tried to suppress the Sikhs but their striking power had increased immensely. In 1764 they seized the territory from the Indus to the districts of Delhi. Ahmad Shah failed to dislodge them and abandoned the design of subduing the Punjab after his campaign of 1767. In Forster's view, the Sikhs were able to establish 'an undivided authority' over the Punjab primarily because of their perseverance and valour. Among the auxiliary causes of their success, the most important was the declining power of the Mughals, Kauṛa Mal's diplomatic support to the Sikhs at a critical juncture, and the fact that Ahmad Shah Abdali put an end to the power and authority of the Mughals in the Punjab without firmly establishing his own. Like his European contemporaries, Forster described the polity and resources of the contemporary Sikh rulers.[10]

II

In the early nineteenth century, the East India Company's contact with the Sikh rulers became much closer in terms of both space and diplomacy. This change was directly reflected in the increasing volume of literature on the Sikhs. That this interest was primarily inspired by the politics of the East India Company is evident from the synchronization of important publications with important events. John Malcolm's *Sketch of the Sikhs* appeared soon after the Treaty of Amritsar between the East India Company and Maharaja Ranjit Singh in 1809. H.T. Prinsep's book on Ranjit Singh was published soon after the Indus Navigation Treaty of 1832. W.L. M'Gregor's *History* was meant to glorify the deeds of British officers and to justify the Anglo-Sikh war of 1845-6. J.D. Cunningham addressed himself to the British nation, rather than the East India Company, expecting nevertheless to influence British policy towards the Sikhs. Much of this literature related to the political history of the Sikhs and to Anglo-Sikh relations. Interest in the early Sikh tradition was reflected mainly in the works of John Malcolm, H.H. Wilson and J.D. Cunningham.[11]

Religion was professedly the most 'curious and important' aspect of the Sikhs for John Malcolm. Guru Nanak's creed was 'pure deism' grounded on the most sublime general truths. At the same time, it was blended with 'the fables' of Islam and 'the absurdities' of Hindu mythology. Guru Nanak was opposed to the bigotry of the Muslims and the superstition of the Hindus. His aim was to reconcile 'the jarring faiths' of Muhammad and Brahma. In support of equality and tolerance Guru Nanak adopted the maxims of the Sūfīs. He called upon the Hindus to discard polytheistic beliefs and idol-worship and he called upon the Muslims to discard cow-slaughter and religious persecution. Guru Nanak had a common message for both Hindus and Muslims but not an altogether a new message. Malcolm looked upon Guru Nanak on the whole as a reformer who made 'no material invasion of either the civil or religious usages of the Hindus'; his only desire was to restore the original worship of One God among them. Quite unambiguously, Malcolm sees Guru Nanak 'more in the light of a reformer, than subverter of the Hindu religion'.[12]

Guru Gobind Singh presents a contrast to Guru Nanak in Malcolm's presentation. Whereas Guru Nanak taught philanthropy and benevolence in a peaceful manner, Guru Gobind Singh made the pursuit of arms a religious duty and inspired his followers with a spirit of hostility towards the Muslims. At the same time he admitted followers from all castes and inspired them with a spirit of equality. He gave a new orientation to the Sikh community and to Sikh history. The political activity of the Khalsa and their polity in the eighteenth century flowed from the measures of Guru Gobind Singh. Consequently, the Khalsa became predominant in the Sikh community during the eighteenth century.[13]

H.H. Wilson discussed the 'civil and religious institutions' of the Sikhs to identify those which distinguished the Sikhs from the

Hindus. He bracketed Guru Nanak with the Hindu reformers of medieval India. Generally unlearned, they were thoughtful and benevolent individuals. Dissatisfied with the religious practices of their countrymen, they tried to reform their defects. They reduced the existing systems of belief to 'a few simple elements of faith and worship in which the Brahman and Shudra, the Muhammadan and the Hindu might cordially combine and from which they might learn to lay aside their uncharitable feelings towards each other'. Though not deeply versed in the Vedas or the Qurān, these reformers were well grounded in both Hindu and Muslim tenets and sought to amalgamate them. They combined the doctrine of transmigration and the Vedantic principle of emanation with the ideas of Islam as represented by the Sūfīs. They addressed the common people in their own language. The literature they produced was influential among the agricultural population in northern India.[14]

The religious 'sect' founded by Guru Nanak was transformed into a nation by 'political events'. Sikhism differed from other movements of reform only in its later development. Wilson had little appreciation for the Sikh movement. In the creed of Guru Nanak One divine cause and essence of all things was acknowledged but this creed was transformed into something quite different by his successors, especially Guru Gobind Singh. What distinguished the Sikhs from the Hindus more than anything else was abolition of the distinctions of caste among the former. But this was not necessarily a gain. In ethical terms, Sikhism was scarcely 'a religious faith'. Wilson wrongly thought that Guru Nanak defined God in negative terms. Consequently he assumed that Guru Nanak's conception of God could not have any moral effect on the believers. Their only worship consisted in chanting of hymns which contained allusions to a powerful and benevolent being. Their belief in divine intervention exercised little influence on their practices. Wilson does not hesitate to conclude that 'the worship of the Book and of the Sword' among the Sikhs led to 'great laxity of conduct and utter disregard of both religious and moral obligations'. Sikhism brought no improvement in 'the superstitious beliefs and multiplied ceremonial of the Brahmans'.[15]

To underline rupture between the early and later Sikhism, Wilson refers to Guru Nanak as 'the nominal founder' of the Sikh religion and the Sikh 'nation'. The original elements of Sikhism were a mystical deism, contemplative worship, peace and goodwill, and amalgamation of Hindus and Muslims. The doctrines of Sikhism were inculcated through mystical and moral verses rather than dogma and precept. Guru Nanak admitted followers from all castes but 'he does not seem to have formally abolished caste'. He treated the Qurān with reverence and acknowledged 'the whole scheme of Hindu mythology'. They who professed 'the pure Sikh faith' still subscribed to the scheme of Hindu mythology. The true followers of early Sikhism, thought Wilson, were the Udāsīs and the Nirmalās of his time. There was little difference between a Nirmalā Sikh and a Hindu of the Vaishnava sect 'except in the mode of performing public worship, and in the profession of benevolent sentiments for all mankind among the true Sikhs'.[16] Wilson wrote on the basis of what was available to him in print, which did not amount to much. His assessment was inspired more by his own theological assumptions than by scholarship. But he was a reputed 'orientalist' and Bodin Professor of Sanskrit when he published his views on Sikhism. His views were bound to command respect.

Nevertheless, Wilson's interpretation of Sikhism was contested by J.D. Cunningham. He was the first British writer to have some understanding of Sikh literature – the *Ādi Granth*, the *Vārs* of Bhai Gurdas, the *Dasam Granth* and the *Rahitnāmas*. He placed the medieval reformers in the context of the history of religion in India to bring out the significance of their ideas and attitudes; he placed Guru Nanak in the context of medieval reform to bring out his distinctive contribution. In his view, Gorakh Nath and Ramanand had preached religious equality in opposition to traditional Hinduism; Chaitanya had taught that faith levelled caste; Kabir had denounced idol-worship and addressed people in their own language; and Vallabhacharya had shown that devotion was compatible with the ordinary duties of the world. However, these reformers were so impressed with the nothingness of life that they attached no importance to improvement in the social condition.

They formed pious and quietist associations with no aspiration to free themselves from the debasing corruption of ages; they perfected forms of dissent but failed to plant the germs of nations.

It was reserved for Nanak to perceive the true principles of reform, and to lay those broad foundations which enabled his successor Gobind to fire the minds of his countrymen with a new nationality, and to give practical effect to the doctrine that the lowest is equal with the highest, in race as in creed, in political rights as in religious hopes.[17]

This thesis finds ample elaboration in Cunningham's *History of the Sikhs*. Guru Nanak combined the excellences of other reformers and avoided their errors. He equated God with Truth and advocated uncompromising theism. He addressed the Pandit and the Mulla, the Hindu ascetic and the Muslim Sūfī, and told them to devote themselves to the Lord of their lords. Knowledge of God mattered more than anything else, and it depended on God's grace. At the same time Guru Nanak emphasized the importance of good works and upright conduct. He regarded himself as the successor of all the inspired teachers of the past and rendered his mission applicable to all times and places. Yet he declared himself to be a humble messenger of God, with universal truth as his only instrument. He declared that the devout householder and the pious hermit were equal in the eyes of God. In this way, Guru Nanak extricated his followers from 'the accumulated errors of ages' and impressed upon them the importance of 'devotion of thought and excellence of conduct'. In its immediate effect his reform was religious and moral, but he left his Sikhs erect and free, unbiased in mind and unfettered by rules. He chose a successor to continue his mission in order to prevent his followers from contracting into a sect or narrowing his comprehensive principles into monastic distinctions. The Sikhs believed that the spirit of Guru Nanak had become incarnate in all his successors.[18]

The work of Guru Nanak served as the base for his successors to give concrete shape to his ideas. Cunningham takes up the work of each successor, commenting on the significance of what they did to carry their heritage further. In his summing up, Guru Nanak disengages his little society of worshippers from Hindu idolatry and Muslim superstition, and provides them with a broad basis of religious and moral purity. Guru Amar Das preserves the infant community from declining into a sect of quietists or ascetics. Guru Arjan gives his increasing followers a written rule of conduct and a civil organization. Guru Hargobind adds the use of arms and a military system. Guru Gobind Singh bestows upon them a distinct political entity, and inspires them with the desire of being socially free and nationally independent. 'No further legislation was required; a firm persuasion had been elaborated, and a vague feeling had acquired consistence as an active principle'.[19] On this hypothesis, success was only a matter of time:

> The last apostle of the Sikhs did not live to see his own ends accomplished, but he effectually roused the dormant energies of a vanquished people, and filled them with lofty although fitful longing for social freedom and national ascendance, the proper adjuncts of that purity of worship which had been preached by Nanak.[20]

Cunningham did not see any conflict between religion and race. 'The characteristics of race and religion are everywhere of greater importance than the accidents of position or the achievements of contemporary genius; but the influences of descent, of origin and worship, need not be dwelt upon in all their ramifications'.[21] The characteristics of race were 'perhaps more deep-seated and enduring' than those of religion but the results of 'birth and breeding, of descent and instruction, must be held jointly in view'.[22]

Whereas Malcolm and Wilson looked upon Guru Nanak as a Hindu reformer, Cunningham looked upon him as the founder of a new faith. Indeed, the movement initiated by Guru Nanak was rather unique in terms of the social relevance of his ideas. It stood distinguished not only from traditional Islam, whether orthodox or Sūfī, and traditional Hinduism but also from the movements initiated by the medieval reformers. Furthermore, the successors of Guru Nanak could build upon his legacy precisely because of the social relevance of his religious and moral ideas. The Sikh movement for Cunningham was one single movement from Guru Nanak to Guru Gobind Singh. The establishment of Sikh rule was a logical and historical extension of this movement. Cunningham was unique among the British historians of the Sikhs to appreciate the role of Sikh ideology in shaping Sikh history.[23]

III

We can see that the primary interest of the late eighteenth-century writers was in the present, and centred in the military resources of the Sikhs and their political organization. They were interested also in the character of the contemporary Sikh 'nation' or 'sect'. They looked upon the Khalsa as distinct not only from Muslims but also from Hindus because of their external appearance, their attitude towards the caste system and their sacred scriptures; they tended to equate the turban wearing *keshdhāri* Singhs with the Sikh community. A few of them tended to equate the Sikh with the Jat Sikh.

The late eighteenth-century writers interpreted Guru Nanak's faith in different ways. Browne thought of it as 'reform' but Forster thought of it as a new religion. The dichotomy between the 'pacifism' of the Nanak-Panthīs and the 'militancy' of the Khalsa also began to emerge in this early phase. Forster was the first writer to bring the role of Guru Gobind Singh into high relief by presenting him as the founder of the Khalsa and the author of the Khalsa code of conduct.

Notwithstanding the differences in their interpretation, all the early writers shared the assumption that knowledge of the past could be grounded only on empirical evidence, written and oral, Sikh and non-Sikh. It could be accepted or rejected only on rational grounds.

The writers of the early nineteenth century tried to collect more information on the past as well as the contemporary history of the Sikhs. They could use the *Dabistān-i Mazāhib* and the *Siyar al-Mutākhirīn*, both of which had been translated into English. They 'discovered' Sikh sources like the *Ādi Granth*, the *Vārs* of Bhai Gurdas, the *Dasam Granth*, and the *Rahitnāmas*. They were more or less agreed that the Sikh movement was theistic. They also saw the relevance of the presence of Islam for the ideas and attitudes of Guru Nanak. Two opposing interpretations of the Sikh tradition began to crystallize: one, that Guru Nanak was a Hindu reformer and Sikhism was a form of Hinduism; the other, that Guru Nanak founded a new faith which was distinct from both Hinduism and Islam. All the writers were inclined to look upon the Khalsa as socially and politically distinct from the rest of the Indian people. Malcolm and Wilson saw a dramatic contrast between the pacifist and the militant phases of Sikh history. Cunningham tended to see a steady evolution from the foundations laid by Guru Nanak to the edifice raised by Guru Gobind Singh. It may be added that Cunningham's work proved to be a source of inspiration for quite a few Indian historians of the Sikhs during the twentieth century.

NOTES

1. Ganda Singh (1962), pp. 45-51.
2. Grewal (1975), pp. 1-11.
3. Ganda Singh (1962), pp. 53-66.
4. Ibid., pp. 101-07.
5. Ibid., pp. 69-75.
6. Browne's observations on the contemporary Sikhs belong to the same category of information as that of Polier or Thomas.
7. Ibid., pp. 13-14.
8. Forster (1970), I, pp. x-xiii and 291-306.
9. Ibid., pp. 306-10.
10. Ibid., pp. 310-40.
11. Grewal (1992), pp. 3-6 and 11; Grewal (1972), pp. 125-30.
12. *The Sikh Religion: A Symposium*, pp. 90-91 and 128-29.
13. Malcolm (1812), pp. 145, 147, 148, 174-79 and 192.
14. Wilson (1958), p. 54.
15. Ibid., pp. 54-55 and 56
16. Ibid., pp. 64 and 68-69.
17. Cunningham (1955), pp. 24-34.
18. Ibid., pp. 38 and 40-43.
19. Ibid., p. 80.
20. Ibid., p. 75.
21. Ibid., p. 9.
22. Ibid., p. 12.
23. Grewal (1972), pp. 123-37 and 190-93.

2. Colonial Rule and 'Orientalist' Dialogue

British administrators and army officers continued to write about the Sikhs after the annexation of the Kingdom of Lahore in 1849. They were interested more in the contemporary Sikhs than in their past. How to handle them as a subject people and how to use their support and services was the main concern. Lepel Griffin published three books from 1865 to 1870 and a fourth one in 1892. It was followed by A.H. Bingley's *Sikhs* in 1899. John J.H. Gordon published his *Sikhs* in 1904, followed by C.H. Payne's *Short History of the Sikhs* in 1915. R.E. Parr's *Sikhs of the Punjab* appeared in 1921, followed in 1928 by A.E. Barstow's *The Sikhs: An Ethnology*. G.B. Scott published his *Religion and Short History of the Sikhs* in 1930. With the exception of Griffin, all these writers based their books largely on the earlier writers: John Malcolm, H.T. Prinsep, W.G. Osborne, G.C. Symth, W.L. M'Gregor and J.D. Cunningham. To these were added Trumpp and Macauliffe later.[1]

By far the most important writer among the administrators was Lepel Griffin. In 1865 he published *The Punjab Chiefs*. In 1869 appeared his *Law of Inheritance as Observed by the Sikhs Previous to the Annexation of Punjab*, followed by *The Rajas of the Punjab* in 1870. These works related to the former and contemporary Sikh rulers and the former *jāgīrdārs* and their descendants in the contemporary Punjab. These were the people with whom the colonial administrators were primarily concerned for government and administration. Griffin did not undertake any research for writing his *Ranjit Singh*: it was based on his earlier books. The scope of the volume as a whole is apparently wide and comprehensive but it suffers from two basic limitations: no theme is treated in any depth, and there is no serious attempt to see any interrelationships between the themes treated.

Both in its form and content Griffin's *Ranjit Singh* reflects the nature of information available in his own earlier publications. He thought that his contemporaries would not be interested in the campaigns and conquests of Ranjit Singh; they would rather know something of the character of the chiefs who surrounded him. For the army of Ranjit Singh, he points out the basic change. Ranjit Singh made infantry the most important arm of his forces and developed good artillery. Though he did not stop using the traditional cavalry of the *jāgīrdārs*, he raised 'regular' units of cavalry as a part of his standing army. For the civil administration of Ranjit Singh, Griffin simply states that it was meant for 'squeezing out of the unhappy peasant every rupee that he could be made to disgorge'. Griffin missed no opportunity of justifying British rule in the Punjab while writing on Ranjit Singh. Griffin's contemporary Sikhs, formed mainly by the 'the great Jat caste', get equated with the Khalsa Singhs. Besides agriculture, their 'natural profession' was the army. For the Sikh faith, Griffin based his observations on Ernest Trumpp's *Adi Granth*, published in 1877.[2]

I

The first important work to appear after the annexation was Dr. Ernest Trumpp's *Adi Granth.* He was a trained theologian who had worked with a Christian mission in India as a linguist before he was commissioned to translate the Granth by the India Office towards the end of 1869. However, his knowledge of Sanskrit and the North Indian vernaculars proved to be inadequate for the task. Besides help from some native scholars in the Punjab, Trumpp was able to prepare a grammar and a dictionary of his own. Having prepared his tools and gone through the entire Granth once, he returned to Europe in the spring of 1872. He worked for a few more years to produce a manuscript which was published in 1877.

Trumpp's *Adi Granth* was a monumental work. His translation covers more than 700 folio pages in print, though he did not translate the whole Granth. The reason he gives for his deliberate omissions is interesting: the Sikh Granth was 'incoherent and shallow in the extreme'.[3] It was painful for the Europeans to read even a single *Rāg*. Therefore, it would have been 'a mere waste of paper to add also the minor Rags, which only repeat, in endless variations, what has already been said in the great Rags over and over again, without adding the least to our knowledge'.[4] It is quite clear in retrospect that he did not understand the original in all its nuances. A part of the difficulty which he ascribed to the original sprang from his own limitations.[5]

Trumpp did not confine himself to translation. He added five 'introductory essays' of about 140 pages to the translation: one each on the life of Guru Nanak, the lives of the other Sikh Gurus, the religion of the Sikhs, the arrangement of the contents of the Granth, and its language and metres. Thus, the scope of Trumpp's work is much more than that of a translation. His *Ādi Granth* may be regarded as the first important attempt at an interpretation of the early Sikh tradition. Trumpp looked upon his knowledge of the *Ādi Granth* as a great advantage over all earlier writers, none of whom in his view had read the Granth personally, not even the Boden Professor, H.H. Wilson.[6]

Trumpp was the first European scholar to study the *Janamsākhīs* for the life of Guru Nanak. During his stay at Lahore in 1870-72 he came upon a lithographed edition of the *Janamsākhī* associated with Bhai Bala and compared it with various other versions in manuscript. He felt convinced that the usual Sikh tradition concerning Guru Nanak 'could by no means be trusted'. He could detect very few historical facts in 'the rubbish of miraculous and often absurd stories'. The image of Guru Nanak which appeared to emerge from the *Janamsākhīs* did not correspond to the image emerging from his compositions. When Trumpp returned to Europe the authorities of the India Office brought to his notice a manuscript acquired originally by H.T. Colebrooke. The contents of this manuscript and its idiom suggested that it was very old. Trumpp surmised that this was 'the fountain' from which all other *Janamsākhīs* were largely drawn. He gives a summary of the events of Guru Nanak's life from this *Janamsākhī*, indicating at places how later versions embellished and enlarged the stories.[7] A full translation in English follows. Extracts from the later *Janamsākhīs* are also given in translation for comparison.[8] Trumpp got the impression that myths about the life of Guru Nanak had already progressed far when the original *Janamsākhī* was compiled. Later versions introduced the supernatural element on a much larger scale and tended to deify Guru Nanak. Thinking in terms of possibilities, probabilities and certainties, Trumpp was inclined to reject much even from the Colebrooke *Janamsākhī*.[9]

Trumpp gives the lives of Guru Nanak's nine successors in thirty pages, making use of published works. His account of the Gurus from Guru Angad to Guru Tegh Bahadur is very brief, and even Guru Gobind Singh gets no more than eight pages. His comments on the Gurus reflect not merely his irreverant scepticism but also his desire to mark significant developments. Had Guru Nanak not appointed a successor before his death, his followers would have gradually dispersed and disappeared. Guru Amar Das built a *bāolī* at Goindwal with eighty-four steps. His verses are 'conspicuous for simplicity and clearness'. Guru Ram Das built the tank called *amritsar*, the temple called Harmandar, and the town called Ramdaspur, giving the Sikhs a fixed central place of worship. 'This was of the greatest importance for the firm establishment of Sikhism'. His verses formed 'the better compositions' of the Granth but there was no originality of thought in them. Guru Ram Das chose his son Arjan as his successor, and succession became hereditary, 'which added greatly to increase the wealth and the authority of the Gurus'. The Sikhs began to look upon them as 'their actual sovereigns'.[10]

Guru Arjan compiled the Granth which gradually supplanted the authority of the Vedas and the Puranas, and separated the Sikhs from the mass of the Hindus. He instructed his followers to accept the Granth alone as authentic and authoritative, and not any other composition even if it bore the pen-name 'Nanak'. The tradition regarding the space left vacant for the compositions of Guru Tegh Bahadur later was of course 'a prophecy *ex eventu*'. As a measure of great importance, Guru Arjan replaced voluntary offerings by a kind of tax to be regularly collected by his deputies called Masands. He engaged in trade in a grand style; he kept an establishment like a grandee; and he meddled with politics. In his time the Sikhs became accustomed to 'a kind of government of their own'. Guru Arjan's execution became a 'great turning-point in the development of the Sikh community'. It changed 'the whole character' of the movement initiated by Guru Nanak.[11]

For the history of the later Gurus, Trumpp felt specially handicapped by the paucity of sources and the character of the evidence available to him. Nevertheless, he highlighted the degree of transformation before Guru Gobind Singh appeared on the scene. Guru Hargobind was a man of warlike spirit and kept a strong band of armed followers. He entered the service of Jahangir and Shah Jahan before he fought battles against the Mughal administrators. He changed *faqīrs* into soldiers, replacing the rosary with the sword. Guru Hargobind attracted a large number of warlike Jats as his followers. He thus gave a different appearance to the Sikh community. His successor, Guru Har Rai, joined the rebellion of Prince Dara, giving Aurangzeb the chance to interfere in the affairs of the Sikhs. Guru Tegh Bahadur was taken prisoner on account of his predatory proceedings and executed 'as a rebel against the Government'.[12]

Guru Gobind Singh matured his plans in the early years of his Guruship to avenge himself on the murderers of his father, to subvert the Muhammadan power, and to found a new empire. He invoked the Goddess at Naina Devi through a ceremony which involved human sacrifice. On his return to Anandpur he asked his followers to offer heads for sacrifice. The five who offered themselves were given the baptism of the true religion (*sachche dharam kī pahul*) with water in which sugar was stirred with a two-edged dagger. They were given the name 'Khalsa', signifying that they were 'the Guru's own special property'. The epithet Singh was added to their names. Whoever accepted this baptism was required to observe the Khalsa *rahit*, including the 5Ks. The caste system was abolished altogether and people from all castes were admitted to the order of the Khalsa on a footing of equality. The men of lower orders, among whom the Jats were predominant, felt attracted to the Khalsa, while the upper caste people decided to remain aloof. The latter, referred to as 'Sikhs', differed 'very little from the Hindus'. Guru Gobind

Singh compiled the *Dasvīn Pātshāhī dā Granth* in 1696. Its greater portion was 'made up by court poets'. It was meant to instill a new spirit in the Khalsa. Trumpp's account of Guru Gobind Singh's battles is brief, and rather confused. He then refers to the removal of the Masands who had become 'a regular plague to the Sikhs'. After this, Guru Gobind Singh went to the Deccan where he virtually invited attack from a Pathan and subsequently died deliberately by bending a strong bow. He did not succeed in his objective of overthrowing the Mughals, but he contributed substantially to their downfall by creating 'a distinct nation of fanatical soldiers'.[13]

Trumpp's 'sketch' of the religion of the Sikhs starts with a general observation on the Sikh doctrines. Guru Nanak was not 'an independent thinker', and he did not deliberately start a new religious sect. He followed the Hindu philosophy of his day in all essential points, and he was particularly indebted to Kabir whose writings in the language of the people were accessible to the unlearned masses. The obligation which Guru Nanak and his successors owed to Kabir is acknowledged by the inclusion of his compositions in the Granth compiled by Guru Arjan. Guru Nanak's successors did not deviate from his doctrines. These doctrines were never called into question after the compilation of the Granth which was held sacred 'as an immediate divine revelation'. The innovations introduced by Guru Gobind Singh did not touch the doctrines so much as the practical course of life. If anything, Guru Gobind Singh 'relapsed in many points' again into Hinduism, being a special votary of Durga. Trumpp's sketch of the religion of Guru Nanak is based on the *Ādi Granth* as a whole.[14]

The chief point in Guru Nanak's doctrine, according to Trumpp, was the unity of the Supreme Being which had already been familiarized by the Hindu philosophical systems and the Bhagats like Kabir. Creation in Sikhism means 'the expansion of the same into a plurality of forms'. There is no teleological principle involved in this conception. There is a gross pantheism in the *Ādi Granth* which identifies all things with the Absolute. However, there is also a fine pantheism which makes a distinction between the Absolute and finite beings; it 'borders frequently on Theism'. The supreme in its essence is light which, though diffused into all creatures, remains distinct. Trumpp sees a contradiction between gross pantheism and the conception of the Supreme as a 'self conscious personality'. Though intellectual and moral qualities are attributed to this personality, Trumpp believed that logically there was no room for such qualities in the system of Guru Nanak.[15]

Emphasis on the unity of the Supreme Being did not mean that Guru Nanak forbade the worship of other gods. They became less important. Guru Nanak took over the whole Hindu pantheon and subordinated it to the Supreme. Only occasionally is idolatry ridiculed in the *Ādi Granth*. It would also be wrong to assume that Guru Nanak attempted to unite the Hindu and Muslim ideas about God. He remained 'a thorough Hindu'. If Muslims became his followers, it was essentially because Sūfism was nothing but pantheism derived from Hindu sources and only outwardly adapted to the forms of Islam. 'On these grounds tolerance between Hindus and Turks is often advocated in the Granth and intolerance on the part of the Turks rebuked'.[16]

As the light emanating from the Absolute, the human soul is immortal. The aim of human life is to be reabsorbed in the fountain of light from which the human soul emanated. What keeps the human beings bound to the cycle of death-and-rebirth, and therefore to perpetual misery, is the influence of 'the three qualities' (*guṇas*) and *māyā*. Only the soul purified from all earthly desires can be reabsorbed in the eternal light. Man cannot attain to liberation unless he is freed from the error of duality. Trumpp brackets Guru Nanak with the *bhaktas* and looks upon their conception of emancipation as a clear proof of the pantheistic character of Sikhism. They all conceived of emancipation in terms of 'total dissolution of individual existence by the reabsorption of the soul in the fountain of light'. This aim is no different from the Buddhist Nirban. It is the final proof of 'the pantheistic character of the tenets of the Sikh Gurus'.[17]

Guru Nanak announced that the name of Hari was the only means of final emancipation in the Kaliyuga. 'The name of Hari is the universal medicine for mankind; whoever mutters it, is saved in a moment'. The Sikh Gurus took good care to underline that the true Guru alone 'can bestow the right initiation and communicate the mantra of the name of Hari'. Renunciation, austerities, bathing at sacred places, and giving of alms were not denied to be meritorious acts; they were insufficient for gaining complete emancipation. Furthermore, emancipation is restricted to the elect who are chosen not according to their meritorious acts but according to the pleasure of Hari. Strict predetermination was mitigated by the contradictory idea that men have the free-will to come to the Guru. Neither Guru Nanak nor his successors give any proof of his being the true Guru. But the Guru is 'the only infallible guide' and the mediator between Hari and mankind'. Indeed, he is 'the very fulness of Hari himself'. The actual teaching imparted by the Guru for final emancipation was 'contained in a few meagre sentences'. There were only three injunctions: muttering the name of Hari, singing his praises, and getting rid of the 'I'. The pantheistic 'I am that, I am identical with the Supreme' is the culmination of the Guru's teaching. The possibility of obtaining emancipation was there 'whilst being yet in the body'.[18]

Sikhism was not a 'moralising Deism' for Trumpp. Nevertheless, he enumerates the moral duties enjoined upon the Sikhs: obedience to the Guru, service of the saints, remembering the name and giving alms and practising ablutions (*nām, dān, isnān*), abstaining from falsehood and slander, not coveting another's wife, purifying the heart from the five vices: lust, wrath, greediness, infatuation and egotism (*kām, krodh, lobh, moh* and *hankār*). Charity to animals is frequently inculcated in the *Ādi Granth* but only on pantheistic grounds. No sanctity is attached to the cow, but abstinence from animal food is inculcated. In due course, the Guru in Sikhism came to be identified with God. The abolition of Guruship by Guru Gobind Singh was good for a free and moral development of the Sikh community. The Sikhs did not become a narrow-minded sect of *faqīrs* and developed instead into a political commonwealth because of the sound principle of Guru Nanak that there was no need to abandon secular occupation for emancipation.[19]

The goal of emancipation was not confined to the higher castes; it was made accessible to all men, even to the *chandāls*. Guru Nanak received all men as his disciples without any regard to caste, recognizing the dignity of all human beings. However, he did not assail the institution of caste directly. It was left for Guru Gobind Singh to abolish caste altogether for his Khalsa. Though the teaching of the Brahmans and the authority of the Vedas and Purānas was often reproved, the dignity of the Brahmans as family priests was left untouched by Guru Nanak and his eight successors. It was left for Guru Gobind Singh to prohibit the employment of Brahmans in any capacity.[20]

It is important to underline that Trumpp's interpretation was not acceptable to all European writers. Frederic Pincott argued against 'the able translator of the Adi Granth' in a special article contributed to the *The Dictionary of Islam.* Trumpp's opinion that Sikhism had 'only an accidental relationship' with Islam was not acceptable to Pincott. In his view the religion of Guru Nanak was really intended as 'a compromise between Hinduism and Muhammandanism'. Pincott went so far as to speak of Sikhism as 'a religion of a Muhammandan sect'. What he wanted to emphasize was that the doctrines preached by the Sikh Gurus were 'distinctly Sufiistic'. The early Gurus assumed the manners and dress of *faqīrs*, 'thus plainly announcing their connection with the Sufiistic side of Muhammandanism'. Pincott tried to establish a close link between Sūfism and Sikhism on the basis of several other points.[21]

It must be pointed out that Pincott was not consistent in his interpretation of Guru Nanak's religion. He says at one place that Guru Nanak's intention was to do away with the differences between Islam and Hinduism 'by instituting a third course which should supersede both of them'.[22] He states elsewhere that Guru Nanak never openly seceded from the pale of Hinduism; in fact in some of the *sākhīs* it is explicitly stated that he was 'a Hindu'. However, he struck a heavy blow on Hinduism by his rejection of caste distinctions. The belief in metempsychosis, a necessary complement to pantheism, was essential to 'the creed of a Hindu, a Buddhist, and a Sufi'. In Sikhism, as in Buddhism, the prime object of attainment is the total cessation of individual existence. In moulding the thoughts of the founder of Sikhism, certain surviving relics of Buddhism had a share, notably the Sikh institution of the Sangat and the concept of Nirban. In Pincott's final analysis, Sikhism was 'based on Hinduism, modified by Buddhism, and stirred into new life by Sufism'. Guru Nanak succeeded in effecting 'a large amount of reconciliation' between Hinduism and Islam and left behind him 'a system designed to carry on the good work'. The later feud between Sikhs and Muslims was due to political causes and to 'a steady departure from the teachings of the Founder of Sikhism'.[23]

Pincott modified his view of Sikhism about fifteen years later. He placed Guru Nanak in his historical context more or less as J.D. Cunningham had done in his *History of the Sikhs*. According to Pincott, Guru Nanak clearly perceived the errors of his predecessors and boldly proclaimed the truth. His principles could be reduced to a single formula: 'the Unity of God and the Brotherhood of man'. There was only one God, not in the likeness of man like Rama, nor a creature of attributes and passions like the Allah of the Prophet, but one, sole, indivisble, self-existent, incomprehensible, timeless and all-pervading creator and sustainer of the phenomenal world. Guru Nanak's conception of God 'levelled all distinctions of creed and caste'. The great truth of the brotherhood of man swept away the barriers of caste, tribe and nation. There are echoes of Cunningham in Pincott's characterization of Sikhism. 'Nanak taught that all men are equal before God; that there is no high, no low, no dark, no fair, no privileged, no outcaste; all are equal both in race and in creed, in political rights and in religious aspirations'. Furthermore, the practical application of Guru Nanak's doctrines of God and man 'led to the formation of new nationality'. Accepting the essential originality of Guru Nanak's faith, Pincott now expresses the view that Hindu, Buddhist and Islamic ideas gave Sikhism only its subordinate or minor features.[24]

II

The most comprehensive work on the early Sikh tradition was produced by Max Arthur Macauliffe. His *Sikh Religion* covers nearly 2,500 pages. About half of these are given to the lives of the ten Gurus and all the 'Bhagats' whose compositions are included in the *Ādi Granth*. The space devoted to the compositions of the Gurus and the 'Bhagats' is more or less equal to the space given to their 'lives'. The first volume contains about eighty pages of 'preface' and 'introduction'. The rest of the volume is devoted to Guru Nanak. The third volume is devoted entirely to the life and compositions of Guru Arjan. The life and compositions of Guru Gobind Singh are given in the fifth volume. Among the Bhagats, the maximum space is given to the compositions of Kabir, followed at a great distance by Namdev and Farid. Macauliffe looks upon Shaikh Ibrahim, the Second Farid, as the author of these compositions.[25] Ravidas comes next, with more than twenty pages for his compositions. Most of the others get only five to one or even less than one page – Beni, Trilochan, Dhanna, Jaidev, Parmanand, Sadhna, Ramanand, Pipa, Sain, Bhikan, Sur Das and Mira.[26]

Macauliffe used a much larger number and volume of source materials than any of his predecessors. It is quite remarkable that the bulk of Macauliffe's evidence consists of original sources. Much of this original evidence comes from Sikh sources : the *Ādi Granth*, the *Dasam Granth*, the works of Bhai Gurdas, the *Janamsākhīs*, the *Gurbilāses* and the works of Bhai Santokh Singh. From amongst his Sikh contemporaries Macauliffe used the works of Giani Gian Singh and Bhai Kanh Singh of Nabha, among others. He also used the well known Persian works like the *Dabistān-i Mazāhib*, the *Khulāsat ut-Tawārīkh* and the *Siyar al-Mutākhirīn*, apart from the works translated by Elliot and Dowson in the *History of India*. Macauliffe relied very little on his predecessors.[27]

Macauliffe's work was meant to replace Trumpp's which in his view was 'highly inaccurate and unidiomatic' and which gave 'mortal offence' to the Sikhs because of the German missionary's *odium theologicum.* 'Whenever he saw an opportunity of defaming the Gurus, the sacred book, and the religion of the Sikhs, he eagerly availed himself of it'. Macauliffe wanted to give a simple and accurate translation. Above all, he wanted to give a translation which should be acceptable to the Sikhs. Therefore he submitted every line of his translation to 'the most searching criticism' of learned Sikhs. He was also convinced that the language of the *Ādi Granth* was exceptionally difficult to master for a single scholar. For this reason too he took help from Sikh scholars. Among them were eminent Sikh writers like Bhai Kanh Singh of Nabha, Giani Hazara Singh of Amritsar and Bhai Ditt Singh of Lahore.[28]

Like Trumpp, Macauliffe wanted to avoid repetition in his translation but on an altogether different argument. The Gurus used to address the crowds who clustered around them and repetitions served to impress on them the instruction meant to be conveyed. In a printed work, on the contrary, repetition was not so necessary. Consequently, Macauliffe's work does not contain translation of the entire *Ādi Granth.* He felt, in fact, that 'orthodox' Sikhs did not like the *Ādi Granth* to be translated into another language 'in the order of the original' because of their fear that the respect which was due to the Guru Granth would not be accorded to the translated work. Therefore, he could intersperse many of the sacred hymns in 'the lives of the Gurus'.[29] The number of such hymns in his work is quite considerable indeed.

Macauliffe's understanding of Sikhism was different from Trumpp's. Whereas for Trumpp the inclusion of the compositions of the 'Bhagats' in the *Ādi Granth* was one of the proofs that there was no difference between them and the Gurus, Macauliffe puts forth the view that Guru Arjan included their compositions in the *Ādi Granth* to indicate 'the historical development of the Sikh reformation'.[30] In other words, 'the last great religion of the world' was not an extension of but a further improvement upon what was done by others. The Gurus spoke to the people in their own language, and not in Sanskrit which was deemed to be 'the language of the gods' in Hinduism. Carefully preserved from the very beginning, the sacred hymns of the Gurus were the most authentic records in the world. The religion they embodied was totally unaffected by Semitic or Christian influence. Based on the unity of God, Sikhism rejected Hindu formularies and adopted an independent ethical system, ritual, and standards which were totally opposed to the theological beliefs of Guru Nanak's age and country. Macauliffe was convinced that the *Ādi Granth* embodied all the elements of a new religion. Indeed, 'it would be difficult to point to a religion of greater originality or to a more comprehensive ethical system'.[31]

Religion in India received its 'monotheistic consummation' from Guru Nanak. The idea of one God was known since the Rigveda. Guru Nanak gave 'expansion' to this idea. The conception of God can be anthropomorphic, pantheistic or theistic. Logically, however, it is difficult to dissociate one from the other. In the writings of Guru Nanak 'Pantheism' is distinctly implied in some passages, and in other passages 'matter is made distinct from the Creator' as an emanation from Him. Macauliffe suggests that anthropomorphic theism which belongs strictly to 'religion' and pantheism which belongs strictly to 'philosophy' are inextricably blended by all sacred and profane writers. It was not a peculiarity of Guru Nanak, or even of the Indian writers. We cannot help feeling that Macauliffe is trying here to correct the view presented by Trumpp. In his discussion of Nirban too, Macauliffe appears to be improving upon Trumpp's view. Nirban and Sach Khand were practically the same, suggestive of the union of the human soul (*jīvātmā*) with the Supreme (*Parmātmā*), like light blending with light or water blending with water. Nirban could be attained through meditation and conforming one's life to the teachings of the Guru. Only those who are sufficiently purified can be absorbed in the Absolute, or 'the all-dazzling fount of God's infinite perfection and love'.[32]

Unlike Trumpp, Macauliffe saw many 'moral and political' merits in the Sikh religion. It prohibited idolatry, hypocrisy, caste exclusiveness, the concremation of widows, the immurement of women, the use of wine and other intoxicants, tabacco-smoking, infanticide, slander, pilgrimages to the sacred rivers and tanks of the Hindus; it inculcated loyalty, gratitude for all favours received, philanthropy, justice, impartiality, truth, honesty, and 'all the moral and domestic virtues known to the holiest citizens of any country'.[33] Macauliffe differed with Trumpp on the bearing of the teachings of the Gurus on moral life as well as the nature and character of Sikhism, its relationship with Hinduism, the conception of God in Sikhism, and the Sikh idea of emancipation. Far from looking at Sikhism as a form of Hinduism, Macauliffe wanted to see the comparatively young religion to escape the deadly embrace of Hinduism. He was opposed to the idea of the Sikhs being declared to be Hindus because this idea was in direct opposition to the teachings of the Gurus.[34]

Initially, Macauliffe had thought only of translating the *Ādi Granth*. After the work on translation was over, he found it 'absolutely necessary' to give an account of the Sikh Gurus, and of the saints whose compositions were included in the *Ādi Granth* even for a correct interpretation of their writings. The current accounts of the Gurus were overladen with 'puerile, heterodox, or repulsive details' which were 'inconsistent with their sacred writings'. This was no less true of Bhai Santokh Singh's works than of the current *Janamsākhīs*. However, Macauliffe's idea was to accommodate the 'orthodox' Sikh point of view. Even miracles find a place in his narratives. Just as in his interpretation of the Sikh faith his aim was to omit 'the debased superstitions and heterodox social customs of Sikhs who have been led astray from their faith by external influences', his aim in narrating the lives of the Gurus was to omit whatever was inconsistent with their true teachings.[35]

Macauliffe tried to work out a compromise between his own critical assessment and the Sikh attitude towards the sources for the life of Guru Nanak. The oldest authentic account was written by Bhai Gurdas not much more than sixty years after the demise of Guru Nanak. The detail given in his first *Vār* could therefore be utilized rather unreservedly. Bhai Mani Singh expanded this *Vār* in his *Gyān Ratnāvalī*. After his death, however, the copyists 'interlarded several Hindu ideas in his works. Tinctured with Hinduism from his early education and environment, Bhai Santokh Singh 'invented' several stories discreditable to the Gurus and their religion. 'His statements accordingly cannot often be accepted as even an approach to history'.[36]

The *Janamsākhīs*, which profess to be biographies of Guru Nanak, were written at different times after his death and they give 'very different and contradictory details of his life'. All of them record 'miraculous acts and supernatural conversations'. They show the extent to which 'pious fiction' can fabricate details of the lives of religious teachers in all ages and countries. One of the most popular *Janamsākhīs* was lithographed at Lahore as a large volume of 588 folio pages. Its editor claimed to have worked hard for collecting and collating materials for this compilation which, he claimed, could not have been produced by anyone else. It was apparently based on Bhai Santokh Singh's *Nanak Prakāsh*.

Attributed to Bhai Bala, it was said to have been dictated to Paiṛa by Guru Angad's order. But its language was not old, and no manuscript copy of the original was available. In fact Bala was not even mentioned by Bhai Gurdas, or Bhai Mani Singh in his *Bhagat Ratnāvalī*. The *Janamsākhī* was professedly written in 1535 or even in 1525. Macauliffe does not say so, but the implication is clear enough. This *Janamsākhī* was not what it claimed to be.[37]

Macauliffe explains 'the falsification of old, or the composition of new Janamsakhis' in terms of 'schisms' in the religion of Guru Nanak. The life of Guru Nanak written by an Udāsī, Anand Ghan, presents Sri Chand as an incarnation of God and the only true successor of Guru Nanak. Miharban wrote a *Janamsākhī* of Guru Nanak to glorify his own father, Prithi Chand, the eldest son of Guru Ram Das. Bhai Bala finds a place in this *Janamsākhī* for the first time. Bidhi Chand compiled a Granth and a *Janamsākhī* to exalt his father Handal and to degrade Guru Nanak by introducing fictitious narratives. Favoured by the Mughal administrators of the province, the Handālīs apparently had sufficient influence to destroy nearly all older accounts of the life of Guru Nanak. The Mughal administrators on their own destroyed Sikh manuscripts in the process of persecuting the Sikhs.[38]

Of all the known *Janamsākhīs,* Macauliffe placed the greatest reliance on the one written by Sewa Das in 1588. Its language was that of Pothohar and its characters were unmistakably older than that of any other known work in Gurmukhi. It mentioned Mardana but not Bhai Bala. It was not free from 'mythological matter' but it was much more 'rational, consistent, and satisfactory' than any other narrative of Guru Nanak's life. It was beyond dispute 'the most trustworthy' record in existence. Macauliffe proposed to make 'this ancient Janamsakhi' the basis of his own account of the life of Guru Nanak. It could be supplemented, when necessary, by 'cullings' from the later accounts of Guru Nanak's life. Though conscious of the idea that the *Janamsākhīs* provided settings for the compositions of Guru Nanak, Macauliffe himself makes ample use of his verses. Though he gives preference to early writings, he supplements his narrative by later materials. He does not entirely excise even the supernatural elements. But he keeps out elements which appeared to contradict Guru Nanak's teachings. His account of Guru Nanak becomes a sanitized *Janamsākhī*.[39]

For the life of Guru Gobind Singh, the main authorities mentioned by Macauliffe are the *Bachittar Nātak*, Bhai Sukha Singh's *Gurbilās* and Bhai Santokh Singh's *Sūraj Parkāsh*. He rejects the *Sau Sākhī* as unauthentic, and finds Giani Gian Singh's *Panth Prakāsh* rather useful. He uses Bhai Nand Lal's *Zindgī Nāma* and his *Dīwān* also for his account. He quotes at length from the *Zafarnāma*. He refers to the letter of Guru Gobind Singh addressed to Tilok Singh and Ram Singh, and to Khafi Khan's work, probably on the basis of Elliot and Dowson's *History of India*. Several compositions of Guru Gobind Singh (other than the *Bachittar Nātak* and the *Zafarnāma*) are also used by Macauliffe. There is no doubt that he was the first European writer to use all this evidence for an account of Guru Gobind Singh.[40]

Macauliffe's attitude towards his sources is quite interesting. He was not uncritical but he tended to select evidence in support of what he regarded as the orthodox position. The Khalsa had no regard for *pīrs* and miracle-workers, whether Hindu or Musalman. Guru Gobind Singh inaugurated 'a new system' and the world was astonished on seeing 'a third religion'. The *Krishan Avtār* was not a work of Guru Gobind Singh but of a bard named Shyam. Macauliffe refers to the report of a newswriter on the institution of the Khalsa, quoted by Ghulam Muhiyuddin, in which Guru Gobind Singh invites members of all the four castes to accept baptism of the sword and to discard the worship of Hindu deities in favour of the path shown by Guru Nanak and his successors.[41]

Macauliffe's account of the invocation of the Goddess by Guru Gobind Singh is not based on Sukha Singh or Santokh Singh but on Giani Gian Singh's *Panth Prakāsh*. In this account it is emphasized that Guru Gobind Singh did not adore any gods or goddesses. He agreed to invoke the Goddess to expose the Brahmans. The people erroneously believed that the Goddess had appeared because Guru Gobind Singh had ordered all the materials to be thrown into the fire and, consequently, a great flame shot up towards the heavens. There is enough of evidence in the *Akāl Ustat*, *Bachittar Nātak*, *Thirty-Three Sawaiyās*, and the *Chandī*

Charitar to prove that he was no worshipper of gods and goddesses. Macauliffe argues that Bhagauti in the writings of Guru Gobind Singh meant the sword and not the Goddess. The sword was further equated with God because the sword, like God, subdued enemies. Guru Gobind Singh used Sanskrit literature for translation in order to inspire bravery and valour: 'he rendered in the vulgar dialect the tenth chapter of the Bhagwat with no other object than to inspire ardour for religious warfare'. Macauliffe accepts Bhai Ditt Singh's view that these translations could at the same time demonstrate that Hindu sacred writings were inferior to the compositions of the Gurus.[42] Enunciation of the *rahit* continued after the institution of the Khalsa. On one such occasion Guru Gobind Singh told his Sikhs not to associate with those who worshipped Sakhi Sarwar, Gugga, or any other *pīr.* Guru Gobind Singh instructed Banda in the tenets of his religion and baptized him according to the new rite. Though he continued to be known as Banda he had been given the name Gurbakhsh Singh. Macauliffe relates the incident in which Guru Gobind Singh 'departed bodily to heaven'. Probably the contemporary Sikhs had no objection to this idea.[43]

Macauliffe's references to the *Ādi Granth* appear to reflect the orthodox Sikh position. Guru Gobind Singh dictated the Granth Sahib to Bhai Mani Singh at Talwandi Sabo, adding for the first time the hymns and *shaloks* of Guru Tegh Bahadur, and his own *shalok*. There were two other recensions of the Granth Sahib, one written by Bhai Gurdas and the other associated with Bhai Banno. The former was still at Kartarpur in the Jalandhar district and the latter was at Mangat in the district of Gujrat. However, the recension prepared under the superintendence of Guru Gobind Singh, which was the most complete, was destroyed or taken away as booty by Ahmad Shah Durrani when he despoiled the Golden Temple.[44] Presumably, this was the recension that Guru Gobind Singh had opened just before his death, placed five paise and a coconut before it, and solemnly bowed to it as his successor. He then circumambulated the sacred volume and said: 'O beloved Khalsa, let him who desireth to behold me, behold the Guru Granth. Obey the Granth Sahib. It is the visible body of the Guru. And let him who desireth to meet me diligently search its hymns'. At the same time, Guru Gobind Singh told the Khalsa that 'the Guru shall be the Khalsa and the Khalsa the Guru'. The mental and bodily spirit of the Guru was thus infused into 'the Granth Sahib and the Khalsa'.[45]

Macauliffe was aware that the authenticity of the *Dasam Granth* was being debated by the contemporary Sikhs. In his view it was compiled by Bhai Mani Singh in 1734 from 'various materials'. Macauliffe's references to its contents indicate that he accepted the authenticity of the *Jāp*, the *Bachittar Nātak*, the *Zafarnāma*, the *Akāl Ustat*, and the *Thirty-Three Sawaiyās*, but he was not sure about the translations from Sanskrit works. Selections from the *Dasam Granth* for translation show that, apart from the works mentioned above, he looked upon the following compositions as authentic : the *Gyān Prabodh*, remarks on the *Rām Avtār*, *Krishan Avtār* and *Parasnath Avtār*, the *Hazāre Shabad* and the *Benatī Chaupaī*. All these compositions are believed by Macauliffe 'to represent the Guru's own opinions and acts'. There were 'many defects of arrangement' in the *Dasam Granth*. An early Sikh view was that the Persian tales (*Hikāyāt*) and the stories illustrating the deceit of women (*Triā Charitar*) should not have been included in the Granth.[46]

Macauliffe includes post-eventum prophecies in his narrative without showing any scepticism. The Sikhs believed in those prophecies, and it suited his purposes as well. Guru Gobind Singh gave a written acknowledgement of debt to a Pathan, telling him that his Sikhs would pay this debt when they would come into power thirty years after his death. 'The debt was duly discharged by the Sikhs under happier and more prosperous circumstances'. Sikh rule in the future was implied also in Guru Gobind Singh's acknowledgements of 'the spiritual benefactions of the founder of his religion': 'Guru Gobind Singh obtained from Guru Nanak hospitality, the sword, victory and prompt assistance'. More suitable from Macauliffe's viewpoint were prophecies in which advent of the British was forecast. Guru Tegh Bahadur had alluded to this in Delhi before his martyrdom. Conversation could turn to this subject in the time of Guru Gobind Singh who tells his Sikhs that the English would defeat the Sikhs in hard fought battles when 'the

Sikhs become entangled in the love of mammon', become self-seekers, unjust and corrupt, abandon the Guru's hymns to follow Shāstras and the religion of the Brahmans, and when the Sikh rulers allow their states to be governed by 'evil influences'.[47] Such prophecies could be of advantage to the colonial state. Another prophecy of Guru Gobind Singh is to the effect that, after the arrival of the English, 'in every house there shall be wealth, in every house religion, in every house learning, and in every house happiness'. Macauliffe quotes a Sikh writer who underlines the loyalty of the Sikhs to their rulers even more than their unmatched bravery in the world. Macauliffe has no hesitation in supporting the British policy of baptizing the Sikh recruits according to the rite prescribed by Guru Gobind Singh in spite of the professed civil policy of 'religious neutrality'. Punjabi could be recognized as an official or optional official language of the Punjab as 'a most powerful means of preserving the Sikh religion'.[48]

Macauliffe mentions several other objectives of his study. Of particular interest is his idea that Sikh studies could throw light on 'the state of society in the Middle Ages'. Sikh studies could be useful also to the student of 'comparative theology'. The administrators could formulate correct policies on the basis of a better understanding of the Sikhs. Above all, a knowledge of the excellence of their religion throughout the world could be of 'political advantage' to the Sikhs. Thus, Macauliffe's work could serve practical as well as academic purposes, to the advantage of both the rulers and the ruled.[49]

Macauliffe's work found ready acceptance among Sikh scholars and Sikh organizations. A Giani of the Golden Temple and two other eminent Bhāīs wrote that his translation conformed to the religious tencts of the Sikhs. The editor of the *The Khalsa* expected his work to introduce 'a new era' in Sikh history. The 'traitors' to the Panth would not be able to misrepresent the Sikh tradition in order to please their 'wealthier and more influential neighbours'. This oblique reference to the Sikh supporters of Hindu identity in the Hindu-Sikh controversy indicates that the editor was a supporter of an independent Sikh identity. The Singh Sabha of Amritsar felt gratified that Macauliffe's work would fulfil the great need of 'an accurate version' of the Sikh scripture, especially because Trumpp's translation was not only generally incorrect but also 'injurious to our religion'.[50] Macauliffe's anxiety to present an orthodox version of the Sikh tradition is understandable in this context. It is also understandable why many a Sikh scholar has been appreciative of Macauliffe and rather indifferent or hostile to Trumpp.

Macauliffe's work displaced Trumpp's for the non-Sikh scholars as well. The tone was set by Dorothy Field soon after the publication of the *Sikh Religion*. A reading of the hymns of Guru Nanak and his successors in Macauliffe's work convinced her that 'Sikhism should be regarded as a new and separate world religion' and not a reformed sect of the Hindus. Guru Nanak was critical of the three cardinal principles of Hinduism: the Vedas, the caste system, and priesthood. One could talk of borrowings from Hinduism and influences of Islam, but 'his religion remains distinct and complete in itself'. It was in no way 'dependent' on Hinduism.[51] Despite some contradictory ideas in Dorothy Field's presentation of Sikhism, she remains close to Macauliffe.[52]

III

With the exception of Lepel Griffin, the administrators and army officers of the colonial period used published works for their books on the Sikhs. The use even of these secondary sources was not thorough. For most of them, Malcolm first and then Trumpp provided ready information and ideas. A few of them in the early twentieth century relied partly on Cunningham and Macauliffe. They were interested primarily in the contemporary problems of politics, government and administration, both civil and military. They tended to justify British rule in the Punjab as much as its annexation, praising all administrative measures and underlining peace and prosperity. In this situation, it was not possible for them to take any serious interest in Sikh politics of the past, and far less in Sikh achievement. Their interest in the early Sikh tradition was marginal. Their general attitude towards the Sikhs was anything but sympathetic. They had little appreciation for the Sikh tradition.

Ernest Trumpp brought the *Ādi Granth* and the *Janamsākhīs* to the centre of Sikh studies. He gave great importance to the earliest known *Janamsākhī*, the Colebrooke manuscript, and suggested that this was the original work to which myths and miracles were added later on a much larger scale. He was highly sceptical about the use of *Janamsākhī* materials for the historical life of Guru Nanak. For the lives of Guru Nanak's successors he used sources like the *Bachittar Nātak* and the *Sakhi Book*, in addition to the *Dabistān-i Mazāhib*, the *Siyar al-Mutākhirīn* and Shardha Ram Philauri's *Sikhān de Rāj dī Vithiā*. Trumpp's comments on certain developments in the Sikh Panth indicate that he saw a movement towards politicization. He looked upon the objectives of Guru Gobind Singh as clearly political. Trumpp accepted the current view that Guru Gobind Singh invoked the Goddess for instituting the Khalsa, and the view that he promulgated an elaborate *rahit*, including the 5 Ks; he abolished all distinctions of caste and dispensed with all services performed by the Brahmans; he removed the Masands; and he got Sanskrit works translated to be incorporated in the *Dasam Granth* in 1696 to serve as a source of martial inspiration.

In Trumpp's view, all these changes had nothing to do with the doctrines of Guru Nanak. His successors had made no change in the doctrines, and there was little scope for innovation after the compilation of the Granth by Guru Arjan. Guru Nanak was indebted to Hindu philosophy for all his important doctrines. For theistic ideas he was especially indebted to Kabir. Guru Nanak's insistence on the unity of God, thus, was not a new thing. He did not discard the gods of Hindu pantheon; he only made them subordinate to the Supreme Being. Guru Nanak was soft on idolatry. In his essentially pantheistic system, there was no teleological principle. Emancipation conceived as Buddhistic Nirban was a further proof of pantheism. There was no room for ethical life in this system. The attainment of Nirban did not affect one's attitude towards moral life. Guru Nanak, like the other reformers, adopted new means for attaining the old goal. It was little more than muttering the name of God and singing his praises. Traditional acts of piety were not discarded; they were looked upon as insufficient for emancipation. The Guru became indispensable; he demanded complete surrender;

and prayers were offered to him. Abolition of Guruship, largely explained the emergence of the Sikhs into 'a nation'. Sikhism strictly was neither theistic nor ethical. That was why it was wrong to see it as 'moralizing Deism'. Guru Nanak discarded neither the Hindu scriptures, nor the caste system, nor the Brahmanical priesthood. In short, Trumpp bracketed Guru Nanak not only with the medieval reformers but also with the Hindu thinkers in general.

Trumpp's interpretation of Sikhism found little acceptance among scholars. Pincott insisted that Guru Nanak's system was clearly theistic, and the gods of Hindu pantheon were virtually non-entities in the governance of the universe. The influence of Islam, especially of Sūfism, accounted for Guru Nanak's uncompromising theism. He gave a serious blow to Hinduism by discarding caste. His egalitarian conception of God led to the ideal of brotherhood of man. Despite plausible borrowings from Hinduism, Buddhism and Islam, the system of Guru Nanak was essentially original. The ideology of Sikhism had serious social and political implications.

Macauliffe widened the scope of the study of the early Sikh tradition on the basis of original sources, especially Sikh sources. That he was quite critical of the sources is evident from his rejection of certain sources as unauthentic, his analysis of the *Janamsākhīs*, particularly his view that their composers looked for appropriate settings for the verses of Guru Nanak, and his analysis of the *Dasam Granth*. However, in his own narratives he not only used these verses but also included post-eventum prophecies and a few supernatural elements. He tried to find a middle ground between his own critical assessment and the 'orthodox' Sikh views. In actual practice, therefore, he proved to be far less critical than Trumpp.

Macauliffe thought of his work as useful for comparative study of society and theology, for formulating correct state policies, and for promoting Sikh interests. He was particularly keen not to offend Sikh susceptibilities. By and large his work can be seen as reflecting the views and attitudes of the Sikh scholars of his day who were generally associated with the Singh Sabha Movement. This can be seen in his opposition to Trumpp, his view of Sikhism as a totally independent world religion, his support for distinct

Sikh identity, his advocacy of Punjabi as the official language of the province, his rejection of the current belief that Guru Gobind Singh invoked the Goddess for instituting the Khalsa, his view that Guru Gobind Singh was opposed to the worship of gods and goddesses, demons, spirits, *pīrs* and cemeteries, and his view that Guru Gobind Singh vested Guruship in the Granth and the Panth. Like the contemporary Sikh scholars of the Singh Sabha Movement, he believed that there were three recensions of the *Ādi Granth* which could be regarded as authentic: the one prepared by Guru Arjan which was at Kartarpur, the Banno recension which was with his descendants at Mangat, and the Damdami recension which was actually lost but its copies were current. That appears to be the reason why he included Mira Bai among the 'Bhagats' of the *Ādi Granth*. Macauliffe was more acceptable to Sikh and non-Sikh scholars not merely because he was 'orthodox'. His translation appeared to be close to the original and his interpretation of the Sikh tradition appeared to be faithful to the sources he used.

NOTES

1. Grewal (1992), pp. 16-20.
2. Griffin (1957).
3. Trumpp (1989), pp. v-vii.
4. Ibid., p. vii.
5. Grewal (1995), and Grewal (1992), pp. 21-27.
6. Trumpp (1989), xcvii.
7. Ibid., pp. i-vii.
8. Ibid., pp. vii-lxxvii.
9. Trumpp's preference for the Colebrooke *Janamsākhī* made it important for Sikh studies. *Abstracts of Sikh Studies* (Oct-Dec 1996), pp. 55-60.
10. Trumpp (1989), pp. lxxvii-lxxx.
11. Ibid., pp. lxxx-lxxxii.
12. Ibid., pp. lxxxii-lxxxix.
13. Ibid., pp. lxxxix-xcvi.
14. Ibid., p. xcvii.
15. Ibid., pp. xcvii-ci.
16. Ibid., pp. ci-cii.
17. Ibid., pp. cii-cvi.

18. Ibid., pp. cviii-cxi.
19. Ibid., pp. cix-cxi.
20. Ibid., pp. cxi-cxii.
21. *Dictionary of Islam*, pp. 583 and 584-87.
22. Ibid., p. 594.
23. Ibid., pp. 586, 588, 589-90 and 590-91.
24. *The Sikh Religion: A Symposium*, pp. 70-83.
25. Macauliffe's view of the authorship is not acceptable any more to a large number of scholars who have argued that Shaikh Farid, and not Shaikh Ibrahim, was the author.
26. Macauliffe himself says that Mira's hymn was included in the Banno recension but not in the Granth prepared by Guru Arjan: Macauliffe (1995), VI, p. 342. Presumably, he accepted both the recensions as equally authentic.
27. Macauliffe refers only twice each to the works of Wilson and Trumpp, and only once each to the works of Malcolm and Cunningham: Ibid., I, pp. xv and 82 n 3; IV, p. 21 n 1; V, p. 35 n; VI, pp. 104 n 3 and 140 n 1.
28. Ibid., I, pp. vii, ix and xxix-xxx.
29. Ibid., I, pp. xvii-xviii.
30. Ibid., I, p. xxxii.
31. Ibid., I, pp. xl-xlix, lii-lv and p. l. Macauliffe quotes from the *Vārs* of Bhai Gurdas to show that in his view the Sikh religion was 'distinct, and superior to other religions': Ibid., IV, pp. 241-74.
32. Ibid., I, pp. lviii-lxix.
33. Ibid., I, p. xxiii.
34. Ibid., I, pp. xxiii and lvii.
35. Ibid., I, pp. ix, xiv-xvii.
36. Ibid., I, pp. lxxiii-lxxvii.
37. Ibid., I, pp. lxxvii-lxxviii.
38. Ibid., I, pp. lxxix-lxxxvi.
39. Ibid., I, pp. lxxxvi-lxxxvii.
40. Ibid., V, pp. 1, 103-14, 201-06, 224 n 1 and 254.
41. Ibid., V, pp. 22 and n 1, 93-94, 97 and 241.
42. Ibid., V, pp. 60-65 and 67-84.
43. Ibid., V, pp. 62, 122, 458-59, 238 and 245.
44. Ibid., V, p. 223.
45. Ibid., V, p. 244. Macauliffe tended to accept the *Prān Sangalī* as authentic, though it was not included in the *Ādi Granth*: Ibid., I, p. 156; III, pp. 53-55 and n 1. The *Rāgmālā* was regarded as a part of the *Madhava Nal Sangīt* written in 1583 by a Muslim poet named Alim. But the list of *Rāgs* and *Rāginīs* and their subdivisions given by Alim do not correspond with the *Rāgs* of the Granth Sahib: Ibid., III, pp. 64-65.
46. Ibid., I, pp. li-lii; V, p. 223 and n 1, pp. 260-61 and n 1.

47. Ibid., V, pp. 107, 240 and 245 n l.
48. Ibid., I, pp. vii-viii, xxiv, xxv and 18-20.
49. Ibid., I, pp. vii and x-xxiii.
50. Ibid., I, pp. x-xiv.
51. Field (1914), pp. 10, 36 and 42.
52. Grewal (1992), pp. 34-36.

3. Sikh Entry into Sikh Studies

By the beginning of the twentieth century educated Sikhs had begun to respond to the 'Orientalist' interpretations of the Sikh tradition. They had good knowledge of the Sikh sources, and they were not uncritical in their attitude towards them. But they were sympathetic to the Sikh tradition. In fact, their faith served as a source of inspiration for their scholarship. However, they did not address themselves to the Sikhs alone. They turned a European dialogue in Sikh studies into a Western-Sikh dialogue.

I

The first major Sikh writer to appear on the scene was Sewa Ram Singh. His *Critical Study of the Life and Teachings of Sri Guru Nanak Dev, the Founder of Sikhism* was published in 1904. As he says in the 'preface', this work needed no apology. Western writers had begun to see that Sikhism had made remarkable progress in a relatively short time, and the Sikhs had established a powerful state. In other words, the Sikh tradition had become a respectable subject of study. However, the European writers like John Malcolm, W. L. M'Gregor and J.D. Cunningham had concentrated more on the political history of the Sikhs than on the earlier Sikh tradition. Their work did not clarify issues related to the early tradition. Indeed, there was 'good deal of misunderstanding regarding the origin and development of the Khalsa Church'. Sewa Ram Singh was keen to clarify issues related to the early Sikh tradition, starting with Guru Nanak. [1]

Sewa Ram Singh was aware of the difficulties involved. The

original sources for the life and work of Guru Nanak were 'chaotic and misleading'. The authenticity of the *Janamsākhīs* had been seriously questioned. Their evidence could not be accepted in its entirety or on its face value. 'Many of them are full of mythological descriptions and fictitious tales'. None of the different versions of the *Bhāī Bālā Janamsākhī* appeared to be 'quite authentic'. The Colebrooke manuscript un-earthed by Trumpp was free from many later 'inventions', but could not be treated as 'perfectly correct'. This 'huddle muddle sort of material' obliged Sewa Ram Singh to be 'very cautious' in using evidence of the *Janamsākhīs*.[2]

It is not without significance that Sewa Ram Singh's book was well received. Sikhs and Europeans alike wrote appreciative letters to him. Maharaja Hira Singh of Nabha sent a robe of honour (*khil'at*) for him. The book was sold out in a few years. There was a great demand for literature on Sikhism in English in the late 1920s, and the Chief Khalsa Diwan wanted to reprint Sewa Ram Singh's book. However, more materials had become available to him, and Bhai Vir Singh had written extensively in Punjabi. Aware of all these developments, Sewa Ram Singh, now a District and Sessions Judge, decided to take leave from his duties to revise his work. The revised version became virtually a new book. He published it in 1930 as *The Divine Master: Life and Teachings of Guru Nanak*.[3] It has been reprinted on the assumption that the author raised 'certain crucial issues' which have continued to engage the attention of scholars.[4]

Sewa Ram Singh's *Divine Master* is quite remarkable for its use of Sikh literature. He tried to use three *Janamsākhī* traditions: Bhai Bala, Bhai Mani Singh and Colebrooke (also called 'Hafizabad' or 'Walaitwali'). In addition to these he used the work of Bhai Santokh Singh and Giani Gian Singh, and the compositions of Guru Nanak and Bhai Gurdas. Besides the Baghdad inscription, he used personal observation at some places. For the teachings of Guru Nanak, understandably, he used his compositions. At the same time, he took the work of his European predecessors quite seriously, but not uncritically.

At a few places, Sewa Ram Singh takes his readers into confidence about the way he treated his evidence. For example, one

Janamsākhī gave the middle of April as the date of Guru Nanak's birth but the November date was observed by the Sikhs everywhere as the date of Guru Nanak's birth. Therefore, Sewa Ram Singh rejects the *Janamsākhī* evidence.[5] He rejects the view projected by the late *Janamsākhīs* and Bhai Santokh Singh that Bhai Bala accompanied Guru Nanak on his travels. Bhai Santokh Singh himself looks upon the *Bālā Janamsākhī* as full of interpolations introduced by the Handālīs, including the story of Bala, but he appears to accept it. More crucial for rejecting Bala as a companion of Guru Nanak on his travels was the silence of the earliest known sources on the point: the *Vārs* of Bhai Gurdas and the Colebrooke *Janamsākhī.*[6]

Sewa Ram Singh refers to the oldest *Janamsākhī* mentioning Sajjan's meeting with Guru Nanak in the southern Punjab before his first travel, while Bhai Santokh Singh specifically mentions Tulamba and places the incident after the four principal travels of Guru Nanak. Sewa Ram Singh does not decide in favour of one view or the other about the time of the incident, but he does point out that this evidence showed the kind of people Guru Nanak met and redeemed.[7] In spite of the statements of Bhai Mani Singh and Bhai Santokh Singh on the point, Sewa Ram Singh rejects the idea that Guru Nanak met any Sultan named Karun, either in Turkey, or Egypt, or Sudan or Arabia, because no such Sultan finds mention in authentic histories of these countries. The *Nasīhatnāma*, said to have been addressed by Guru Nanak to Karun, is not included in the *Granth Sahib*; its language and sentiments do not inspire any confidence in its authenticity. Therefore, the *Nasīhatnāma* is also rejected.[8] Guru Nanak's visit to Mecca is accepted, but the *Makke dī Gosht* is suspect because all the verses it contained are not included in the *Ādi Granth.*[9] The visit to Baghdad is accepted on the basis of the Baghdad inscription.[10] Guru Nanak's meeting with Sultan Ibrahim Lodhi in Delhi is accepted on the basis of the Colebrooke *Janamsākhī*.[11] It must be pointed out that Sewa Ram Singh's references to the *Bālā Janamsākhī*, though the most numerous, are less than a score in the whole work.

The chronology of Guru Nanak's travels presented a great difficulty to Sewa Ram Singh. The *Janamsākhīs* give 'disconnected and mixed description'. The earliest authentic account, the first *Vār* of Bhai Gurdas, is 'meagre and scrappy' and lacks chronological exactness. The chronology given in the Colebrooke *Janamsākhī* cannot be accepted in its entirety. Its author had not paid that regard to the sequence of events 'which one would expect from a modern historian'. The later writers like Bhai Santokh Singh and Giani Gian Singh tried 'to formulate a connected account' but they seem to have drawn on conjecture and given no information about their sources, and no reasons for their formulation.[12] Sewa Ram Singh came to the conclusion that only the incidents recorded in the earliest sources and supported by Guru Nanak's compositions in the Granth Sahib could be accepted as authentic. Allusions to contemporary events could be helpful in assigning dates to some of the incidents of his life. External evidence could be used for fixing the dates of some events. There was some scope for surmise based on 'geographical position' of the places visited. Sewa Ram Singh held the view that the most important evidence for the incidents of Guru Nanak's life was provided by his own words. Nevertheless, though one could be almost certain about incidents, one could not be so sure about their sequence.[13]

We find a large number of references to the *Ādi Granth* in Sewa Ram Singh's work. Indeed, such references are far more numerous than all the other references put together. At several places he uses the evidence of Bhai Gurdas, and at a few places he refers to Bhai Banno's *Bīṛ*. Occasionally, he is wrong in attributing verses to Guru Nanak, or Guru Gobind Singh. At a few places he refers to verses which are not included in the *Ādi Granth*. By and large, however, he makes use of the authentic compositions of Guru Nanak, giving his own translation in English.[14]

The outline of Guru Nanak's life that emerges from Sewa Ram Singh's treatment of his sources is clear and plausible. He may appear to have met the challenge implicit in Trumpp's *Ādi Granth* that a biography of Guru Nanak could not be written on the basis of the existing materials. However, the relative clarity and plausibility of this biography of Guru Nanak is gained by compromising a few known principles of historical research. First of all, the dates given by Sewa Ram Singh do not come from his sources in most cases and he does not advance any reasons for giving these dates. Secondly, he simply takes for granted that the compositions of Guru Nanak were his response to the situations in which he places them. This assimilates his biography actually to the *Janamsākhīs*, with the only difference that he uses the compositions of the *Ādi Granth*. Thirdly, he retains many such elements in his account that can be regarded only as supernatural. He looks upon them as a proof of the 'divine' personality of Guru Nanak.[15]

Sewa Ram Singh gives a separate chapter to Guru Nanak's 'creed'. Three more chapters relate to his 'church', his 'method' and his 'personality'. The chapter on his stay at Kartarpur in the 1530s is devoted largely to the institutions he founded. According to Sewa Ram Singh, Guru Nanak did not indulge in any philosophical discussions about the existence of God. 'He felt God within him and with him, and thus spoke of him with the authority of an eye-witness'. Therefore, he simply declares the existence of God and commands his disciples to accept it as the Reality. This meets Trumpp's demand for a proof of Guru Nanak's divine mission. Guru Nanak was a prophet 'in the highest and truest sense of the word'. He wanted to rescue Hinduism from gross polytheism and Islam from aggressive unitarianism, to free both of them from barren ceremonialism and mechanical conventionalism. At the same time, he wanted to preach 'a more exclusive monotheism, a nobler doctrine and a purer morality, based on solid foundations of Divine Grace'. His noble ideals had 'a practical and social meaning'.[16]

The first fundamental principle of the religion of Guru Nanak is the unity of God. As enụnciated in the *mūlmantar,* 'there is but one God, whose name is True, the Creator, the all-pervading, devoid of fear and enmity, Immortal, Unborn, Self-begotten'. Whatever the epithet used for Him – Brahm, Hari, Ram, Govind or Allah – God is incomprehensible, invisible, uncreated, eternal, and alone possessing real existence. He alone is the true object of worship. The second fundamental principle of Guru Nanak's creed is the brotherhood of man, without distinctions of colour, race, caste or tribe. He knew that spiritual development, religious reform and social progress were not possible 'under a system of privileges, which vested the monopoly of spiritual evolution and religious sanctity in the higher castes, and debarred those of the lower castes from these advantages'. He denounced caste in unmistakable terms and established the equality of man before God. Emancipation, in theory, was open to all.[17]

Emancipation for Guru Nanak meant the attainment of everlasting happiness: it consisted of 'living with God and in God'; it could be attained 'even in this life'. Only they with whom God is pleased and on whom he bestows his favours are saved, but it is necessary to strive for salvation. Training one's consciousness (*surt*) for constant communion with God may lead to unfoldment of the soul. But this cannot be done without restraining the mind from indulgence in earthly cravings and low appetites. Devotion to God and meditation on His True Name with a heart full of faith were the means by which the grace of God may be deserved. Guidance of the Guru was essential. This implied strict obedience to the Guru's Word. By loving admiration of God, humility and self-surrender, one may become worthy of God's grace.[18]

Ethical living, like meditation, is an essential requirement. 'Man must bring all his actions into line with the will of the Supreme Lord of the Universe'. Without this, all austerities and good deeds are fruitless. The disciple whose mind is fixed on the ideal is called Gurmukh. The disciple of the Guru should seek the company of Gurmukhs. At the opposite end is Manmukh. Even his benevolent deeds are of no merit. The path suggested by Guru Nanak is not easy to pursue. For stepping on it, one has to place one's head on the palm of one's hand; one had to be prepared for 'the supreme sacrifice'.[19]

Individual and congregational prayer found a prominent place in the discipline evolved by Guru Nanak precisely because emancipation was ultimately a matter of Divine Grace. With the bestowal of grace all past sins were washed away. The world was not an illusion or a dream; its existence was real. 'It is in this real universe that individual soul has descended to work up its elevation and it is not by spurning it that the elevation can be attained'. The spirit should continuously remain in 'communion' with God and pray for mercy. Forgiveness of sins may then come of Divine Grace. In this lies 'the consolation of Sikhism'.[20]

Both for the life of Guru Nanak and his creed, Sewa Ram Singh wrote with reference to the work of European and Indian authors who had written before him. Unlike Muhammad Latif, he does not accept the statement of the author of the *Siyar al-Mutākhirīn* that Guru Nanak had passed his early life in the company of Sayyid Husain and learnt the moral maxims and doctrines of Islam to be subsequently expressed in his own language and formed into a book called the Granth. No Sayyid Husain is known to have been Guru Nanak's contemporary. The well known mystic Shah Husain lived at Lahore in the time of Akbar, and his compositions are not consistent with the Sikh doctrines. The view expressed by some European writers that Kabir was Guru Nanak's teacher is not acceptable to Sewa Ram Singh; there was no evidence to support this view. Guru Nanak is likely to have met Kabir at Banaras but by then he was fairly well advanced in his mission. About the position of the reformers who had gone before Guru Nanak, Sewa Ram Singh gives a long quotation from Cunningham's *History* which ends with the statement that it was reserved for Nanak to perceive the true principles of reform and to lay the foundation of a nationality.[21]

On the unity of God, Sewa Ram Singh quotes Cunningham and refutes Trumpp's lengthy argument that Guru Nanak believed in the Hindu Pantheon. He quotes Cunningham also to refute Wilson's view that the doctrines of Guru Nanak were based on the abstractions of Vedanta and Sūfism. He refutes Trumpp's view that the institution of caste was not directly assailed by Guru Nanak. Trumpp's work was marked by contradictions and inconsistencies; his conclusions and unwarranted opinions point to 'his scanty information and want of keen insight'. His study of the *Granth Sahib* was too 'superficial' to comprehend the meaning of Guru Nanak's teachings. The 'absurdity' of Trumpp's remarks on Sikh ethics brings his grave errors into high relief. He was totally wrong in viewing Sikhism as devoid of ethical values. Trumpp had to be refuted because 'more than one European writer, and some of the Indian writers also, who have ever needed something to support a misrepresentation of the Sikh religion, have often drawn upon Dr. Trumpp's authority'.[22]

Sewa Ram Singh looked upon Guru Nanak as a unique person. That he was commissioned by God is clear from the character of his message and the influence he exerted on the lives of his followers. He himself says in his hymns that he was instructed by God. That he set up a new dispensation and founded 'the true religion' in its pristine glory and purity goes without saying. As regards other religious systems, 'he followed none and denounced none'. A perfectly spontaneous spiritual movement, Sikhism struggled for four hundred years 'for liberty of conscience'. To refresh itself it returns to the Master in the form of the Holy Book. Guru Nanak 'came from the Divine' and enabled his fellow men to take 'the greatest step towards the Divine'. That is why he is 'the Divine Master'. Among sons of men, 'none was born greater than Nanak'.[23]

According to Sewa Ram Singh, Guru Nanak established a number of centres *(manjīs)* in different parts of the country, and even outside, before settling down at Kartarpur finally in the 1530s. There, he established a pattern of individual and congregational worship in which some of his compositions were used. A common kitchen was maintained for community meals on the basis of contribution made by the disciples themselves. Guru Nanak himself worked on a farm, and his wife and sons lived with him. Before his 'ascension', the spirit which had 'come unto him from above' was passed on to Guru Angad. The master remained at the head of his Church in the bodies of his successors for nine generations. After the tenth Master, the Word, as contained in the *Granth Sahib*, was installed in the supreme command of the Church.[24]

The congregation (*sangat*) was next to the Master in commanding respect in the Church. It was in the congregation that the Gurmukh imparted illumination to others. 'These Sangats were the noblest examples in history of assemblies of pious and spiritual enthusiasts, of truthful and mutually confiding seekers after Truth, and the humble and sincere servants of humanity'. The link between the sangats and the Guru was provided by his representatives who presided over the sangats. They were known as Bhāīs or Bābās. In the Church of Guru Nanak, married life was no bar to spiritual progress. The householder who meditated on the name of the Lord was of equal merit with the hermit. No special virtue was attached to asceticism. The path was open to women. In the time of Guru Amar Das, women were allowed to preach as 'Mothers' (*Māīs*). A ceremony of initiation was instituted for all novices. Instruction in the principles of the faith and *charanghāl* (water in which the toe of the Master was immersed) constituted the basic features of initiation, and served as the prototype of the more elaborate baptism of the sword adopted by Guru Gobind Singh.[25]

Guru Nanak enunciated the basic principles for the guidance of his disciples. In matters of diet, for example, all food was pure as a gift from God. But eating for pleasure was 'impure' and the food which produced ailment in the body or evil thoughts in the mind was 'impure'. No ceremonials were set up, but when the need was felt by his successors the ceremonies introduced conformed to the principles of their Master. The composition *kītā loṛiyey kamm*, for example, could be appropriately adopted for the Sikh rite of marriage. The *Kīrtan Sohilā* or 'the wedding song' could similarly be used on the occasion of death because of its metaphor for union. The sacred thread and the practice of *sūtak* could be discarded on the basis of Guru Nanak's hymns. He was a man among men, a living example that could be followed: nowhere does he give the impression that 'his standard is beyond approach by mortal man'. Even today he speaks to men and women through his 'songs'.[26]

II

The first Sikh biographer of Guru Gobind Singh was Bhagat Lakshman Singh, a teacher of History and English Literature at Gordon Mission College at Rawalpindi. He edited *The Khalsa* before he thought of writing a book in English on the Guru who was acknowledged by millions of men in the Punjab as their 'saviour'. He felt convinced that no European writer had given 'a comprehensive account of the life of Guru Gobind Singh', and the majority of the Indian writers had assumed that his principal role was of a political nature. Bhagat Lakshman Singh wanted to show that the great and lasting work of Guru Gobind Singh was 'to preach the Fatherhood of God and the Brotherhood of man .

The tenth Guru was a divine poet, a sage, and a reformer as much as a patriot.

Lakshman Singh's work was remarkable for its rational and humanistic approach to the life of Guru Gobind Singh. All miracles attributed to him were deliberately left out. Lakshman Singh believed that such miracles were never performed. The working of the laws of nature cannot be prevented. Guru Gobind Singh had openly discarded the theory of miracles, and characterized miraculous performances as 'trickeries'. Lakshman Singh was opposed to deifying heroes. Once deified, they ceased to be realizable ideals. They became objects of worship, creating an impassable barrier between them and their worshippers. Guru Gobind Singh clearly told his people to look upon him only as their spiritual father, a man among men. He took pride in acknowledging that his victories were due to his devoted disciples. The only object of adoration was the Timeless one.[27]

Guru Gobind Singh's achievement was made possible by the work of his predecessors. Guru Nanak had rejected 'ritualism', emphasized the importance of right living in complete dedication to God, and demonstrated that all human beings were equal in the eyes of God. With response from the lowly and the meek to this message of equality, a brotherhood was formed. A successor was needed to guide this brotherhood. Guru Angad, and his successor Guru Amar Das, faithfully followed Guru Nanak to consolidate 'the Church' established by him. Guru Ram Das added benevolence and charity. Guru Arjan built the Harmandar, requesting Hazrat Mian Mir to lay its foundation, and compiled the Sikh scripture, which included the compositions of Hindu and Muslim saints. In the history of religions, this was the first example of equal honour being accorded to godly men of other creeds. Guru Hargobind infused military spirit in his followers, took active part in politics, and fought and won battles. Guru Tegh Bahadur followed his example in displaying acts of bravery, culminating in the supreme sacrifice of his life. Guru Gobind Singh gave 'the finishing touch' to the dispensation of his predecessors by instituting the Khalsa.[28]

The Sikhs were different from the Hindus even before the institution of the Khalsa but mostly in doctrinal matters. Guru

Gobind Singh sought to organize his followers into 'a real brotherhood' united by worldly interests as well as by common beliefs. He wanted to inspire his people, with the feelings of love, manliness and a sense of sacrifice. He evolved a 'new creed', the pure way or the *Khālsā Panth*.[29]

Lakshman Singh gives a 'rational' explanation of the origin of the idea that Guru Gobind Singh invoked the Goddess for instituting the Khalsa. The Pandit who used to narrate stories of the *Mahābhārata* to the Sikhs of Guru Gobind Singh dwelt generally on the blessings that all the great warriors had received from the Goddess. To show the absurdity of the notion the Guru gave his consent to the performance of *havan*. Despite elaborate preparations and profuse expenditure there was no result. The cunning priest fled during the night for fear of his life. All the ingredients of *havan* were thrown into the fire. The unusual illumination was attributed by the people to the appearance of the Goddess. But they were soon informed of what had actually happened.[30]

Guru Gobind Singh thought deeply about the predicament of his people. A voice from on high told him that he had been commissioned to save humanity from sin and suffering as God's anointed son. With a naked sword in his hand he addressed a large assembly of his followers, telling them that this was the goddess that had appeared to him. He asked if any one was ready to sacrifice his life for the Guru and the community. The call had to be repeated before Daya Ram, a Khatri of Lahore, stood up. He was taken into the adjoining tent. Down came the sword and the sound of a thud. The Guru came out and demanded another head. Dharma, a Jat, came forward. He was taken into the tent and the thud was heard again. Three more Sikhs offered themselves for sacrifice: Himmat the water-carrier, Sahiba the barber, and Muhkam the washerman. A few minutes later all the five stood in new attire before their bewildered brethren. In their place, five goats had been killed. On the following morning, which was the first day of Baisakh, 1699, all the five volunteers were administered *amrit* of the two edged sword prepared by the Guru. Among other things, the epithet Singh was added to their names and they were duty bound to carry arms on their person. The Guru drank *amrit* from the same vessel and partook of sacred food offered by them. These 'five beloved' (*panj piāre*) formed the nucleus of the Khalsa. The hitherto neglected and down-trodden sections of the populace joined this order to contest power and position with the erstwhile privileged sections.[31]

Guru Gobind Singh taught belief in one God, rejected the theory of incarnation and worship of images, put no faith in austerities, and emphasized the efficacy of the Name of the Lord. Lakshman Singh quotes the well known passage from Ghulam Muhiyuddin's *Tawārīkh-i Punjab* to the effect that Brahmans, Chhatris, Vaishas and Shudras were to be regarded as equals, that no place of Hindu or Muslim pilgrimage was to be visited, that Rama, Krishna, Brahma and the Goddess were not to be worshipped, and that all could learn from one another without any regard for caste. Many Brahmans and Chhatris refused to abandon the old religion of their ancestors and left the place. But twenty thousand persons accepted baptism (*pahul*). Within a century, the low-caste Jats began to rule over Chhatris and Brahmans and to employ them 'as their gate-keepers and orderlies'.[32]

Personal Guruship ended with the death of Guru Gobind Singh. When he saw that his strength was failing and his dissolution was approaching he collected his disciples and told them to regard the *Granth Sahib* as their Guru, and to submit all matters of moment to an assembly of five representative elders and to abide by their decision. Elsewhere Lakshman Singh states that the Guru left his *gaddī* to the whole community which consisted of men with brave souls united by noble ties, investing them with power 'to govern in matters spiritual and temporal'.[33] All were free to aspire to the highest rank in society. No one was deprived of the solace of religion because of his low origin. Hope was held out to all that God lifts all who seek his aid.[34]

Lakshman Singh's interpretation of the mission of Guru Gobind Singh was interlinked with his view of the political and social problems in his own day. Guru Gobind Singh had lived for the people, worked for the people and died for the people. He was no friend of the Brahmans and no enemy of the Muslims. He inculcated 'a distinct creed, organized his followers into a distinct community with distinct symbols and distinct ways and beliefs'. However, diversity in matters of belief was no bar to an exchange of courtesies in matters social and political. A just Sikh social order and humanitarian relations of its members with others were issues of great importance.[35] The members of a religious denomination did not 'necessarily form one nationality'. Lakshman Singh visualised an 'Indian Nation' which would be neither Hindu nor Muslim, nor Christian, nor Sikh: it would include all the religious communities of India. True patriotism was based on the fatherhood of God and the brotherhood of man. Guru Gobind Singh had laboured to ensure 'harmonious development of his country' as 'a patriot'. His patriotism was of 'a higher type', concerned with the down-trodden of the society and their uplift. His example could serve as a source of inspiration for 'every Indian patriot of whatever race or creed'.[36]

Lakshman Singh was not happy with the insistence that all Sikhs should take *pahul* and observe the Khalsa *rahit* on the argument that Guru Gobind Singh had made it obligatory for all Sikhs. This insistence was historically conditioned, he maintained. Like many of his contemporaries, Lakshman Singh believed that the Sikh creed was 'Hinduised' after the establishment of Sikh rule. The high caste Hindus had made advances for reconciliation with the new power and a compromise was effected by which the Sikhs abandoned their 'revolutionary programme' and the Hindus included the Gurus in the list of Vishnu's incarnations. Sikhism began to lose its distinct identity. The Nirmalās, who were mostly responsible for this, had virtually gone over to Hinduism in Lakshman Singh's view. It was in this situation that the Sikh reformers had begun to insist more on the outward form than inward purity. In Lakshman Singh's view the Sikhs who took *amrit* and observed the five symbols (*kaṛā, kachhā, kirpān, kesh* and *kanghā*) declared their determination to make sacrifices for the Panth. Guru Gobind Singh did not insist that all his followers must take *amrit*: the baptismal ceremony 'was not forced upon any one'. The insistence merely on the form with total disregard for the spirit could not serve the larger purposes of the Sikh community.[37]

III

The first comprehensive work on the history and religion of the Sikhs was produced by Khazan Singh, an Extra Assistant Commissioner. He was aware that many Sikhs and non-Sikhs had written on this subject. He had a lot of appreciation for the 'splendid work' of Macauliffe, and he looked upon the work of Giani Gian Singh as extremely useful. However, most of the works published by English writers were 'extremely defective' and 'in many ways misleading'. A systematic account of the religion and history of the Sikhs, a truer and a fuller account, was needed. Towards this end, Khazan Singh published his work History and Philosophy of Sikhism in two volumes in 1914 on the basis of nearly all the important sources available at that time.[38]

Khazan Singh was not satisfied with the materials available to him. The Persian writers had their own biases and limitations. The *Janamsākhī* dictated by Bhai Bala and inscribed by Paiṛa Mokha for Guru Angad did not have a large circulation because the Gurmukhi script was not known to many. Before long, the disciples of Kabir corrupted and mutilated the *Janamsākhī* to show that Kabir was much higher in spiritual status than Guru Nanak. The Handālīs introduced interpolations in the original *Janamsākhī* to exalt Handal. Eventually, the original *Janamsākhī* was destroyed and the corrupted one was made current. The Colebrooke *Janamsākhī,* compiled by a private individual independently of Bhai Bala, was not a continuous chronicle but a mass of isolated and detached *sākhīs*. The extant *Janamsākhīs* were either apocryphal, or corrupted, or incomplete. In spite of excision of interpolations by the editors, their texts contained much that should be discarded.[39]

The biographies of the sixth and the tenth Gurus, one written in the early decades of the eighteenth century and the other around 1800, and Bhai Santokh Singh's *Nanak Parkāsh* and *Sūraj Parkāsh* appeared to have been written more or less 'under the influence of the priestly classes'. Bhai Santokh Singh, who was helped by many able Pandits commissioned by the Sikh Chief of Kaithal, could not escape their conservative 'suggestions and insinuations'. Imperfection of knowledge among the Sikhs gave ample opportunity to polytheistic Pandits to mislead the Sikh authors who were not well educated. They were obliged to put 'wrong or misleading constructions' on the hymns of the Gurus. The compositions of Guru Gobind Singh, which have a peculiar style and rhyme, demanded a very deep and extensive knowledge.[40]

The nature and character of the original source materials dictated critical approach. Khazan Singh suggests that the 'touchstone' for assaying any work on Sikhism was available in the *Ādi Granth* and the *Vārs* of Bhai Gurdas. The latter, which depicts the condition of Sikhism up to the time of Guru Hargobind, appears to be 'free from any foreign influence'. In the Granth associated with Guru Gobind Singh his genuine compositions were 'few in number'. The rest of the book consisted chiefly of 'biographies' of the incarnations of Vishnu based on Sanskrit works. The Guru's personal remarks at the end of each translation indicate that he believed in the Lord God and not in these incarnations. Then there were abstracts from the *Rāmāyan* and the *Bhāgvat*. About two-fifths of the book dealt with the viles of women. These three subjects occupied nearly two-thirds of 'the so-called Granth'. It was not 'a Holy Scripture in the true sense of the word'. It was a collection of scattered and unconnected fragments which fell into the hands of its unknown compiler.[41]

The *Ādi Granth* prepared by Guru Arjan contained the hymns of the first five Gurus and other votaries of God, irrespective of their caste or religion. Some space was left vacant at the end of each *Rāg* to be filled up with the hymns of the Guru who should sacrifice his head for the sake of righteousness. This explanation of the inclusion of the compositions of Guru Tegh Bahadur in the Granth, which was characterized by Trumpp as a post-eventum prophecy, comes from the *Gurbilās Chhevīn Pātshāhī*. This also explains for Khazan Singh why the hymns of Guru Gobind Singh were not included in the *Ādi Granth*. Guru Arjan got books from Mohan, the son of Guru Amar Das, which contained hymns of the first three Gurus. Khazan Singh holds the view that all the hymns of the Gurus were not included in the Granth compiled by Guru Arjan, either because they were not procurable or because they were deliberately left out. The *Prān Sangalī*, for instance, was procured from Ceylon but it was not included in the Granth because Guru Arjan found it 'too difficult and complex for laymen to follow'.[42]

Khazan Singh believed that the process of selection was started by Guru Nanak himself, and there were various considerations for exclusion. The existence of authentic but not canonized compositions is thus postulated by Khazan Singh. A historian could utilize the genuine compositions not included in the *Ādi Granth* 'for the purpose of illustration or explanation of facts'. For all writings, the ultimate criterion was whether or not an idea or a practice attributed to the Gurus was contrary to the teachings of the *Ādi Granth*. Since the Gurus practised what they taught, their acts were never at variance with their teachings.

Bhai Banno's recension was 'brackish' (*khārī*) because it contained hymns which did not have the prior approval of Guru Arjan. The Guru accepted his copy, signed it and sealed it, but he also remarked that it was *khārī*. The volume prepared by the Guru was kept at Amritsar and Bhai Banno was allowed to take the other volume to his village Mangat in the district of Gujrat.[43]

Khazan Singh was interested far more in the early Sikh tradition than in the political history of the Sikhs. Within the early Sikh tradition he gives great prominence to Guru Nanak and Guru Gobind Singh. Virtually, therefore, he covers the ground covered by Sewa Ram Singh and Bhagat Lakshman Singh. His interpretation of the early Sikh tradition is not radically different from theirs.

For the life of Guru Nanak, Khazan Singh pays special attention to the date of his birth. Karam Singh had argued at some length in favour of the Baisakh date. Khazan Singh points out that the various versions of the *Bhāī Bālā Janamsākhī* gave the Kattak date. These *Janamsākhīs* were not free from interpolations, but they were not forgeries. Bhai Santokh Singh gives the Kattak date in his *Sūraj Prakāsh*. After a careful study of Sikh sources Giani Gian Singh also comes to the same conclusion. The Kattak date was celebrated by the descendants of Guru Nanak at Dera Baba Nanak from the very beginning. The Baisakh date is given in the Colebrooke *Janamsākhī*, but this work was based on hearsay and not on 'any authority'. The strongest evidence in support of Baisakh appears to come from Bhai Gurdas who uses the word *vasoā* in his *Vār*: this was interpreted as a reference to the celebration of Guru Nanak's birth on the first of Baisakh. In Khazan Singh's view this interpretation takes the word *vasoā* literally. But it was used by Bhai Gurdas metaphorically, to suggest that every day was treated like the new year day (Baisākhī) for singing the praises of God. Khazan Singh comes to the conclusion that there was no clear or credible evidence against the *pūranmāshī* of Kattak as the date of Guru Nanak's birth.[44]

For the teachings of Guru Nanak, Khazan Singh repeats the view expressed by Cunningham that the reformers like Shankarāchārya, Gorakh, Ramanand and Kabir, had failed to promulgate the much desired 'reform' and it was left for Guru Nanak to remove oppression, to raise the morals of the people, and to direct them to righteousness. Guru Nanak and his successors insisted on the worship of the only True Lord, excluding all other objects of worship. The fatherhood of God and the brotherhood of man were the two cardinal principles of Guru Nanak. He never recognized any distinctions of caste or class, and he addressed himself to all classes of Hindus and Muslims. Khazan Singh elaborates three ideas in particular: the doctrine of the Divine Order, the theory of transmigration, and the law of *karma*. He emphasizes that Sikhism was meant to supersede all earlier religions. Designed for 'the whole world', the Sikh gospel was 'the essence' of all revelations: Hindu, Muslim, Jewish, Christian, and others. There was no difference between Guru Nanak and his successors, and in their teachings. It is a mistake to think that 'Khalsa was an innovation of Guru Gobind Singh' on the faith of Guru Nanak.[45]

Guru Nanak's successors had prepared the way for the adoption of the Khalsa faith by Guru Gobind Singh 'on the lines chalked out by Guru Nanak'.[46] Indeed, everything was 'pre-arranged' by Guru Nanak, even the end of personal Guruship after the tenth Guru and the vesting of Guruship in the Khalsa theocracy and the Holy scripture.[47]

The Khalsa Panth was meant to be distinct in all its 'domestic, social and political' functions but not necessarily sovereign.[48] The Gurus themselves had inculcated that there are 'always two sovereigns' in the world, and obedience to them was binding: 'The successors of both Baba Nanak and Babar, were created by God Himself. Recognize the former as the spiritual and the latter as temporal kings'. Khazan Singh goes on to add that the successor of Baba Nanak was now the Granth Sahib and that of Babar 'the British Government'. The Sikhs were 'enjoined' to be loyal to both.[49] This loyalty was not passive either. The Sikhs should help their sovereigns in 'carrying out the administration of the country'. Indeed, for a Sikh to be guilty of disloyalty was to fall from the faith of the Gurus.[50]

IV

All the three Sikh writers belonged to the new middle class. One was a lawyer who later became a Judge; another was a teacher and a journalist; and the third was a civil servant. They were aware of the context of Sikh studies in which they were writing. They were dissatisfied with the existing work on the Sikh tradition. To improve upon it, they turned to original sources in addition to the work of Sikh and non-Sikh scholars. Reliance on Sikh sources became a remarkable feature of their work. Their attitude towards these sources was by no means uncritical, but they were far more sympathetic to the Sikh tradition than the non-Sikh scholars, whether Indian or European. In fact, they tended to look upon Sikhism and the Sikh Gurus as essentially unique. Thus, their interpretation of the Sikh tradition was closely linked to their faith in Guru Nanak and his successors.

According to Sewa Ram Singh, the existence of God for Guru Nanak was a matter of experience and not of proofs. His creed was monotheistic, egalitarian and ethical. Emancipation in Sikhism meant essentially living with God and in God. Devotion to God, meditation on the Name, and ethical living in accordance with the teachings of the Gurus embodied in the *Ādi Granth* could lead to emancipation, but never without the grace of God. Guru Nanak emphasized the importance of congregational worship and prayers, and he established a number of centres for this purpose. The one at Kartarpur had a regular pattern of daily worship, and the whole community (*sangat*) ate in the common kitchen (*langar*) maintained by contributions made by the individual Sikhs. Guru Nanak chose Angad as his successor to continue his work. The local communities of Sikhs (*sangats*) elsewhere were guided by Bhāīs (Brothers) and Māīs (Mothers) appointed by the Guru. Novices were baptized through *charan pahul*. The Sikhs being house-holders needed social institutions. These were evolved in due course on the basis of principles enunciated by Guru Nanak. The question of a Kabir or a Shah Husain influencing Guru Nanak did not arise. In any case, there was no evidence to support such contentions. Sewa Ram Singh appreciated Cunningham's view of Sikhism as a new and original dispensation, and he disagreed with Trumpp on several important issues – Guru Nanak's conception of God and His attributes, the effect of Sikh beliefs on ethical living, the role of the Guru, and the conception of emancipation.

Bhagat Lakshman Singh looked upon the work of Guru Gobind Singh as the culmination of the work of Guru Nanak and his eight successors. Under them the differences between the Sikhs and the Hindus were of religious nature. The egalitarian order of the Khalsa brought in differences which were social and political as well. Guru Gobind Singh agreed to invoke the Goddess only to expose the Brahmans. He gave the awesome call for sacrifice much later, gave a new kind of *pahul* to the five beloved, and enunciated the *rahit* of the 5Ks. All those who accepted the baptism of the double edged sword were told to believe in one God and not to worship Hindu gods and goddesses, not to worship idols, not to go to the sacred places of the Hindus, not to observe austerities of any kind, and not to observe any distinctions of caste. After the death of Guru Gobind Singh, they were to believe in the Guruship of the Granth and the Panth.

Khazan Singh believed that Guru Angad had prepared a *Janamsākhī* of Guru Nanak which was eventually lost because of the envy of the Kabir-Panthīs and the Handālīs and the enmity of the Mughal administrators. Besides this official biography so to speak, *Janamsākhīs* were compiled by private individuals – like the Colebrooke *Janamsākhī*. Just as *Janamsākhīs* were corrupted by the rivals of the Gurus, much of the other Sikh literature was vitiated by the insidious influence of the conservative priestly class of Brahmans. Nevertheless, Khazan Singh accepted post-eventum prophecies found in the early nineteenth century Sikh literature. For him, all the genuine compositions of the Gurus were not included in the *Ādi Granth*. These could be used by the historian as authentic evidence. Khazan Singh believed in the divinity of Guru Nanak and the originality of his creed. Guru Nanak was the seal of the prophets, and his revelation was the essence of all previous revelations. As the essence of all previous revelations, Sikhism was meant to transcend all earlier faiths. Without saying so, Khazan Singh tried to refute Trumpp in his exposition of the divine governance of the universe, the law of *karma*, and the doctrine of transmigration. He saw the work of the successors of Guru Nanak leading inevitably towards the institution of the Khalsa and the vesting of Guruship in the Panth and the Granth.

All the three writers appear to have cherished the Sikh tradition. Therefore, they were keen to correct what they regarded as 'misrepresentation' or 'misunderstanding'. They wanted to project their own understanding and interpretation of the Sikh tradition for Sikhs and non-Sikhs alike. All their concerns were not the same as the concerns of the European writers. They had no interest in what was regarded as 'comparative study'. Their concern for the uniqueness of the Sikh tradition was linked with their understanding of their own situation. The question of Sikh identity was important for all of them. Sewa Ram Singh, who looked upon the Udāsīs as a part of the Sikh tradition, was nonetheless clear that Sikhism was basically different from Hinduism. Bhagat Lakshman Singh believed that Sahajdhārīs were a part of the Sikh Panth, but his preference for the Singh identity was quite marked. Khazan Singh appears to equate the Sikh with the Singh.

For all the three writers, the Sikhs had a distinct identity of their own, which marked them off from Hindus as well as Muslims. For Khazan Singh, there was no contradiction between the distinct identity of the Khalsa Panth and Sikh cooperation with and loyalty to the British Government. In Lakshman Singh's view, Guru Gobind Singh's aim of social revolution was arrested by the political success of the Sikhs. His message was still relevant for social revolution, and it had a close bearing on the relations of the Sikhs amongst themselves and with non-Sikhs. The distinct and separate identity of the Sikhs did not mean that the Sikhs were a nation in the political sense. No religious community of India constituted a nation. The Indian Nation of the future would embrace all such communities. The position of the Sikhs within this nation appeared to be a rather distant question. Nevertheless, concern for the Sikh present and future was not divorced from concern for the Sikh past for any of the three writers.

In retrospect we can see the limitations of the work of these three Sikh writers, but it is more relevant to see them in the context of the developing Sikh studies for appreciating their positive contribution. Their attitude towards the Sikh sources was critical but not cynical. In fact they brought Sikh sources into high relief by a more or less critical use of these sources. Whatever their personal beliefs about Guru Nanak and Guru Gobind Singh, they tried to write their biography in human and rational terms. It is not surprising that they produced biographies which can be treated as 'secondary works' by a present day biographer of Guru Nanak or Guru Gobind Singh. They presented cogent arguments for treating Sikhism as a new faith with some important social implications. They tried to show that the institution of the Khalsa cannot be regarded as a rupture with the earlier Sikh tradition. They underlined the significance of the concept and the institution of Guruship in the Sikh tradition – its unity, continuity, and indivisibility leading to the doctrines of Guru-Granth and Guru-Panth. They emphasized the importance of the norm of equality in relation to caste and gender. They insisted on looking at the pre-Khalsa as well as the Khalsa Panth as a distinct entity. None of them was inclined, however, to make Sikh identity the basis of Sikh politics, and much less of Sikh nationalism.

NOTES

1. Sewa Ram Singh (1988), pp. xi-xii.
2. Ibid., pp. xii-xiii.
3. Ibid., Preface to the second edition, pp. ix-x.

4. Ibid., Editor's Note, p. v.
5. Ibid., pp. 11-12 and 14-15.
6. Ibid., pp. 49-50. Sewa Ram Singh accepts the existence of Bala but rejects the view that he accompanied Guru Nanak on his travels.
7. Ibid., p. 62.
8. Ibid., pp. 101-02.
9. Ibid., pp. 102-03.
10. Ibid., pp. 104-08 and 110-11. A photographic reproduction of the Baghdad inscription is given. Sewa Ram Singh also states that the cloak (*cholā*) received by Guru Nanak at Baghdad was still in the possession of his descendants at Dera Baba Nanak.
11. Ibid., pp. 117-19.
12. Ibid., pp. 53-54.
13. Ibid., p. 54.
14. Ibid., pp. 123, 145, 146, 185, 191 and 204.
15. Ibid., pp. 20, 36-38, 109, 117-19 and 155. Conversely, the 'divinity' of Guru Nanak induces Sewa Ram Singh to accept that he composed in his childhood verses like a learned and mature man; he could bodily ascend to the court of God; he could leave on a rock the impression of his palm; he could revive a dead elephant; a mill could grind without being handled by him; and his dead body could vanish after his death. The consistency of character and personality which Sewa Ram Singh discerns in the whole life of Guru Nanak also gets explained on the assumption of his 'divinity': Ibid., p. 213.
16. Ibid., pp. 157-60.
17. Ibid., pp. 160-70.
18. Ibid., pp. 170-75.
19. Ibid., pp. 170-82.
20. Ibid., pp. 183-84.
21. Ibid., pp. 10-11, 23-24 and 25.
22. Ibid., pp. 164-66 and 176. According to Sewa Ram Singh, Trumpp misunderstood the idea of obedience to the Guru. Insistence on obedience was meant to teach humility: Ibid., p. 171.
23. Ibid., pp. 207-16.
24. Ibid., pp. 147-55.
25. Ibid., pp. 147-55 and 193-97.
26. Ibid., pp. 201-04 and 208.
27. Lakshman Singh (1963), pp.184-85 and 193-94.
28. Ibid., pp. 190-92.
29. Ibid., pp. 28, 30 and 48.
30. Ibid., pp. 30-31.
31. Ibid., pp. 32-37.
32. Ibid., pp. 39-55.

33. Ibid., pp. 136 and 166.
34. Ibid., pp. 139-46.
35. Ibid., pp. 146-48.
36. Ibid., pp. 149-64.
37. Ibid., pp. 167-77 and 181.
38. Khazan Singh (1970a), pp. i-v.
39. Ibid., pp. 8-22.
40. Ibid., pp. 191-221.
41. Ibid., pp. 22-23 and 24-25.
42. Ibid., pp. 26-28.
43. Ibid., pp. 28-29.
44. Ibid., pp. 211-34.
45. Khazan Singh, (1970b), pp. 31, 63-69, 103-91, 193, 204-06, 213 and 218.
46. Ibid., pp. 224-27.
47. Ibid., p. 229.
48. Ibid., p. 323.
49. Ibid., p. 188.
50. Ibid., p. 178.

4. Advance in Western and Sikh Scholarship

The early Sikh writers transformed Sikh studies from a European dialogue into a dialogue between Western and Sikh scholars. Other Sikh and non-Sikh as well as European scholars entered the field of Sikh studies before the end of colonial rule in 1947. Some of the important scholars of this phase continued to write after 1947. New writers appeared on the scene to enlarge the scope of Sikh studies. It is not possible to treat all this vast literature in detail, but it is possible to notice general trends during the middle quarters of the twentieth century. It would be necessary, however, to analyse a few works in some detail to form an idea of the dialogue during this half a century.

I

Bhai Kanh Singh Nabha, the most eminent scholar of the Singh Sabha Movement, published his *Encyclopaedia of Sikh Literature* (*Gurshabd Ratnākar Mahān Kosh*) in 1930. He had started work on his magnum opus in 1912 to be completed in 1926. All the words of the *Ādi Granth* and the *Dasam Granth*, besides a dozen other works of Sikh literature, were included and explained in the *Encyclopaedia*. With more than 62,000 entries, it has been reprinted twice by the Punjab Languages Department, once in 1960 and then in 1974. Bhai Kanh Singh Nabha's *Encyclopaedia* came as the culmination of his *Gurmat Prabhākar*, and *Ham Hindū Nahīn*. The posthumously published *Gurmat Sudhākar* makes it quite clear that Bhai Kanh Singh Nabha was keen to correct or reject all such notions that did not accord well with the ideas of the *Ādi Granth.* Essentially a product of the Singh Sabha Movement, the *Encyclopaedia* came to be seen as the most authentic representation of Sikhism and Sikh history.[1]

For the interpretation of Sikhism, Bhai Kanh Singh's work was carried forward by Professor Teja Singh who had assisted Bhai Kanh Singh in finalizing the *Encyclopaedia.* Its warmly appreciative Foreword was in fact written by Teja Singh.[2] He was intimately connected with the Gurdwara Reform Movement. His *Gurdwara Reform Movement*, published in 1922, reflected some of the ideas he had expressed in *Guru Nanak and His Mission.* He brought out *Āsā dī Vār* in English translation in 1924, followed by an English translation of the *Japjī.* In 1937, he published an English translation of the *Sukhmanī.* At the same time, he published his *Sikh Religion* and the better known *Sikhism: Its Ideals and Institutions.* Teja Singh's *Growth of Responsibility in Sikhism* came out in 1942, and his *Essays in Sikhism* in 1944. In all these publications, he had two concerns: to interpret Sikhism as an original system and to propagate this interpretation among Sikhs and non-Sikhs alike. The most scholarly work of Teja Singh was the *Shabadārth Srī Gurū Granth Sāhib Jī.* His only systematic work on Sikh history was *A Short History of the Sikhs,* published jointly with Ganda Singh.

Bhai Jodh Singh too was intimately connected with the Gurdwara Reform Movement. He published his *Religion and Religious Life as Conceived by Guru Nanak* in 1925. Seven years later came out his well known *Gurmat Nirnai.* A very different kind of work appeared in 1947, *Prachīn Bīṛān Bāre Bhullān dī Sodhan.* It was written in response to G.B. Singh's *Srī Gurū Granth Sāhib diān Prachīn Bīṛān*, published in 1944 as a textual study. Bhai Jodh Singh continued to publish after 1947, bringing out *Some Studies in Sikhism* in 1953 and *The Japji* in 1956. But more interesting in retrospect is his *Srī Kartārpurī Bīṛ de Darshan*, published in 1968. It was written in response to the controversial issue of the *Rāgmālā* in Guru Granth Sahib and published partly in response to a scholarly demand for a textual study of the Kartarpuri Bīṛ. Bhai Jodh Singh was deeply interested in Gurbāṇī and its interpretation, a subject on which he was regarded as a great authority since the 1930s. His interest in the Bhagat-Bāṇī was equally serious. Printed posthumously for the third time in 1993, his *Bāṇī Bhagat Kabīr Jī Steek* bears ample evidence of his scholarship in this area of Sikh studies.

Interest in biographical, philosophical and scriptural studies in the last quarter of colonial rule in the Punjab was reflected in the works like Sir Jogendra Singh's *Thus Spake Guru Nanak*, Kartar Singh's *Life of Guru Nanak Dev*, Gyani Sher Singh's *Philosophy of Sikhism*, Bishan Singh's *Srī Gurū Granth Sāhib Steek*, Narain Singh's *Dasam Gurū Granth Sāhib Steek*, and the anonymous *Srī Dasam Granth Sāhib Jī*. In this context we can appreciate the publications of Professor Sahib Singh. He published his *Gurbāṇī Viākaran* for the first time in 1939. This work, he thought, was essential for a proper understanding of Gurbāṇī. He wrote a number of articles on the *Ādi Granth*. The manuscript of his *Ādi Bīṛ Bāre* was completed in 1950, though it was actually published in 1970. It contains a new hypothesis about the compilation of the *Ādi Granth*. In Professor Sahib Singh's view, Guru Nanak recorded his own *bāṇī* and left it for Guru Angad. His example was followed by all his successors so that Guru Arjan had the *bāṇī* of all his predecessors with him for compiling the Granth in 1604. Professor Sahib Singh is known to the scholarly world primarily for a work which is really monumental: *Srī Gurū Granth Sāhib Darpan*. It was published in ten volumes in 1962-64 on the basis of his understanding of the grammar of Gurbāṇī.[3]

Interest in Sikh history before 1947 was represented most eminently by Ganda Singh who looked upon Karam Singh 'the historian' as his predecessor. Karam Singh had published his *Kattik kih Visākh* in the opening decade of the twentieth century, and brought out his *Bandā Bahādur* and *Mahārāja Ālā Singh* in the second decade. Ganda Singh had great appreciation for Karam Singh's interest in empirical evidence and his open minded research.[4] Ganda Singh published three works in 1935: *The Life of Banda Singh Bahadur*, with an exhaustive bibliography; the *Mīrāt ut-Tawārīkh-i Sikhān*, a bibliographical work; and the *History of the Gurdwara Shahidganj, Lahore*, which related to a contemporary issue. In 1938, he published three more works: the Persian text of

Qazi Nur Muhammad's *Jangnāma*, an English translation of the *Dabistān-i Mazāhib's* section on the Nanak-Panthīs; and the *Contemporary Sources of Sikh History (1469-1707)*. In 1939, Ganda Singh contributed three articles to *Maharaja Ranjit Singh: First Death Centenary Memorial Volume* which he co-edited with Teja Singh. Before 1947, he published six more books, all in Punjabi: *Mahārāja Kaurā Mal Bahādur, Sardār Shām Singh Attārīwāla, Kūkiān dī Vithiā, Sikh Itihās Bāre, Punjab diān Vārān*, and *Sikh Itihās Wal*. This detail of Ganda Singh's early works highlights his basic interests as a historian: biography, original source materials, and issues or themes of contemporary interest.

These major interests stayed with Ganda Singh throughout his long and productive academic life. In 1949, he published *A History of Khalsa College*, besides Persian sources in the *Mākhiz-i Tawārīkh-i Sikhān*, and the *Aurāq-i Parīshān*. At the same time he brought out his *Mukhtasar Nanak Shāhī Jantarī* as a useful tool for comparative chronology. In 1950, came out *A Short History of the Sikhs*, written jointly with Teja Singh. Though Teja Singh was a senior scholar, this work appears to have been the result of Ganda Singh's interest in history. It must be added, however, that the two scholars formed an admirable combination of twin interest in Sikhism and Sikh history. Ganda Singh could not take up a systematic history of the Sikhs after 1765, the year with which *A Short History of the Sikhs* ended.[5] He continued to publish original sources, bibliographies, and biographical studies. His doctoral thesis was published in 1959 as *Ahmad Shah Durrani*.

New Sikh writers appeared on the scene after 1947. Ganda Singh was succeeded at Amritsar by Kirpal Singh who produced a biographical study of Maharaja Ala Singh, and published the texts of Ganesh Das's *Chār Bāgh-i Punjab* and Miharban's *Janamsākhī*. For his doctoral thesis, however, he chose to work on the partition of the Punjab in 1947. He has continued to publish original sources and to write on themes of Sikh history. Sardar Kapur Singh published his *Parasharprasna or the Baisakhi of Guru Gobind Singh* in 1959. Its third edition was brought out in 1989. With an erudition which marks all his works, Kapur Singh tries to demonstrate how Sikhism of Guru Nanak and his successors, especially the Khalsa of Guru Gobind Singh, represented a complete departure from all the religious systems associated with 'Hinduism' and from the social order envisaged and sought to be upheld as *Varnashram-dharma*.[6] Khushwant Singh published the first general history of the Sikhs in two volumes in 1963 and 1966 as *A History of the Sikhs*, repeating the title of Cunningham's book and looking upon him as his predecessor. Harbans Singh brought out his *Heritage of the Sikhs* in 1964, followed by his *Guru Gobind Singh* in 1966, and *Guru Nanak and the Origins of Sikh Faith* in 1969.

Neither before nor after 1947 were the Sikh scholars writing in isolation from the other Indian, or European, scholars. G.C. Narang had published his doctoral work, *Transformation of Sikhism*, as early as 1918. Sita Ram Kohli published his *Catalogue of the Khalsa Darbar Records* in two volumes in 1919 and 1927. He also published a few seminal articles relating to the reign of Ranjit Singh, in addition to a paper on a 'book of *parwanas*' containing more than 450 orders of Maharaja Ranjit Singh issued to Tej Singh as the Commander of the Kampū-i-Mu'allā in less than a year and half. The Persian text and English translation of the 'book of *parwanas*', prepared by him for publication, was posthumously revised and published as *The Civil and Military Affairs of Ranjit Singh* in 1987. Kohli wrote his *Maharaja Ranjit Singh* in Punjabi after 1947. Two more scholars covered the reign of Ranjit Singh and his successors on the basis of their doctoral theses: G.L. Chopra with his *Punjab as a Sovereign State* and B.R. Chopra with his *Kingdom of the Punjab (1839-45)*. Hari Ram Gupta wrote four volumes on the history of the Sikhs and the Punjab during the eighteenth century before 1947 and, besides several other studies, covered the Guru period and the reign of Ranjit Singh, after his retirement from the Panjab University in the early 1960s. Scholars from outside the Punjab also wrote on Sikh history, like Indubhushan Banerjee who published his *Evolution of the Khalsa* in two volumes before 1947. He was not alone. N.K. Sinha published his *Rise of the Sikh Power* and his *Ranjit Singh*. The Indian Institute of Advanced Study, established at Shimla in 1965, organized a seminar on 'Sikhism and Indian Society' and published its proceedings. Niharranjan Ray, the Director of the Institute, gave

Guru Nanak Lectures at the Punjabi University, Patiala, which were published in 1970 as *The Sikh Gurus and Sikh Society*. A different kind of work was published by D.P. Ashta in 1959 as the *Poetry of Dasam Granth.*[7]

Scholarly input into Sikh studies was re-inforced by scholars in the departments of social sciences and humanities at the universities of the Punjab. To cite a few examples, Surinder Singh Kohli published his *Critical Study of the Adi Granth* in 1961, followed by his *Outlines of Sikh Thought* in 1964. Fauja Singh brought out the *Military System of the Sikhs* in 1964, followed by his *Kuka Movement* in 1965. In 1967, a historical study of Guru Gobind Singh was published by J.S. Grewal and S.S. Bal as *Guru Gobind Singh: A Biographical Study* (reprinted in 1987). J.S. Grewal's *Guru Nanak in History* and S.S Bal's *Life of Guru Nanak* came out in 1969. S.S. Bal tried to show that a historical biography of Guru Nanak could be attempted with the help of the *Janamsākhī* materials. J.S. Grewal tried to demonstrate the originality of Guru Nanak's system of ideas and practices by analysing his response to his political, social and religious milieu during the late fifteenth and the early sixteenth century.[8]

Two Western scholars published their work on Sikhism before and after 1947. One of them was Hobber Professor of Comparative Religion at Yale University – John Clarke Archer. He brought out *The Sikhs in relation to Hindus, Moslems, Christians and Ahmadiyyas* in 1946. It was followed in 1949 by an article entitled 'The Bible of the Sikhs'. The other scholar was C.H. Loehlin who was associated with Baring Union Christian College at Batala. He published *The Sikhs and their Book* in 1946. Its revised and enlarged version was published in 1958 as *The Sikhs and their Scripture*. In 1966 his short paper on the Kartarpur Granth was published in the *Proceedings* of the Punjab History Conference. His doctoral thesis, completed in 1957, was published in 1971 as *The Granth of Guru Gobind Singh and the Khalsa Brotherhood.*

On the whole, thus, we find that the middle quarters of the twentieth century witnessed an increasing interest in Sikh studies among the Sikh and other Indian and Western scholars. Much of this interest centred on the rediscovery and publication of original sources in Persian, Gurmukhi and English. Biographical and historical studies became more important than before. The bulk of the work on Sikh history related to the pre-colonial centuries. Sikhism and Sikh scriptures came to form a prominent part of Sikh studies. The contribution of scholars formally trained in research became increasingly important. We may look at the *Short History* of Teja Singh and Ganda Singh and the works of J.C. Archer and C.H. Loehlin in this broad context.[9]

II

The first thing to note about *A Short History of the Sikhs* is its comprehensive bibliography. Nearly all the major works in Gurmukhi are listed, some of them available only in manuscripts, besides the works of Bhai Kanh Singh Nabha and Karam Singh. Nearly all the contemporary works in Persian are also listed. To be listed among the European writers are James Browne, George Forster, John Malcolm, H.H. Wilson, J.D. Cunningham, Lepel Griffin, and M.A. Macauliffe. Among the Indian writers are G.C. Narang and Indubhushan Banerjee, besides Sewa Ram Singh, Teja Singh, and Ganda Singh. In the footnotes figure also Ernest Trumpp, J.C. Archer, and G.B. Singh.

The primary concern of Teja Singh and Ganda Singh was to provide a meaningful account of Sikh history from the time of Guru Nanak to the declaration of Sikh sovereignty in 1765. The book is divided into three parts. The first part deals with 'religious foundations' under the ten Gurus. The second part deals with Banda Bahadur alone, summarizing Ganda Singh's work on Banda Bahadur, under the title 'political foundations'. The third part covers the political history of the Sikhs from 1716 to 1765 in four clearly demarcated phases, showing how 'persecution leads to power'. Teja Singh and Ganda Singh feel concerned not with authors but with issues. They point out the inadequacies of their predecessors on the basis of fresh evidence, better linguistic competence, and understanding of the original sources.[10] Forster, Malcolm, Cunningham, Trumpp, Narang and Banerjee are sought to be corrected on various points.[11] Teja Singh and Ganda Singh try not only to correct the factually wrong statements of Narang and Banerjee but also their inadequate interpretations.[12]

Teja Singh and Ganda Singh state their own position at the outset. The Sikh Gurus were temporal as well as spiritual guides, and the political institutions of the Sikhs grew out of their religious origins. 'The whole movement was gradual and at no stage was there any sudden or uncalled for departure from the original aim'. The dichotomy between 'saintly' and 'worldly', between 'peaceful' and 'military', was not justified. The Sikh movement was harmonious and many-sided. Sikh history reveals 'the gradual making and development of a nation' in the hands of ten successive Gurus. They had in mind 'the duties of a nation as much as the duties of an individual'. From this point of view, all apparent contradictions begin to vanish. For Teja Singh and Ganda Singh, the appropriate term for this development in Sikh history is 'transfiguration'and not 'transformation'.[13]

Teja Singh and Ganda Singh accept 15 April 1469 as the date of Guru Nanak's birth, and underline the importance of his early education which made him 'a scholarly writer'. Many of the *sākhīs* which became current were 'only settings provided for the word-pictures drawn by him in his verses'. The *sākhī* of Guru Nanak's spiritual experience at Sultanpur is taken by Teja Singh and Ganda Singh as his communion with 'the spirit pervading the whole universe'. Guru Nanak 'felt' that he stood before the throne of the Almightly, and received from him the message of his mission. 'There is no Hindu, no Musalman' proclaimed his mission 'to reconcile the two warring communities of India into one brotherhood'. This was 'a turning point' in his life. He travelled far and wide in India and abroad. Against Trumpp's scepticism about Guru Nanak's visit to the South and Ceylon, Teja Singh and Ganda Singh refer to the evidence of *Hakīkat Rāh Makām.* For Guru Nanak's visit to Baghdad, the evidence of the Baghdad inscription is cited. One of his own hymns makes him an eye-witness to the sack of Saidpur by Babur.[14] For most of the incidents of Guru Nanak's life, Teja Singh and Ganda Singh use the evidence of the *Janam-sākhīs*, interpreting it as rationally as possible.[15]

Guru Nanak was not only 'a man of devotion and peace' but

also a leader who thought of 'the worldly needs of the people'. He felt concerned with their 'social and political disabilities'. He declared that woman, having an equal responsibility for her actions before God, was not inferior to man. To give a practical shape to the idea of equality, Guru Nanak 'instituted the custom of inter-dining in a common mess attached to every place of worship'. He roused 'the national sentiment of the people' by adopting their spoken language for religious purposes. 'That the Guru was not a mere reformer but the founder of a new religion is clear from the fact that he travelled abroad to non-Hindu countries, established Sangats or Sikh organizations in different centres under the charge of Manji-holders, and took special care to test and appoint a successor who should continue his work after him'. Guru Nanak actually installed Guru Angad in his own place and 'saluted him' as the Guru before he died on 22 September 1539.[16]

Guru Angad explained the mission of Guru Nanak through 'regular meetings', wrote on the same themes, maintained the common kitchen, and 'gave definiteness and distinction to the general ideals laid down by Guru Nanak'. He got the *bāṇī* of his master recorded in a special script called Gurmukhi. Thus, a nucleus of the Sikh Scripture began to be formed, leading to the consciousness that the Sikhs were 'distinct from the mass of Hindus'. Like his predecessor, Guru Angad chose his successor before he died on 29 March 1552.[17] Guru Amar Das told his Sikhs 'to reject the path of renunciation' and to think of the life of householder as 'the only' approved way of practising religion. When Goindval became a big religious centre, Guru Amar Das constructed a *bāolī* with 84 steps 'for the use of visitors'. The *langar* became a great institution: Guru Amar Das asked all visitors to sit in a line and eat together. 'No distinction of caste or creed, high or low, was made'. Guru Amar Das prohibited the practice of becoming *satī*. He divided his spiritual domain into twenty-two provinces (*manjīs*) and appointed his representatives to each of these. His own compositions and selections from the compositions of some *bhagats* were added to the compositions of his predecessors and put together by his grandson Sahansar Ram. These volumes were later used by Guru Arjan for the compilation of the Holy Granth. Ceremonies of marriage and death came to be performed with the help of Gurbāṇī. Guru Amar Das wanted only the praises of God to be sung on his death. He consecrated his son-in-law, Ram Das, as his successor before he died on 1 September 1574.[18]

Guru Ram Das laid the foundation of the city of Amritsar, then called Chak Guru, Chak Ramdas or Ramdaspur. He invited traders and craftsmen to reside in the town. 'Possession of wealth was no longer to be considered as Maya, but as a very salutary and helpful thing in the conduct of human affairs'. Guru Ram Das died in Goindval on 1 September 1581 to be succeeded by his youngest son. Guru Arjan completed the work of building the tank and the city with the manual and material help of the Sikhs. Every Sikh was expected to set aside one tenth (*dasvandh*) of his income for the Guru's fund as a voluntary contribution. This could be remitted through an accredited Masand. Guru Arjan laid the foundation of the central shrine, now called the Golden Temple, in the midst of the tank of *amritsar*. He founded Tarn Taran and Sri Hargobindpur not far from Amritsar, and he founded Kartarpur in the Jalandhar Doab. He constructed a *bāolī* at Lahore. Compilation of the Holy Granth was 'the greatest work of his life'.[19]

Teja Singh and Ganda Singh outline the history of the compilation of the *Ādi Granth*. Some work in this direction had already been done by Guru Angad and Guru Amar Das. Guru Arjan went to Goindval personally to borrow the volumes from Baba Mohan and to bring them reverently to Amritsar. He had to consult some other sources too to complete the work. Guru Arjan's own contribution to the Holy Granth was the biggest. He also included selections from the writings of fifteen Hindu and Muslim saints, most of whom belonged to the so-called depressed or untouchable classes. The basis of selection was not doctrinal but 'the lyrical and living values of the pieces'. The idea was inherent in the 'cosmopolitan nature of Sikhism'. Guru Arjan was not the first Guru to think of making a collection of the verses of the *bhagats*. He enlarged the scope of inclusion and gave 'a scriptural position' to their writings. The compositions of men like Kanha, Chhajju, Shah Husain and Piloo were rejected either because of their Vedantic leanings or because of their hatred for the world, or for women.

Guru Arjan 'wanted only healthy optimism and joy in worldly duties and responsibilities and not mere tearful ecstaticism or other-worldliness'. The huge material assembled was reduced to writing by Bhai Gurdas at the dictation of Guru Arjan. The Holy Granth was completed and installed in the Harmandar at Amritsar in 1604. Teja Singh and Ganda Singh refer to the arrangement of the contents of the Holy Granth with some interesting comments. The Granth was brought to its present final form by Guru Gobind Singh at Damdama Sahib (Talvandi Sabo) in 1705. The new recension was prepared, not by dictating it from memory, nor by adding the *bāṇī* of Guru Tegh Bahadur for the first time, but by re-editing an existing recension.[20]

Jahangir had formed a prejudice against the Sikh movement. As he states in his *Tuzk*, he had thought of putting an end to 'this false traffic' or to bring Guru Arjan into the fold of Islam. He got the chance during the rebellion of Prince Khusrau. After the prince was captured and punished, Jahangir was told that Guru Arjan had put a saffron mark on Khusrau's forehead as the mark of his blessings in favour of the rebel. No enquiry was made, nor any trial held. Jahangir asserts that he knew the Guru's 'heresies'. He ordered 'that his house and children be made over to Murtaza Khan, that his property be confiscated, and that he should be put to death with tortures'. The allegation seems to have been concocted by the Guru's enemies, and Jahangir got the pretext he needed. Guru Arjan was handed over to Chandu Shah who had a private grudge against him. Subjected to all sorts of tortures in the burning heat of Lahore, the blistered body of Guru Arjan was thrown into the cold water of the Ravi to be carried away. This occurred on 30 May 1606.[21]

The martyrdom of Guru Arjan convinced the Sikhs that they must arm themselves and fight if they wanted to live. Guru Hargobind wore two swords on the occasion of his accession, one to represent spiritual and the other temporal interests. He asked the Masands and the Sikhs to bring arms and horses as offerings. A fortress, called Lohgarh, was constructed in Amritsar. A meeting place for the Sikhs was also built. It was called Akāl Takht, or the Throne of the Almighty. In the courtyard in its front, physical feats were performed, visitors were received, and complaints were heard and redressed. Jahangir summoned the Guru and sent him to the fort of Gwalior as a state prisoner. Later, however, the emperor seems to have been convinced that he had been misled. Guru Hargobind was released and he resumed his mission. He built the town of Kiratpur in the hills. Jahangir's death in 1627 brought the phase of peace to an end. Shah Jahan, prohibited the conversion of Muslims and ordered the demolition of temples. The *bāolī* at Lahore was filled up and a mosque was erected on the site of the free kitchen attached to it. In this situation even a slight cause could result in a clash of arms. This cause was provided in 1628 by an altercation over a hawk between the Sikhs and some men of the royal hunting party. The Mughal noble Mukhlis Khan was killed. Guru Hargobind left Amritsar for Kartarpur where he was attacked by the Mughal *faujdār* of Jalandhar. The *faujdār* was killed in the battle. Two other commandants, Painde Khan and Kale Khan, were killed in yet another battle fought near Kartarpur in 1632. 'A new heroism was rising in the land, of which the object, then dimly seen, was to create the will to resist the mighty power of the foreign aggressors'. This accorded well with the intentions of Guru Nanak. The Sikh Gurus were practical leaders as well as meditating saints. For them, to propagate religious ideals was not inconsistent with active measures for the service of mankind. The assumption of *mīrī-pīrī* by Guru Hargobind was not a deviation but a logical development.[22]

Teja Singh and Ganda Singh give a factual narrative of events from the death of Guru Hargobind through the martyrdom of Guru Tegh Bahadur to the institution of the Khalsa by Guru Gobind Singh. Going through Puranic literature, he was deeply impressed by the idea that God had been sending a saviour from time to time to uphold righteousness and to destroy evil. He came to feel that he himself was the man required by the times. As he states in the *Bachittar Nātak*, he believed that God had commissioned him 'to advance righteousness, to emancipate the good, and to destroy all evil-doers root and branch'. The keynote of literature preserved in the *Dasam Granth* is optimism, and the heroic deeds of gods and goddesses are glorified 'to inspire ardour for religious warfare'.

On 30 March 1699, he gave the dramatic call for sacrifice and baptized the first five volunteers with sweetened water stirred with a dagger. He spoke to the assembly of his mission. For the speech of Guru Gobind Singh, Teja Singh and Ganda Singh quote Ghulam Muhiyuddin alias Bute Shah. The Guru begged the Five Beloved Ones to baptize him in the same way as he had baptized them. 'After this there remained no difference between him and his baptised Sikhs'. They were 'quite competent to take his place after him'. About 80,000 men were baptized in a few days. Guru Gobind Singh ordered that all those who called themselves Sikhs should get themselves confirmed by receiving the new baptism, and follow the *rahit* he enunciated. Guru Gobind Singh expressed great admiration for the Khalsa. To serve them pleased his heart, and no other service was so dear to his soul. 'All the substance in my house, nay, my soul and body are at their disposal'. The Guru poured his life into the Khalsa and invested them with his own personality.[23]

In the narrative of the post-Khalsa phase of Guru Gobind Singh's life, Teja Singh and Ganda Singh highlight the effect of the *Zafarnāma* on the mind of Aurangzeb, resulting in an invitation for a personal meeting. This is followed by Guru Gobind Singh's meeting with Bahadur Shah at Agra in 1707, his intention to return to Anandpur, disillusionment with Bahadur Shah after a year's stay near his camp, the conversion of Banda Bahadur, and an attack on Guru Gobind Singh by a hired assassin. The wound had not yet fully healed when the Guru tried to bend a stiff bow. The wound burst open. On 7 October 1708, a couple of hours after midnight, he roused his Sikhs from sleep to bid them farewell. There was to be no personal Guru after him. 'The whole Sikh community, in the organised form called the *panth*, was to guide itself by the teaching of the Gurus as incorporated in the Holy Granth, and also by the collective sense of the community'.[24]

Teja Singh and Ganda Singh emphasize that Banda Bahadur was 'baptised as a regular Sikh' and he was raised to the position of 'the commander of the Khalsa'. He was sent to the Punjab to continue 'the struggle with the Mughal rulers'. He sacked towns, won battles, occupied territories and established a government. He assumed 'royal authority' and struck coins in the name of the Guru. The inscription on his official seal is also read by Teja Singh and Ganda Singh as Banda Bahadur's devotion and loyalty to Guru Gobind Singh.[25] According to them, Banda Bahadur abolished the *zamīndārī* system. Bahadur Shah had to move against him personally. Banda remained a source of real danger to Mughal power and authority for several years before he was besieged and captured towards the end of 1715. He was executed in Delhi on 9 June 1716. 'Banda Singh was the first man among Sikhs to think of founding a political raj. He fought battles not to cripple the Mughal power, but to destroy it root and branch'. The hill chiefs supported the Mughals; the general mass of Hindus remained aloof; only the poor classes joined Banda as supporters. Though they were defeated, a will was created in the ordinary masses to resist tyranny. The example set by Banda served as a beacon light for the Sikhs in the darker days to come.[26]

The issue of authority within the Sikh Panth came to the surface in the time of Banda Bahadur himself. Teja Singh and Ganda Singh are anxious to underline 'Banda's faithful adhesion to the doctrines of Guru Gobind Singh'. They admit, however, that Banda introduced 'Fateh Darshan' as the war cry and insisted on vegetarianism. Furthermore, the Sikhs called *Bandeis* apotheosized Banda after his death and looked upon him as the successor of Guru Gobind Singh. There were other claimants to Guruship: Ajit Singh, Gulab Rai and Kharak Singh, besides the *gurus* of the Miṇas, Dhirmallias and Ramraiyyas. Then there were Sikhs of some other denominations, like the Handālīs, the Nirmalās and the Udāsīs. There was yet another category of Sikhs who came to be known as *sahajdhārīs* or slow adopters. 'They believed in the same principles as the regular Sikhs, whom they helped with money and provisions in times of need and whom they would join as baptised brethren as soon as they found themselves ready for sacrifice'. For Teja Singh and Ganda Singh only the baptized Khalsa were the 'genuine' or 'regular' Sikhs.[27]

The Khalsa represented the 'central authority' within the Sikh Panth. Guruship in essence had represented two things: the Word and the Congregation. A mystic unity was established between the

Word and the Guru on the one hand, and the Guru and the Sikh on the other. Greatest respect began to be paid to the incorporated Word, even the Guru choosing for himself a seat lower than that of the Scripture. The Sikh congregations also acquired great sanctity, owing to the belief that the spirit of the Guru lived and moved among them. They began to assume higher and higher authority until collectively the whole body, called the *Panth*, came to be regarded as an embodiment of the Guru. This was the context in which Guru Gobind Singh received baptism from the Sikhs initiated by him. 'What the last Guru did was to separate the personal and the scriptural aspects of the Guruship. The one he gave to the Khalsa and the other to the Holy Granth. Both acquired the title of Guru, and were to be addressed as Guru Granth and Guru Panth'.

In actual practice, the Sikh congregation would sit together, with the Holy Granth in their midst, and deliberate over issues of common interest. The decisions they came to in such meetings were known as *gurmatas*. No Sikh was expected to contravene these 'decisions of the Guru'. The meetings of the Sikh congregation, the *Sarbat Khalsa*, were held twice a year, on the occasion of the Diwali in October and on the Baisakhi day in April. The organization of *rākhī* and the *misaldārī* system of government were important for the rise of the Khalsa into political power but they were not linked with any religious doctrines. The optimistic conviction of the Sikhs about the inevitability of their rule (*rāj karegā Khalsa*) was based on a prophecy attributed to Guru Gobind Singh.[28]

III

In the very title of his work, Archer declares that it is 'a study in comparative religion' though a study in which 'prolonged attention' is given to the Sikhs and their religion. Archer was aware of the work done by Cunningham, Trumpp and Macauliffe; he was also familiar with the work published by Khazan Singh, Bhai Jodh Singh, Teja Singh, and Ganda Singh. But they had not undertaken a 'comparative appraisal'. The distinguishing feature of Archer's study was his approach.[29]

Archer puts forth the familiar hypothesis that Sikhism originated in an effort toward 'reconciliation' of Hindu and Islamic orders and ideas. He goes on to add that, 'somewhat at variance from initial purposes', Sikhism did become 'an independent and conspicuous order of its own', comparable with Christianity, Hinduism and Islam. Paradoxically, therefore, the success of the Sikhs was the outcome of their failure to accomplish the original purpose of Sikhism. Archer observed that half of the Sikhs in the contemporary Punjab, could not readily be distinguished by 'outward signs' from their Hindu kinsfolk. But the other half bore distinctive marks, representing an enduring order which was 'at once non-Moslem and non-Hindu'. Archer's chief concern was with the rise of the Sikhs 'who are distinctive'.[30]

Archer makes a sharp distinction between 'the temporal and the spiritual' concerns of men which somehow do not remain separate. Guru Nanak seemed to give no thought to politics, unless to reject it. But perhaps 'it was politics, primarily, which after a while gave Sikhism a much altered character in relation with the Mughals and the British'. That was why 'Sikhism as venture in the reconciliation of religions' issued ultimately in 'a distinct religious order and a separate political community'. Archer saw for this development some relevance of the Jats too. Ordinarily they were peaceably inclined and yet they were 'independent to a degree of impatience over too immediate government control'. The Jat Sikhs organized the Khalsa, and gave to Sikhism 'most of its stolid and compelling substance'.[31]

For an analysis of 'Sikh origins', Archer thinks of Kabir whose teachings represent 'a reconciliation of the major doctrines of Islam and Hinduism'. About a dozen sects came to share Kabir's inheritance. Of them all, the Sikhs were 'the most conspicuous, alert and virile'. But for the fact that Guru Nanak inaugurated 'a more virile movement nourished partly by Kabir', the memory of Kabir might have faded into the dim light of the common Hindu day. Kabir and Guru Nanak 'shared something of a common vernacular', but they were two 'distinct phenomena'. The Sikh movement was at once related to and distinct from the movement initiated by Kabir.[32]

Guru Nanak is both factual and formless for Archer. 'This may be recognized at once as something common in the history of religions'. Guru Nanak was a 'historical person'; he was also a 'theological construction'. He was a real person and he was also 'a creature of religious fancy'. However, the two Nanaks are not always to be distinguished from each other. 'They are two in one, both in practice and in theory'. The formless Nanak is more important as a typical phenomenon in the total history of religion: 'It was the faith in him which made him a compelling figure'. Whereas the records for the role of Nanak the formless are ample, the records for the factual Nanak are meagre: 'no Sikh has yet examined the career of Nanak by the full means of modern, critical techniques'. What Mohan Singh has done for the life of Kabir, some Sikh 'must do the same one day for Nanak'.[33]

Imaginatively, Archer tries to make the best sense of the materials available to him. The round of Guru Nanak's early life was dictated largely by common custom. He received some formal education in the local elementary school, and learnt many things from observation, including both mosque and temple ceremonial. He seems to have displayed an unusual disposition toward religion. His piety was often more pronounced than his willingness for manual labour. He became acquainted in due course with portions of the Hindu Shāstras and sacred writings, and with portions of the Hadīs and the Qurān, which were in circulation. He may have heard wandering Hindu and Muslim teachers discussing the unity of God. Breathing 'a lively atmosphere', he came under the influence of kindred expressions by different kinds of various devotees. But it would be wrong to insist that 'he was merely acquiring the mind and the manner of imitation', or to say that when he expressed his teachings in any similar phraseology 'he was exhibiting dependence and not initiative'.[34]

Guru Nanak got married and took service, but he remained restless and unhappy. Possibly in his early thirties he took up an exclusively spiritual career. He may have been about fifty years of age when, in response to special vision, he entered the final phase of his career: God offered him the cup of *amrit* as a token of favour and promise of his ultimate success. God commissioned him to 'repeat the Name', to inspire others also to repeat it, and teach all mankind the 'true religion'. The 'basic text' of Sikhism, the *mūlmantar*, was uttered by Guru Nanak after this experience of illumination. He also proclaimed that 'there is no Hindu, nor is there a Musalman'. Archer takes it to mean that all men were 'only brethren under God'. If 'legend' was to be believed, Guru Nanak wandered widely throughout India and abroad. But we may assume that even his actual wanderings were 'extensive'. Informal groups of followers came into existence in 'loose, quasi-monastic bonds'.[35]

Archer attaches special significance to the travels of Guru Nanak. It was outside the Punjab that he had occasion to consider older atheisms of Buddhism and Jainism, to plead for 'a recognition of True Name' as the centre and object of devotion, and the sure ground of spiritual illumination. At Puri, he contended that Jagannath's *āratī* was nothing in comparison with man's recognition of the divinity in all things. In his contest with the Yogīs, he revealed the 'miracle' of the True Name. He had no appreciation for Yogic practices. Similarly, he agreed to one God of Islam but not in 'association' with Muhammad.[36] Guru Nanak had a message which 'revealed the hidden heart of things' and which could serve as a leaven for regeneration. He may be judged, therefore, not as one may judge Muhammad but as one may judge Christ. He left the creedal content of the movement largely undeveloped and its organization vague and incomplete. We have to judge 'this first Sikh in a fuller measure than himself, by other Sikhs and what came after him'. 'Was there something worldly after all in Nanak?'[37]

The psalms of Guru Nanak 'expound a socially and spiritually extensive and inclusive religion' in the name of One who makes no unfavourable distinctions among men, even though they themselves are born 'high and low by His will'. There is an optimistic note in Guru Nanak that was 'unusual in Hindu India'. 'It is Sat Nam that frees the devotee from the control of Karma and from the round of transmigration'.[38] On the basis of his understanding of the *Japjī*, Archer comes to the conclusion that Guru Nanak proposed the superiority of the 'way of truth' over the 'way of knowledge' and the 'way of works'. He commended the way of truth as superior even to the'way of bhakti'. Archer thinks that

Guru Nanak was preaching the way of *bhakti* with the True Name as its inspiration. The *bhakti mārga* was to Guru Nanak 'the true way if pursued in the true Name'. He proposed, 'even though not deliberately, a fourth way of salvation, more instrumental and effective than any one or all of the other three'.[39]

Guru Nanak introduced no formal legal code. Nor did he suggest any specific alterations in the immemorial legal usages of Indian tribes and clans. He took the state for granted. That is why Archer looks upon the appointment of a successor as of crucial importance. The successors of Guru Nanak gave Sikhism a form 'measurably in harmony with Nanak's legacy and his own intention'. The decades between the death of Guru Nanak and the martyrdom of Guru Arjan are seen by Archer as the 'period of adjustment'. Guru Nanak had made the public kitchen 'a distinctive feature of the Sikhs'. All the visitors and disciples ate 'as one family, regardless of race, wealth, sex, caste, occupation or religion'. Guru Angad extended the operation of the public kitchen and enlarged his ministry. Guru Nanak had used essentially 'the language of the village folk' for his hymns. Guru Angad provided for these hymns their distinctive alphabet: 'through his effort arose Gurmukhi as a new language of religion'.[40]

Guru Amar Das's career in office gave further emphasis to the development of Sikhism as 'something more than a mere sect of Hinduism'. His verse became the channel of his message. He denounced the practice of *satī*, giving it a figurative spiritual meaning. Guru Amar Das composed his *Anand* to be commonly used at wedding festivals. In general terms too, the Sikh movement was marked by joy (*anand*) rather than sorrow (*udās*) to distinguish it from the 'mere negative asceticism' of Sri Chand.[41] Archer attributes to Guru Ram Das not only the founding of Ramdaspur but also the construction of the Harmandar amidst the 'pool of immortality'. Sikhism came to assume 'more definite proportions as an actually new community' during the time of Guru Arjan, 'the fashioner of a second sword'. His era was 'a time of utter transformation in the mission of the Sikhs'. Matters creedal, ritual, financial, political and social became public issues for the Sikhs in a special sense. Guru Arjan's noblest achievement was the assembling of the *Ādi Granth* into compact, coherent form, and its elevation as authoritative scripture. The Sikhs became a people of the book (*granth*), like the Muslims with their Qurān and Hindus with their Shāstras. The governing principle was 'the Sikh communal consciousness'.[42] Guru Arjan had to deal with matters of importance other than ritual and scriptural. To meet increased, legitimate expenses, voluntary offerings were no longer adequate. 'A church and even a state were virtually in process of formation'. Every adult Sikh was asked to pay a tenth of his gross income to support the kitchens, the sanctuaries and the office of Guruship. Tithe-gatherers were appointed to work under supervisors (*masands*). 'Sikhs were getting acquainted with and practising self-government'. Then there was trade. Sikhs began to travel freely anywhere, uninhibited by any religious taboo. 'There were political considerations also, with their own social and religious implications'.[43]

The larger world of the Mughals took increasing notice of the Sikhs. Guru Arjan was fined, imprisoned, and tortured to death as 'the first martyr of the Sikhs'. However, it was not the martyrdom alone which made the Sikhs warlike. 'Sikhs were slowly getting organized and as an organism they came to be confronted by some circumstantial need of war'. The 'martial mood' was in the making in a situation of 'competition' between the Sikh church and the Mughal state. 'It was not long before rumor, whether couched in terms of the last "words of Arjun" or in others, began to pass through the Indian bazaars and along the pilgrim routes that a change of mood prevailed among the Sikhs'. In Archer's explanation of how a 'fellowship of reconciliation was assuming martial form', no single event and no single person is pin-pointed. This transformation was the result of 'adjustment' that took place after 1539 in consonance with Guru Nanak's legacy and his intentions.[44]

The Sikh attitude under Guru Hargobind was not aggressive but the principle of mutual antagonism between Sikhs and Muslims by this time was well established. He asked for offerings of arms and horses as well as money. 'The nation in the making must defend itself, he thought, and be ready likewise for offensive, if necessary'. The 'communal consciousness' of the Sikhs made them feel distinct from Hindus as well. In Archer's view, the construction of Akāl Takht ('Throne of the Timeless'), completed by Guru Hargobind, was begun by Guru Arjan. Archer was not interested in the battles of Guru Hargobind. But he does comment on the devotion of his Sikhs to him: several of his followers would have cast themselves into the very flames of his funeral pyre.[45] Archer takes notice of the *Vārs* of Bhai Gurdas as evidence of a heightened sense of Sikh communal consciousness: in them, Sikhism is superior to all other faiths, and the Sikhs are different from all other communities, not just Hindus and Muslims. Archer saw nothing of great significance in the careers of Guru Har Rai and Guru Har Krishan but Sikhism under Guru Tegh Bahadur took on a 'martial character' so that he was more than a 'harmless' guide in spiritual concerns. The orthodoxy of Aurangzeb and the 'party' of Guru Tegh Bahadur were 'incompatible'.[46]

Guru Gobind Singh became a champion of the lowly peoples of North India and 'an irreconcilable foe' of Muslim rule. His measures resulted in 'further integration' of Sikhism and its 'ultimate expansion'. Archer has the institution of the Khalsa in mind in making this observation. In 1699 Guru Gobind Singh was 'a man of forty': 'mature, seasoned and resourceful, with an enhanced sense of divine assistance in his discharge of sacred duty, and enjoying the confidence of a large following and the general public'. He summoned all Sikhs to Anandpur on the Baisakhi day, 'announcing that the goddess Durga has already bestowed her blessing upon his enterprise'. Guru Gobind Singh knew the value of appeal to her. He did not see anything in her worship 'necessarily incongruous with Sikhism'. Nor did this make Guru Gobind Singh 'a Hindu'. He was proceeding 'with some independence and sound judgment of his own'. Several unifying factors made the Khalsa Sikhs 'unique', and there was no violent departure from the earlier Sikh tradition. There was some telescoping in the code ascribed to Guru Gobind Singh. But one thing was certain: 'there was instituted an imposing order, adequately free, on the whole, of contaminations from Hinduism and Islam'. The concept of Guruship too was undergoing change. *Wāhgurūjī kā Khalsa, Wāhgurūjī ki Fateh* suggested to Archer that Guru Gobind Singh was thinking of putting an end to personal Guruship. The *Ādi Granth* was a logical alternative to the personal Guru.[47] However, even after Banda Bahadur's death, the question of Guruship was still 'somewhat indeterminate'. This question was answering itself 'by a gradual but sure process'.[48]

In the early eighteenth century the Sikhs stood divided into a number of sects and parties: the Bandeis, the Handālīs, the Ramraiyyas, the Miṇas, the Dhirmalliyas, the Masandīs, the Nanakpanthīs, the Udāsīs, the Nirmalās, the Sewāpanthīs and the Akālīs-Nihangs-Shahīds (as a single category). Archer looked upon the last as the most important. Regarding themselves as the heirs of Guru Gobind Singh's tradition, the Akālīs rallied many other Sikhs to build the Khalsa of Guru Gobind Singh's conception. Some active unity was forged against the Muslims by these members of the 'third religion'. From the middle of the eighteenth century bands of Sikhs could be found all over the central Punjab. In 1764 a committee of the Akālīs called a diet in Amritsar to proclaim the independence of the Sikh state and religion. A theocracy (*gurmata*) was formed, consisting of a representative assembly sitting as a committee of the whole (*sarbat*) and taking counsel (*mata*) in the name of God the Guru. It provided unity of action, grounded in the theory of Sikh faith.[49]

Archer talks about the *misls* to emphasize the unity of action and sums up the position of the Sikh Panth before the end of the eighteenth century. To an outside observer, Sikhism was 'a loose collection of misls and sardars, of panths and mahants'. Politics among them were more apparent than religion. Observing the Sikhs closely, however, one could see that this loose confederacy was, nonetheless, dominated by 'the ideal of the Khalsa', with religion as perhaps the chief of its ingredients. The men of action moved in a field 'so large and varied that no less than a three-fold standard should be applied to its appraisal, namely, politics, religion and morality'.[50]

Maharaja Ranjit Singh gave Sikhism a state. His own religion was scarcely more than form. He made it political and diplomatic, 'an affair of man and not of God'. Yet he was punctilious in worship, was not only present regularly at public prayers, but listened daily to readings from the *Ādi Granth*. Nevertheless, his Sikhism had something of a Hindu odour. He celebrated Hindu festivals, gave financial aid to Hindu holy places, and he countenanced *satī* among Sikhs. On his own *samādh*, four wives and seven concubines are commemorated as *satīs*. It may be argued that by maintaining *gurdwaras* and their custodians Ranjit Singh had met his obligation towards religion.[51]

For morality, however, Maharaja Ranjit Singh did not escape personal responsibility. He was promiscuous in sex affairs. He was addicted to both liquor and *bhang*. Both liquor and *bhang* were used frequently by the *sardārs* and the rank and file of Sikhs. The Singhs were men of courage but they often simulated bravery with *bhang*. Sikhism had gained much, but at the cost of morals. Even 'the Khalsa' had not been realized in terms commensurate with the larger plan of Guru Gobind Singh in which considerations of politics, morals and religion were held in delicate balance.[52]

Archer had been visiting the Punjab in the 1930s and 1940s. He had the privilege of seeing at Kartarpur in 1946 the original Granth prepared by Guru Arjan. He contributed an article to *The Review of Religion* in 1949, carrying the title 'the Bible of the Sikhs'.[53] This article briefly described the Kartarpur manuscript and ended with the note that 'an altogether comprehensive and intensive study of the Bible of the Sikhs' may be undertaken. Archer was aware that several Sikh scholars were engaged in research 'in the history, composition, and authentic content of the Book' to seek answers to questions raised within the community. The scope of this research could be extended, he argued, to include linguistics and a comparative study of the various versions of the compositions of the *bhagats*. Reputable Sikh scholars could be encouraged to undertake historical and textual criticism of the Kartarpur manuscript.

Though Archer starts with the statement that he assumed the Kartarpur manuscript to be the original Granth, his description was meant to suggest that the 'problem of the book is, of course, acute'. The problem is summed up at the outset: 'it bears no date, nor the name of any scribe. Its history is not altogether clear, nor has the authenticity of all its contents been established'. The two other accepted versions of the *Ādi Granth* did not improve matters. The

Bhai Banno version contained a hymn of Mira Bai, besides being simply a copy of the Kartarpur recension. The Granth authenticated by Guru Gobind Singh contained his own verse and the *bāṇī* of Guru Tegh Bahadur, in addition to what was there in the Kartarpur recension. But the copy authenticated by Guru Gobind Singh was lost. The printed Granth was 'for the most part, an uncritical reproduction of the Kartarpur original' together with the additions made by Guru Gobind Singh. With his subdued scepticism, thus, Archer raised by implication the issue of the authenticity of the Granth at Kartarpur.

C.H. Loehlin reinforced Archer's plea for historical and textual criticism. He had visited Kartarpur twice in 1946 and, like Archer, taken rough notes. Archer's note as quoted by Loehlin is not ambiguous any more: the authenticity of the Kartarpur Granth 'cannot be proved'. Loehlin goes on to add that their observations were not 'superficial'. Both of them were familiar with the 'textual criticism of the Christian scriptures', involving an effort to establish 'the original text with no original manuscripts of it extant'. If the authenticity of the Kartarpur Granth was proved, the Sikhs 'will hold a unique position among the religions of the world'. He suggested that photostatic copies of the entire volume could be made for intensive study.[54]

In his *Sikhs and their Scriptures*, Loehlin starts with the environment of tyranny in which Guru Nanak attempted a reconciliation of the two warring communities on the basis of a synthesis of Hinduism and Islam 'to form a new brotherhood'. The 'sect' of the Sikh Gurus was one of the sects which sprang from the teachings of Kabir. Like Kabir, Guru Nanak represented the Bhakti tradition which was meant 'to synthesize Hinduism and Islam'. The synthesis produced by the Sikh Gurus resulted in an 'intermediate religion'. 'Sufism offered Bhakti Hinduism a congenial field of contact for this fusion'. According to Loehlin, Guru Nanak rejected the Vedas and other scriptures, priesthood of the Brahmans, caste, idolatry, pilgrimages, asceticism, *ahimsa* and animal sacrifice but he retained pantheism, *karma*, transmigration, *māyā*, necessity of the Guru, repetition of the Name, *bhakti*, and salvation by grace. From Islam, Guru Nanak took the idea of One Absolute God, theocracy, repetition of God's name, fatalism, hatred of idolatry, a central shrine and daily prayers. The difference of Sikhism with Christianity related to ten Gurus instead of one Perfect Guru, baptism only of adults, no special recurring day of worship like Sunday, set prayers for every day, and physical symbols. Nevertheless, Loehlin thinks that several ideas and practices could have possibly come from Christianity: salvation by grace, lay readers of scriptures, reality of sin and need of forgiveness, sacrifice in service, baptism and the communion meal, congregational hymn singing and worship by all men and women and children, and organization of local congregations. At the same time Loehlin thinks that congregational worship could have been taken from Buddhism.[55] Loehlin's cataloguing of ideas and practices in terms of 'influences' does not clarify any issue. His interpretation of Sikhism tends to emphasize its similarity with Bhakti.

Loehlin's *Granth of Guru Gobind Singh and The Khalsa Brotherhood* was meant to correct the 'militaristic interpretation' of Guru Gobind Singh's mission.[56] A substantial portion of his book is devoted to the *Dasam Granth.* He discusses its status, purpose, character, form and language in two chapters. He underlines its importance by stating that the Sikhs have 'two books of scripture'. The *Ādi Granth* aimed at developing 'the mystical and contemplative side' of the Sikh character; the *Dasam Granth* aimed at developing 'the martial side of the Sikhs'. These two books 'helped form the Sikh ideal man, the soldier-saint'. However, only 'a handful of extremists regard the Dasam Granth in its entirety as in any way equal to the Adi Granth'.[57]

The writings included in the *Dasam Granth* were composed by Guru Gobind Singh and his fifty-two bards and translators mainly in two phases: at Anandpur and Paonta before 1700, and at Damdama in 1705-06. While the others wrote in Braj, Guru Gobind Singh wrote in Punjabi and Persian as well. The Granth was compiled by Bhai Mani Singh in 1734. After his martyrdom in 1738, Sikh scholars assembled at Damdama expressed doubt about the spiritual value of much of its content. The issue was decided in favour of retaining the Granth as it was, but only because Mahtab Singh succeeded in killing Massa Ranghar and returning alive – a criterion which strictly speaking was extraneous to the terms of the debate and, therefore, arbitrary. The purpose of translating Hindu literature is stated explicitly by Guru Gobind Singh at the end of the *Krishan Avtār*: 'I have rendered in the vernacular the tenth chapter of the Bhagvat with no other purpose than to arouse desire for a holy war'. This militant purpose becomes clear from the various books of the Granth.[58]

Loehlin endorses the general agreement that the *Jāp* was written by Guru Gobind Singh. The idea of incarnation is emphatically rejected in this composition. The *Akāl Ustat*, a jumble of subjects, was a composition of Guru Gobind Singh, but not entirely. Loehlin does not like to believe that Guru Gobind Singh composed the section containing verses with 'amoral flavour'. But he is not surprised to see the Goddess riding the tiger in this 'praise of the Immortal'. Despite its invocations to the God of war, the composition ends with an attitude of universal tolerance. Loehlin is inclined to endorse the general agreement that the *Bachittar Nātak* was composed by Guru Gobind Singh. He has reservations, however, about a section which 'seems far too Hindu in outlook and ideals', such as the exaltation of the Vedas and the sanctity of caste. This could not be 'the guru's own work'. The two-fold nature of Guru Gobind Singh's mission to create the warrior-saint is well exemplified in the *Bachittar Nātak*.[59]

The epic of *Chandī* in Punjabi was another work of Guru Gobind Singh. The first verse of this *vār* is always recited at the beginning of the Sikh prayer (*ardās*). Much of the *Giān Prabodh* seemed contrary to the authentic teachings of Guru Gobind Singh, but it was sought to be authenticated by the use of '*patshahi* 10' at its heading. Loehlin finds it hard to conceive that Guru Gobind Singh was the translator of the *Chaubīs Avtār*. Its great mass must have been produced by the bards, some of whom must have been Hindus and 'probably all had imbibed the culture and mythology of Hinduism'. At the end of the *Rām Avtār*, Guru Gobind Singh makes it clear that he did not accept the opinions of the Purānas or of the Qurān, nor the doctrines of the Smritis, Shāstras or the Vedas. The *Shabad Hazāre* and thirty-three *Sawaiye* were composed by Guru Gobind Singh. Another of his authentic compositions is the

Zafarnāma. Loehlin comes to the conclusion that the *Chaubīs Avtār*, *Shastar Nām*, *Pakhyān Charitar*, and the *Hikāyāt* were probably the work of the bards. These may have been supervised by Guru Gobind Singh who sometimes added verses of his own. Thus, the Guru's authentic compositions cover only about 170 out of over 1400 pages of the *Dasam Granth* compiled by Bhai Mani Singh.[60]

Loehlin compares the two Granths, reiterating that only the *Ādi Granth* has the status of the Guru. In general, both the Granths accept the Hindu theology of the contemplative *bhakti* type. Both express boundless wonder at the Creator and His universe. However, Guru Nanak's God is the God of truth while Guru Gobind Singh invokes the immortal, deathless and unchanging God. Both the Granths reject Hindu practices such as pilgrimages, the sacred thread, caste, asceticism, and idolatry. And both seem at times to be tinged with Hindu pantheism, and with Muslim ideas of the absoluteness of God, and of fatalism. Both take for granted *karma* and transmigration. Both use the vernacular, and both are rhymed poetry. Their main difference is that of purpose. The *Ādi Granth* 'aims at peace of mind, the *Dasam Granth* at readiness for war'. There is nothing in the *Japjī* of Guru Nanak like the hundreds of negative attributes used to describe the immortal One in the *Jāp*, nor like the dozens of Muslim names for God. There is nothing in the *Jāp* like the emphasis of the *Japjī* on God's *hukm* or the mystical realms of Guru Nanak. 'Resting on a common theological foundation, the Adi Granth had taken form as a temple, the Dasam Granth as fortress'.[61]

Loehlin gives a whole chapter to *hukamnamas*, many of which were issued by Guru Gobind Singh. They have not merely a human interest but also historical importance. We may agree with Loehlin that these *hukamnāmas* reveal religious, political, social, literary, and economic conditions 'in the intimate way letters do'. But Loehlin fails to relate this evidence in any appreciable way to either the life of Guru Gobind Singh or his creative writings. The chapter does not integrate with the rest of the book. Loehlin was probably tempted to talk of this fascinating evidence ready to hand in Ganda Singh's *Hukamnāmey*.[62]

Loehlin points out some similarities between the writings of Guru Gobind Singh and the *Gītā*. These similarities relate to the mission of Krishna on the one hand and that of Guru Gobind Singh on the other. Both hold out reward for death on the field of battle; both celebrate the destructive might of God; and both put emphasis on 'a mission of deliverance and mercy, and on a God who is supremely gracious'. Nevertheless, Guru Gobind Singh rejects the teaching of the *Gītā* on caste duties, incarnation, action without desire, *nirvana*, and the value of Yoga and asceticism. Loehlin takes up Guru Gobind Singh's attitude towards Islam in order to correct the widespread opinion that he was an irreconcilable enemy of all Muslims. The Muslim terms used for God in the *Jāp* appear to be relevant here. And so is the Guru's semitic outlook on the subject of incarnation. The dealings of Guru Gobind Singh even with the fanatical Aurangzeb 'show a singular lack of vindictiveness'. The Guru's relations with Bahadur Shah also indicate that he was not opposed to conciliation on fair terms. Loehlin concludes his discussion by referring to the *Akāl Ustat* in which 'the temple and the mosque are the same, puja and namaz are the same'. Allah and Abhekh are the same; the Purān and the Qurān are the same; all are the creation of the One.[63]

Loehlin's Appendix on 'The Need for Textual and Historical Criticism' reproduces the short paper he had presented to the Punjab History Conference in 1965. But he goes on to say:

> If the problem of the Adi Granth is so acute, it should be evident from the preceding account how much more so that of the tenth Granth is. Who wrote it? How really was it compiled ? What is its authentic text ? What is the purpose of its various books? [64]

There was a difference in the order and division of the contents in the various manuscripts of the *Dasam Granth* prepared by Bhai Mani Singh. The need of 'literary criticism' was evident from the fact that there was no general agreement as to what the Guru wrote himself, what he edited, what the bards wrote, and whether he approved of their writings or not. The Sikh as well as Western scholars of Sikhism had noted lack of critical interest on the part of the Sikhs. 'Fortunately, many of their scholars and research experts are doing research on textual and historical problems'.[65] Truth was the main attribute of God for Guru Nanak. Guru Gobind Singh declared that he would not remain silent through fear of mortals. Loehlin saw no reason why the followers of Guru Nanak and Guru Gobind Singh should not pursue truth in a spirit of fearless independence.

IV

The half a century after the Gurdwara Reform Movement was marked by increasing interest in Sikhism and Sikh history. Besides interpretations of Sikhism, annotated texts of both the *Ādi Granth* and the *Dasam Granth* were published, and parts of these texts were studied in some detail. The problem of authenticity was raised, first by Sikh scholars, particularly in relation to the *Rāgmālā* which involved the Kartarpuri Bīṛ, and then by Archer and Loehlin who emphasized the need of historical and textual criticism in relation to both the *Ādi Granth* and the *Dasam Granth*. Bhai Jodh Singh's *Kartarpuri Bīṛ de Darshan* was published in this context to establish the authenticity of the Kartarpur manuscript.

One major issue in the study of Sikhism was its character and its status. This was not a new issue. After the publication of Macauliffe's work, Sikh scholars reinforced the view that Sikhism was an original, independent system of beliefs and practices. The work of Bhai Kanh Singh Nabha, Professor Teja Singh, and Bhai Jodh Singh provided the norm from the Sikh viewpoint. Teja Singh and Ganda Singh take this view almost for granted in their *Short History of the Sikhs*. Both Archer and Loehlin agree that Sikhism eventually emerged as a world religion, but they differ from the Sikh viewpoint regarding the origins of Sikhism. Loehlin makes no distinction between Vaishnava *bhakti* and Kabir and looks upon Guru Nanak as indebted to both. For him, Sikhism is a synthesis of Bhakti Hinduism and Sūfī Islam, and it stands equated essentially with the *bhakti-mārga*. Archer isolates Kabir from Vaishnava *bhakti* and sees his relevance for Guru Nanak. Nevertheless, Guru Nanak is distinguished by his doctrine of the True Name. His movement was distinct from that of Kabir. Indeed, Archer talks of Guru

Nanak's path as the fourth way which was more efficacious than all the other three: *karma*, *giān*, and *bhakti*.

Apart from the character and status of Sikhism, the historians of this phase were interested in the life of Guru Nanak. This interest brought in the question of sources for his biography. It was generally agreed that *Janamsākhīs* were not easy to utilize for a historical biography of Guru Nanak. Teja Singh and Ganda Singh try to see the relevance and significance of *sākhīs* in natural and human terms. Only at one place they seem to accept something supernatural. Archer raises the issue of the *Janamsākhīs* to a different plane altogether by postulating a distinction between the factual and the formless Nanak. This is only another way of referring to 'the Nanak of history' and 'the Nanak of faith'. For Archer's purpose, there was no urgency for isolating the one from the other, but he did emphasize the need of a strictly historical biography of Guru Nanak.

Teja Singh and Ganda Singh, Archer, and Loehlin do not see the Khalsa of Guru Gobind Singh as a sudden departure from the earlier Sikh movement, but they differ in their views of the starting point and, consequently, in their understanding of the development between the time of Guru Nanak and Guru Gobind Singh. Teja Singh and Ganda Singh talk of 'transfiguration' to emphasize the historical and logical links between the ideas of Guru Nanak and the structure raised by his successors. Archer attaches due importance to the *Japjī* as the nucleus of the Sikh scripture and to *langar* as the institution embedded in the idea of equality. The work of Guru Angad, Guru Amar Das, Guru Ram Das and Guru Arjan, in his view, made the Sikh Panth a state within the Mughal empire and brought it into competition with the Mughal state. This view makes Guru Hargobind an integral part of the elan of the Sikh movement. The difference between Archer and Teja Singh and Ganda Singh relates to Guru Nanak's attitude toward politics. Whereas Teja Singh and Ganda Singh underline his concern for the political and the social disabilities of the people, Archer tends to look upon Guru Nanak as more or less apolitical.

Loehlin's latest position on the development of the Sikh Panth is stated in his *Granth of Guru Gobind Singh*. Since each Guru built upon the work of his predecessors, Loehlin summarizes their contribution. When Guru Nanak chose Angad as the Guru in preference to Sri Chand, Sikhism broke with the ascetic tradition. The Sikhs have been a body of house-holders ever since. Guru Angad adapted an existing alphabet of the Punjab into the Gurmukhi script which has remained the sacred script of the Sikhs ever since. Guru Amar Das organized the *manjī* system, bringing the Sikh genius for organization into operation. He started work on the Golden Temple. It was completed by Guru Arjan by a regular system of collecting tithes through the *masands*. He founded Tarn Taran and Kartarpur and he compiled the *Ādi Granth* in 1604. 'The last five gurus had to face an increasingly aggressive and hostile Islamic state, and gradually built up an army of defence'. Guru Arjan and Guru Tegh Bahadur suffered martyrdom. It was left for Guru Gobind Singh 'to complete the development of Sikhism by founding the militant Khalsa Brotherhood which has survived severe persecution by fanatical Muslim emperors, and infiltration by Hindus, and is the main cohesive force of Sikhism today'.[66]

Loehlin bases his short account of Guru Gobind Singh mainly on the works of Macauliffe and Teja Singh and Ganda Singh. His description of the institution of the Khalsa conforms to what his predecessors had published. But he tends to subscribe to the view that Guru Gobind Singh propitiated the Goddess at Naina Devi. Whereas Teja Singh and Ganda Singh maintain that Guru Gobind Singh wanted to disillusion the people, Loehlin remains formally neutral about his belief. Archer appears to subscribe to the view that Guru Gobind Singh believed in the Goddess. All the four writers agree that Guru Gobind Singh went through the ritual of invoking the Goddess, as they agree on nearly all other points connected with the institution of the Khalsa. Archer suggests, however, that the Khalsa *rahit* was not entirely the result of a single pronouncement but of a gradual development extending presumably into the eighteenth century.

None of the four writers suggests that Guruship was vested in either the Granth or the Panth at the time of instituting the Khalsa. Teja Singh and Ganda Singh are quite explicit that Guru Gobind

Singh bequeathed Guruship to the Khalsa towards the close of his life. Loehlin states that Guru Gobind Singh proclaimed the *Granth Sahib* to be the only Guru of the Sikhs. At this time there was no *Dasam Granth*. Therefore the 'Granth Sahib' in question was the *Ādi Granth* finalized by Guru Gobind Singh himself. Archer looks upon the *Granth Sahib* as the logical alternative to personal Guruship and he recognizes the increasing importance of the Khalsa and its authority. But he is vague about the timing. In fact he leaves the impression that the Guruship of the Granth and the Panth came to be established gradually during the eighteenth century. The doctrine of Guru-Granth remains far more important for Archer than the doctrine of Guru-Panth.

All the four writers agree that the Sikh movement was egalitarian. The Khalsa order in particular was an egalitarian social order. But only Loehlin discusses the idea of equality in relation to the system of castes. The Khatri Gurus, according to him, can be seen as rejecting the authority of the Brahmans. The Sikhs themselves 'have an obsession against domination of any kind in their democracy'. Furthermore, there were almost no restrictions on the kinds of food that may be eaten, 'except that they do not eat beef, more from social custom than from religious convictions'. There was no cow-*puja* among the Sikhs. Their whole attitude towards eating with others was embodied in the *langar*, the free kitchen attached to their important *gurdwaras*. It was open to all 'regardless of creed or caste, and all must sit down and eat together'. In making marriage arrangements, however, the Sikhs normally 'do observe caste restrictions'. The Sikh Gurus made converts from the lower castes or even from the outcastes. However, they were not received by the Sikhs of higher castes as 'social equals' and sometimes 'equality of worship' was not accorded to them. Loehlin points out that the inclusion of many hymns from 'low caste Bhagats' is an interesting feature of the *Ādi Granth*. The fact that the Golden Temple was open on all four sides was taken to symbolize that God is everywhere and that Sikhism is open to the entry of all men. 'There is thus much teaching in Sikhism that is against caste distinctions, and the standard of equality set in the Granth is high'. Loehlin goes on to add, however, that in spite of their original protest against caste, the Sikhs do practise caste to some extent, and 'belong in the caste system'. But the war on caste was still going on.[67]

NOTES

1. Pritam Singh (1989).
2. Professor Teja Singh admires Bhai Kanh Singh for his 'profound and unrivalled' knowledge of the Sikh Scriptures, his fondness for minute detail, and his capacity to take large views of subjects, combining, thus, the qualities of 'traditional' and Western scholarship.
3. Professor Sahib Singh takes the reader into confidence about his interest in various subjects and the completion of his studies.
4. Ganda Singh. 'Editorial'. *The Panjab Past and Present*. Volume IV, part 2 (October 1970), pp. i and ii.
5. That Teja Singh and Ganda Singh intended to bring out more volumes on Sikh history is evident from the use of 'Volume One' for the work published in 1950.
6. Kapur Singh (1989). Despite the limited scope suggested by the original title, this work was a fresh interpretation of the Sikh faith, imparting new significance to the baptism of the double-edged sword and the Khalsa *rahit*.
7. Ashta takes the whole of the *Dasam Granth* to be the work of Guru Gobind Singh, with the obvious implication of his acceptance of the 'Hindu' tradition.
8. This book was reprinted in 1979.
9. The Christian-Sikh dialogue in the Punjab was marked by sobriety. In any case, Archer and Loehlin were writing more than half a century after Trumpp. By then, Christian attitudes towards Indian religions had changed a good deal. Denunciation was replaced by serious effort to understand.
10. Teja Singh and Ganda Singh (1989), pp. 26-27 n 1, for example.
11. Ibid., pp. 38 n 1, 39 n 1 and 54 n 1.
12. Ibid., pp. 10 n 5, 12 n1, 34 n 2, 63 n 3 and 73-74 n 2.
13. Ibid., Preface, p. iii.
14. Ibid., pp. 2-5, 9 n 1 and 11-12.
15. We find only one detail accepted literally from the *Janamsākhīs* by Teja Singh and Ganda Singh that involves acceptance of the supernatural: 'red blood of tortured humanity trickling from the rich dainties of Malik Bhago': Ibid., p. 6.
16. Ibid., pp. 13-16.
17. Ibid., p. 18 and n 1.
18. Ibid., pp. 18-23.
19. Ibid., pp. 23-28.

20. Ibid., pp. 28-31 and 68-72.
21. Ibid., pp. 32-34.
22. Ibid., pp. 35-42.
23. Ibid., pp. 44-68.
24. Ibid., pp. 68-75.
25. Ibid., pp. 76-83.
26. Ibid., pp. 84-102.
27. Ibid., pp. 43-44, 104 and 106-08.
28. Ibid., pp. 105-6, 112, 128, 144-45, 148-49 and 173.
29. Archer (1946), pp. v-vii.
30. Ibid., pp. v and 2.
31. Ibid., pp. 3 , 5 and 6.
32. Ibid., pp. 37-56.
33. Ibid., pp. 57-65.
34. Ibid., pp. 65-71.
35. Ibid., pp. 72-87.
36. Ibid., pp. 88-105.
37. Ibid., pp. 105-07.
38. Ibid., pp. 108-17.
39. Ibid., pp. 119-33.
40. Ibid., pp. 134-39.
41. Ibid., pp. 139-41.
42. Ibid., pp. 142-52.
43. Ibid., pp. 152-53.
44. Ibid., pp. 169-71.
45. Ibid., pp. 172-74.
46. Ibid., pp. 174-86.
47. Ibid., pp. 187-98.
48. Ibid., pp. 198-219.
49. Ibid., pp. 221-35.
50. Ibid., pp. 236-37.
51. Ibid., pp. 238-45.
52. Ibid., pp. 245-46.
53. Archer (1977), pp. 22-31.
54. Loehlin (1966), pp. 93-96. The doubts raised by Loehlin were sought to be removed by Bhai Jodh Singh in his 'Note on Kartarpur Granth': Ibid., 97-99.
55. Loehlin (1958), pp. 3 and 4.
56. Ibid., (1958), pp. 3, 4, 10, 35, 43-44, 54, 57-58, 59, 60, 61 and Table III.
57. Ibid., (1971), Preface.
58. Ibid., pp. 9-10.
59. Ibid., pp. 18-20.
60. Ibid., pp. 20-32.

61. Ibid., pp. 9 and 57-59.
62. Ibid., pp. 61-67. Cf. Ganda Singh (1967).
63. Loehlin (1970), pp. 75-79.
64. Ibid., pp. 97-102.
65. Ibid., p. 103.
66. Ibid., pp. 1-2 and 16.
67. Ibid., pp. 10-14.

Part Two

THE RECENT CONTROVERSY

5. Emergence of the Debate

The current debate in Sikh studies can be traced directly to the publication of the *Perspectives on the Sikh Tradition* in 1986. Formally, it was brought out by the Academy of Sikh Religion and Culture from Patiala. It was edited by the President of the Academy, Justice Gurdev Singh, a former Judge of the Punjab and Haryana High Court. It is divided into six parts. The first part contains the editor's Introduction and an essay on 'critical scholarship' by Professor Noel Q. King. The second part consists of five chapters by Sardar Daljeet Singh on comparative study of Nathism, Vaishnavism and Sikhism. The third part, on the birth of the Khalsa, is a single chapter by Professor Hari Ram Gupta. The fourth part, on Guru Granth Sahib, contains two essays, one by Dr. Ganda Singh and the other by Professor Harbans Singh. The fifth part on caste among the Sikhs and the sixth on 'militarization' of the Sikh movement are by Professor Jagjit Singh. The 'foreword' to this volume was contributed by Sardar Khushwant Singh, a well known historian of the Sikhs and known even better as a journalist and creative writer. Both Justice Gurdev Singh and Khushwant Singh look upon this book as primarily a refutation of the works of Professor W.H. McLeod.

I

There was a mixed reaction to W.H. McLoed's *Gurū Nānak and the Sikh Religion* after its publication in 1968. Some of its reviews appeared to be extremely 'hostile'. Dr. Ganda Singh thought it was necessary to examine 'this criticism' because it involved 'certain principles of historiography'. He pointed out that Karam Singh had already conducted a critical appraisal of the *Janamsākhīs* in his *Kattik kih Visākh.* He went on to add that the 'obscurity and darkness about the events of the Guru's life must go, if the real Master has to be discovered'. There could be 'no compromise between history and fiction, between light and darkness and between truth and falsehood'. It was imperative to discard 'fictional traditions' in the interest of 'truthful history' for our own enlightenment and for that of 'the rising generation'. In support of McLeod's treatment of the *Janamsākhīs*, Dr. Ganda Singh observed that there was a good deal amiss in a number of *sākhīs,* 'historically, geographically or chronologically'. The accounts of Guru Nanak's travels are 'so conflicting and confusing' and 'so ungeographically set' that it is 'well nigh impossible' to accept them in all their details.[1]

With reference to the reviews of McLeod's work, Dr. Ganda Singh observed that there could be 'no greater injustice than misquoting an author' or quoting him out of context. A few of the reviewers had doubted the author's intention and his motives. In Dr. Ganda Singh's view, this was 'morally wrong, if nothing else'. In any case, he had known McLeod personally for several years and could say with confidence that his motives were 'honest and pure'. Some of the reviewers were unduly upset over McLeod's observations on Guru Nanak's visit to Mecca and Baghdad. 'Credulousness is not a praiseworthy quality in a research scholar, nor is skepticism a great defect'. Dr. Ganda Singh goes on to add, nevertheless, that Guru Nanak's visit to Mecca was 'not improbable' and his visit to Baghdad was almost certain. As no author is infallible, there is nothing wrong in pointing out mistakes. However, every author expected sympathetic consideration and not unjust criticism.[2] Dr. Ganda Singh also pointed out that most of the reviewers had ignored McLeod's exposition of the 'teachings' of Guru Nanak which was based on the Guru's compositions and given in 'a very lucid and convincing manner'.[3]

The late Professor Attar Singh too was appreciative of McLeod's exposition of the teachings of Guru Nanak as 'the most systematic, the most cogent and the most sympathetic'. In analysing some of the important concepts of Guru Nanak, McLeod had displayed an exceptional kind of 'semantic skill'. Professor Attar Singh had something to say also about the reaction to McLeod's *Gurū Nānak and the Sikh Religion.* The vehemence with which Sikh scholarship reacted 'more against the motives than against the findings and the formulations' of McLeod revealed the limitations of a 'purely scholastic approach' and the difficulties created by 'the identity crisis in which Sikhs as a religious group are caught up today'. Non-Sikh scholars were discouraged by 'the latent hostility of Sikh scholarship towards manifest rational exploration of any theme relating to Sikh faith'.[4]

Sikh scholarly response to McLeod's *Evolution of the Sikh Community*, published in 1975, was no less critical. The late Professor Fauja Singh saw it as a 'very bold interpretation'. The novelty of McLeod's approach lay 'chiefly in his effort to interpret the evolution of the community entirely on the basis of contemporary events and Jat cultural patterns'. Consequently, the ideology of Guru Nanak was given 'no place of importance in shaping the growth of the community'. McLeod appeared to have missed the essential elan of the Sikh movement. He regarded Guru Nanak as the founder of Sikhism in organizational but not in religious terms. One could agree with McLeod that 'the roots of some of the Guru's ideas are traceable in the past Indian religious tradition' but to say that he only followed the Sant synthesis is to go too far. 'In so far as Guru Nanak accepted social concern as central to his religious belief, he broke an independent and new ground and from that point of view he may be regarded as the founder of Sikhism in the full sense of the term'.[5]

McLeod's interpretation of the Sikh past suffered from some other limitations too. His statement that Guru Amar Das 'deviated' from the teaching of Guru Nanak in building the *bāolī* at Goindval was 'unacceptable'. In any system of religious belief it is necessary to establish institutions. Guru Nanak himself had shown the way by founding the institutions of *sangat*, *pangat*, and *dharamsal.* 'This process was accelerated under his successors in response to the requirements of the growing Sikh society'. McLeod attributed militancy to the impact of Jat culture. This too was open to question. The Jats were not the only people in the Punjab to have a martial tradition. They could not have forced Guru Hargobind to adopt militancy. The Guru wore the swords of *mīrī* and *pīrī* on his own. Above all, militancy was not 'a deviation from Guru Nanak's system of thought': it was in full accord with the ideology inherited from Guru Nanak by his successors. The Jats did make a great contribution to Sikh history, but only after the Gurus had taken the decision to meet force with force.[6]

McLeod's view that the institutions of corporate and scriptural Gurus were not established by Guru Gobind Singh, that they were subsequent developments appearing 'gradually in response to contemporary circumstances and cultural patterns of the Jats', was 'contrary to historical facts'. Fauja Singh refers to the *Gursobha* for the vesting of Guruship in the Khalsa. For the scriptural Guru, he does not refer to any definite evidence. But there was a strong belief that 'this too is based on a pronouncement of Guru Gobind Singh. Giani Garja Singh claimed that he had seen an entry to this effect in a *Bhat Vahī*. The earliest reference known to Fauja Singh himself was in the *Gurbilās* of Koer Singh. McLeod's theory of gradual evolution of the Sikh code of discipline during the eighteenth century 'needs to be scrutinized with great care'. His main argument was based on the fact that the *Rahitnāmas* were of later origin.[7]

Stretching his argument, McLeod expressed the view that the different ingredients of the Khalsa code owed their origin to cultural pattern of the Jats who dominated Sikh politics in the eighteenth century.This view was untenable so far as 'the basic code' was concerned. The injunction about uncut hair is found in some of the *hukamnāmas* issued by Guru Gobind Singh after 1699. *Kard* or *kirpān* was an object of high veneration and, therefore, in all probability a part of the original code. *Kanghā* and *kaṛā* go respectively with the uncut hair and *kirpān*. *Kachhā* is mentioned in the *Prem Sumārg*. Fauja Singh thought that confusion on this issue arose 'because all the 5Ks are not found mentioned together in contemporary or near contemporary sources'. McLeod's assumption that Jats wore uncut hair remained unsupported by evidence. 'If the uncut hair was a cherished Jat tradition, then how is it that hundreds and thousands of Hindu and Muslim Jats in the country have no attachment to it'?[8]

Fauja Singh appreciated McLeod's essay on the *Janamsākhīs* as 'probably the best of the whole lot'. It explains their nature, purpose and function and also attempts a historical assessment of the material. The essay on Sikh scriptures was full of useful information. Though McLeod takes cognizance of 'the controversy regarding the three versions of *Adi Granth*', he leaves the problem unsolved. In his short treatment of the *Dasam Granth,* he raises the issue of its value in assessing the impact of the hill culture on the Jats and, through them, on the evolution of the Sikh Panth during the eighteenth century. In McLeod's view, the Sikh Gurus abolished the caste system in the religious sphere completely and in social matters partially. This view is closer to historical realities than the extreme view that the Sikh Gurus abolished the caste system completely and established full equality, or that they abolished caste distinctions only in the religious field. However, McLeod takes 'a static and not dynamic view of things'. The process of 'liquidation of caste differentiations' was started by Guru Nanak. It reached its culmination in the Khalsa which represented a completely casteless society. Pernicious elements of the caste system appeared subsequently, particularly under Brahmanical influences.[9]

Fauja Singh's overall assessment of *The Evolution of the Sikh Community* may be quoted in full in view of the controversy this book has raised:

> To sum up, this is an extremely thought-provoking but tendentious study. The author has made a few far-reaching formulations which if correct are likely to establish a new theory of development of the Sikh community. For the present they are mostly based on conjecturing and some of them may not even serve as good hypothesis. At any rate, they demand thorough investigation from scholars. On the face of it, there is substantial ground to regard them as ill-founded, and known historical evidence contradicts them. Dr McLeod has done well to underscore the role of cultural and social factors in the evolution of the Sikhs but has underestimated the role of ideas in the historical process.[10]

Four years later, Dr. Mohinder Singh observed that McLeod's work had stirred the entire Sikh intelligentsia. His detractors felt very strongly that he had not been able to understand 'the basic spirit' of the Sikh tradition but they were unable to come out with an equally well-argued case in defence of the Sikhs and their Gurus. They were desperately waiting for a Messiah 'to come and present the other side of the picture'. Some of them saw the Messiah 'in the person of Noel Q. King, an American admirer of the Sikh faith'.[11] Significantly, Khushwant Singh refers to 'Dr Noel Q. King, currently Professor of History and Comparative Religion at the University of California, Santa Cruz, and his collaborators' in his Foreword to the *Perspectives on the Sikh Tradition*, giving undue credit of initiative to Professor King.[12]

An obituary notice after the sad demise of Sardar Daljeet Singh in October 1994 tells us that he took initiative to discuss academic matters with like-minded people, particularly with Professor Jagjit Singh and Justice Gurdev Singh, and this resulted in the publication of the *Perspectives on the Sikh Tradition*.[13] Professor Jagjit Singh says that Daljeet Singh's interest in McLeod's work was aroused by a review of his *Evolution of the Sikh Community* by Khushwant Singh which appeared to support McLeod's thesis 'in a manner that provoked Sikh sentiment'.[14] Jagjit Singh gives the impression that this provocation was the cause of Daljeet Singh's interest in Sikh studies, resulting in the publication of his *Sikhism: A Comparative Study of its Theology and Mysticism* in 1979. We know, however, that Daljeet Singh's interest in Sikh studies predates the publication of *The Evolution of the Sikh Community*. The *Journal of Sikh Studies* (February 1974) carries his article 'The Doctrine of *Maya* in Sikhism'.[15] His article on 'The Doctrine of *Naam* in Sikhism' was published in the *Journal* in August 1975.[16] Possibly, Daljeet Singh's intrinsic interest in Sikh studies and his own understanding of the Sikh faith induced him to respond to McLeod's work rather sharply.

Daljeet Singh himself reviewed *The Evolution of the Sikh Community*. Trying to give too much in too short a space and covering five major themes in a little over one hundred pages, McLeod tended to become journalistic and speculative rather than academic and comprehensive. Nearly the whole structure of his book was based on the premise that 'Sikhism had no new religious thesis' to offer. McLeod's equation of Sikhism with 'the Sant tradition' did not explain 'how the quietist mysticism of Sant tradition' suddenly transformed itself into the 'Prophetic Mysticism of Guru Nanak' marked by 'the use of body and blood'. Nor did it tell us how the inert ideal of salvation was changed into the dynamic goal of carrying out the will of God. McLeod completely ignored the role of ideology in Sikh history. Instead of finding the basis of new developments in 'the thesis' of the Gurus, he attributed their socio-political and military activities to 'the influence of Jat elements amongst Sikh ranks'. Empirical evidence did not support his hypothesis. McLeod's hypothesis about the impact of the Shakti cult ignored the glaring fact that 'the age old acceptance of the same cult by the hill people never inspired them to throw off the Muslim yoke'. In his hypothesis about the 5Ks he 'neither shows that these Ks were Jat symbols in the region before their adoption by the Sikhs nor explains why those disappeared from among all the Jats of the neighbouring regions of Haryana, Rajasthan and Pakistan'. Daljeet Singh concluded his review with the pungent remark that the book abounded in originality and historical evidence but only if oddity was equated with originality and conjectural assertions were treated as historical evidence.[17]

McLeod's interpretation had a serious flaw. He made 'the simplistic assumption' that Guru Nanak's mission was the same as that of the *bhaktas*, and then found it difficult to explain 'the exteriority, the organization and the socio-political objective and struggle' of the Sikh Gurus. Instead of revising his premises he proceeded to find props for his fragile structure in entities like Jat culture and Shakti cult. Just as the growth of Christianity cannot be explained without reference to the life and teaching of Christ, the growth of the Sikh Panth cannot be explained without reference to the thesis of the Gurus and their lives. Just as the deep concern of Jesus for the poor cannot be attributed to the presence of poor fishermen among his followers, the socio-political concerns of the Gurus cannot be attributed to the presence of Jats among their followers. It is a common failing of 'persons with mechanistic views' to ignore the role of ideology as 'a cementing and directive force in human history' and to over-stretch and over-estimate the significance of 'ordinary facts and routine events'.[18]

Professor Jagjit Singh tells us that Daljeet Singh prevailed upon him 'to put down in writing' his views 'concerning the history of the Sikh movement'.[19] Jagjit Singh's article on 'The Jats and Sikh Militarization' was published in the *Journal of Sikh Studies* in February 1977. His *Sikh Revolution* came out in 1981. It was followed by the *Perspectives in Sikh Studies* in 1985, with its last two sections devoted to the issue of caste in the Sikh Panth and the role of Jats in the Sikh movement. Thus, whether or not Jagjit Singh's interest in Sikh studies predated the publication of McLeod's *Evolution of the Sikh Community*, he had done his major work on the Sikh movement before the publication of the *Perspectives on the Sikh Tradition*.

II

Returning to the *Perspectives on the Sikh Tradition*, we can safely state that it was the result of deliberations between Sardar Daljeet Singh, Professor Jagjit Singh and Justice Gurdev Singh. About three-fifths of this book consists of contributions made by Daljeet Singh and Jagjit Singh on the basis of the work they had already published. The contributions by Hari Ram Gupta, Ganda Singh and Harbans Singh were similarly based on their published work. The only new contribution came from Noel Q. King. Significantly, Hari Ram Gupta, Ganda Singh and Harbans Singh had nothing to say against McLeod's work. Noel Q. King never forgets the merit of his work in his emphasis on the limitations of the critical method. Jagjit Singh's criticism of W.H. McLeod is scholarly and mild. Only Daljeet Singh's criticism of McLeod's work is brusque and pungent. The editor gives the impression as if all the contributors wrote in reaction to the work of W.H. McLeod. His 'introduction' is trained entirely against McLeod. Consequently, McLeod appears to be the arch villain of Sikh studies. This impression is reinforced by Khushwant Singh in his 'foreword'.[20]

Khushwant Singh refers to Cunningham's pioneering work in the field of Sikh historiography and Macauliffe's work in the field of religion, and adds that much of the recent work on Sikhism and Sikh history is little more than 'a restatement' of their facts and interpretations. Outstanding among the Sikh writers who have made an advance over Cunningham and Macauliffe are Dr. Ganda Singh, Dr. Hari Ram Gupta, Professor Harbans Singh and Professor Fauja Singh. Outstanding among the European writers is Professor W.H. McLeod. Indeed, his works proved to be 'the most challenging event in Sikh historiography'. In his *Gurū Nānak and the Sikh Religion*, McLeod came to the conclusion that 'the life-story of Guru Nanak is based on fiction', and that he 'only stated religious beliefs current during his time and should not be regarded as the founder of a new faith'. In his *Evolution of the Sikh Community*, McLeod carried his 'thesis' forward to maintain that large scale intrusion of the Jats into the Khalsa Panth, rather than something planned out by Guru Hargobind and Guru Gobind Singh, was the main cause of the metamorphosis of the pacifist Nanak-Panthīs into the militant fraternity of the Khalsa. Furthermore, McLeod questioned 'the authenticity of the baptismal ceremony of the Baisakhi of 1699' and discounted the *Rahitnāmas* as 'subsequent compilations'. To Khushwant Singh, it was 'evident' that McLeod was 'on weak ground' and some of his conclusions were 'erroneous'. The record had to be set right in order to establish that the Sikh religious tradition was not 'an edifice built on hot air or make-believe'. This was precisely what the *Perspectives on the Sikh Tradition* had done. The reader is left with the impression that McLeod has been demolished, justly and finally.

Justice Gurdev Singh starts his Introduction with a bold outline of Sikh history to hammer the point that the Sikhs have lived 'in full gaze of history'. After Independence they were concentrated in the Punjab but they settled in the rest of India too, and even in distant countries like Canada, U.S.A. and U.K. Wherever they go they attract attention, not simply because of their distinctive appearance 'but also because of their integrity, hard labour and will to work'. These moral traits evoke interest in their religion, history and social structure. Foreign scholars became interested in Sikhism and Sikh history, and some of them made valuable contribution to Sikh studies. However, though the Sikhs have 'lived, struggled and achieved something in full view of history', some tendentious work has appeared to make them 'victims of distortion, misrepresentation and misunderstanding'.[21] The foremost among the foreign writers to come on the scene in recent decades is W.H. McLeod. Even a hurried glance through his *Gurū Nānak and the Sikh Religion*, his *Evolution of the Sikh Community*, and his *Early Sikh Tradition* would reveal that he is 'at pains to propagate that Sikhism, which has recently been gaining a foothold in the West, does not deserve much consideration as it is only a rehash of an effete Hindu creed'. He is said to have done this deliberately out of a design:

> Having been involved in the Christian Missionary activities for a number of years in the Punjab, the homeland of the Sikhs, McLeod seems to be deeply conscious of the fact that after 1947 Partition of India in this part of the country, the Christian Missionary work has no future unless the faith of the new generation in its own traditions is undermined. For that purpose a fresh study, with a non-believer's approach accepting nothing that is not established to his satisfaction, of the founder of Sikh religion and Sikhism assumes importance.[22]

Justice Gurdev Singh feels convinced that McLeod has written his book with an eye on the growing Sikh generation and on the Western people 'among whom the Sikhs have recently spread and who feel attracted to the Sikh tenets'. The message gets across that 'the image of Guru Nanak hitherto projected by his numerous biographies and studies on Sikhism is not real but legendary or a myth, and Sikhism has nothing new to offer'. Whereas Khushwant Singh talks of McLeod's erroneous conclusions, Justice Gurdev Singh attributes evangelist motives to him. On the first count, McLeod is not a sound historian; on the second, he is not an honest scholar. He is out not to understand but to undermine the Sikh tradition.

According to Justice Gurdev Singh, the slow reaction of the Sikhs to his first 'tendentious work encouraged McLeod to come up with his *Evolution of the Sikh Community* in 1975'. In this book he attacks 'most of the Sikh traditions, institutions and beliefs' and questions their validity in order 'to create doubt about the others'. Eight propositions are attributed to McLeod: one, that he places Guru Nanak within the Sant tradition; two, that the successors of Guru Nanak did not preach one set of doctrines, giving up at one stage his teachings in favour of militancy; three, that the Panth got armed not because of any decision of Guru Hargobind but because of Jat influx; four, that the traditional account of the founding of the Khalsa cannot be accepted; five, that the Sikh code of discipline and Sikh symbols were evolved during the eighteenth century and not promulgated by Guru Gobind Singh on the Baisakhi of 1699; six, that the Gurus denounced caste system but they were not sincere or serious in removing caste differences; seven, that the succession of Granth Sahib as the Guru after Guru Gobind Singh was a subsequent adoption and not due to his injunction; and eight, that the authenticity of the current version of Guru Granth Sahib is open to question. These salient propositions 'belittle the Sikh faith and doctrines in the eyes of the English speaking people and other non-Sikhs'; they also tend to shake 'the faith of the younger generation of the Sikhs in their religion, Gurus, scriptures, institutions and all that they inherit'.[23]

Justice Gurdev Singh thinks that Sikh scholars in the universities of the Punjab have not cared to refute McLeod or to examine his thesis. His influence is allowed to spread by default. Sikh scholars and researchers are prone to accept McLeod's work 'in the absence of any challenge by the Sikhs themselves'. The propositions put forward by McLeod are clearly in conflict with 'the basic beliefs and long unbroken traditions of the Sikhs'. The unmistakable trend of his writings is 'to undermine the Sikh faith'. His sweeping observations tend to denigrate the mission of the Sikh Gurus. This situation called for a thorough refutation.[24]

On some of the propositions attributed to McLeod, Justice Gurdev Singh had 'studies made by well-known Indian scholars and historians', besides an essay by 'the eminent Professor of Comparative Religion and History, Dr. Noel Q. King'. Justice Gurdev Singh presents the views of the contributors in some detail to claim that McLeod stands refuted on all the major issues. Noel Q. King's essay underlines the basic fault in McLeod's methodology; Daljeet Singh's essays establish the originality and the uniqueness of the Sikh faith; Hari Ram Gupta establishes the authenticity of baptismal ceremony on the Baisakhi of 1699; Ganda Singh and Harbans Singh prove that Guru Gobind Singh abolished the system of personal Guruship by vesting Guruship in the *Granth Sahib*; Jagjit Singh demonstrates that caste distinctions were abolished by the Gurus in both theory and practice, and that 'militarization' of the Sikh movement was not due to the influx of Jats, nor to any economic crisis or any impact of the Shakti cult; it was a logical outcome of Sikh ideology and deliberate decisions of the Gurus.[25]

III

In retrospect we can see that Dr. Ganda Singh and Professor Attar Singh had positive appreciation for McLeod's *Gurū Nānak and the Sikh Religion*. Professor Fauja Singh disagreed with McLeod on several important points in his interpretation of the evolution of the Sikh Panth but he appreciated McLeod's analysis of Sikh literature and his treatment of caste. He never doubted McLeod's *bona fides* as a scholar. Professor Noel Q. King, as we shall see, regards McLeod as the greatest 'western' scholar of Sikhism and the most critical scholar of the Sikh tradition. Only two other contributors to the *Perspectives on the Sikh Tradition* have expressed some disagreement with McLeod: Sardar Daljeet Singh and Professor Jagjit Singh. Justice Gurdev Singh alone has argued the whole case against McLeod and he alone has attributed extraneous motives to him. That McLeod could possibly have some unconscious biases, like all social scientists, can be readily conceded. But Justice Gurdev Singh asserts that McLeod's deliberate purpose is to undermine Sikh tradition. We feel obliged to satisfy ourselves that Justice Gurdev Singh has presented McLeod's position accurately. We have to see further that McLeod's critics have presented his position accurately. We have also to see whether or not the contributors to this volume have performed the task which Justice Gurdev Singh attributes to them. This is the only way to clarify the issues under debate.

Two major issues appear to emerge from McLeod's *Gurū Nānak and the Sikh Religion* and its criticism: the faith of Guru Nanak, and Guru Nanak of faith. The issues which emerge from *The Evolution of the Sikh Community* and its criticism relate to the relative role of ideology and environment in the development of the Sikh Panth: institutionalization in and militarization of the Sikh movement, the Khalsa *rahit*, and the doctrines of Guruship. The question of caste in the Sikh Panth also gets related to the idea of equality and social environment. We shall take up these issues in the next four chapters .

NOTES

1. *The Panjab Past and Present.* Volume IV, part 2 (October 1970), pp. i-iv.
2. Ibid., pp. v-vi and viii-x.
3. Ibid., p. vii.
4. Ibid., Volume VI, part 1 (April 1972), pp. 234 and 237.
5. Ibid., Volume XI, part 1 (April 1977), pp. 178-79.
6. Ibid., pp. 179-80.
7. Ibid., pp. 180-81.
8. Ibid., pp. 181-82.
9. Ibid., pp. 182-84.
10. Ibid., pp. 184-85.
11. Ibid., Volume XV, part 2 (October 1981), pp. 498-500.
12. Without this context Khushwant Singh's statement does not make any sense, unless the mere fact that Professor King's article heads the book is assumed to make others his 'collaborators'.
13. *Abstracts of Sikh Studies* (January 1995), p. 4.
14. Ibid., p. 18.
15. *Journal of Sikh Studies.* Volume I, Number 1 (February 1974), pp. 57-58.
16. Ibid., Volume II, Number 2 (August 1975), pp. 27-65.
17. Ibid., Volume IV, Number 1 (February 1977), pp. 166-69.
18. Ibid., pp. 168-69.
19. *Abstracts of Sikh Studies* (January 1995), p. 18.
20. Khushwant Singh leaves the impression as if Professor Harbans Singh wrote in response to Dr. McLeod's book. A revised edition of his *Heritage of the Sikhs* appeared in 1983 but the book was first published in 1964. Even the revised edition made no attempt to set any records right.
21. *Perspectives on the Sikh Tradition,* 'Introduction', pp. 3-5.
22. Ibid., p. 5.
23. Ibid., pp. 8-10.
24. Ibid., p. 10.
25. Ibid., pp. 14-15.

6. The Faith of Guru Nanak

The faith of Guru Nanak is one of the oldest themes in Sikh studies. Interest in his ideas and practices involved the issue of their relationship with the contemporary systems, both Hindu and Muslim. Greater attention in this regard came to be given to Bhakti and Sūfism. The awareness of distinction between Vaishnava Bhakti and what is called the Sant Tradition is a recent development. The question of the status of the faith, message, teachings or ideology of Guru Nanak has also been raised from the very beginning of Sikh studies. Different answers were given to this question. One simply was that the Sikhs represented a Hindu 'sect'. Another was that Sikhism represented a mixture, a syncretism, of Hindu and Islamic beliefs, especially of Bhakti and Sūfism, carrying the implication that there was little original in it. Yet another view was that Sikhism represented a new faith, a new religion. This view was presented by a number of Western writers before it came to be expounded and projected by Sikh scholars as a divine dispensation. The recent controversy regarding the faith of Guru Nanak can be appreciated in the context of this background.

According to Justice Gurdev Singh, W.H. McLeod propagates that Sikhism has nothing new to offer.[1] Guru Nanak did not originate a new set of teachings or a new school of thought. All that he offers is a clear expression of the *nirguṇa sampradāya*. The following which gathered around Guru Nanak was certainly the original nucleus of the Sikh Panth, but that does not make Guru Nanak the founder of Sikhism. McLeod holds the view that Guru Nanak stands firmly within the so-called Sant Tradition of Northern India.[2] Justice Gurdev Singh feels concerned about McLeod's view of the origins of Sikhism but not with McLeod's exposition of the teachings of Guru Nanak. This partial presentation becomes a source of misunderstanding.

I

McLeod discusses the teachings of Guru Nanak in terms of (a) the nature of God, (b) the nature of unregenerate man, (c) the divine self-expression, and (d) the discipline. We may sum up his ideas on each of these aspects for a proper understanding of his position.

The figure 1 at the very beginning of the *mūlmantar* declares the unity of God. In His primal aspect God in *nirguṇ* – absolute, unconditioned, devoid of all attributes. He is formless (*nirankār*). He is boundless and infinite; he is ineffable; he is eternal, without beginning, beyond time, unborn, non-incarnated; he is unknowable, completely beyond the range of human comprehension. However, of his own volition, he became *sāguṇ* in order that man might know him. He is the creator of the universe and a participant in the life of the universe, watching, directing and upholding it as its sustainer. He is the sovereign Lord, the wielder of absolute authority. God is immanent in the universe. He is everywhere and in everything. He is the bestower of liberation. He unites the worshipper with himself through his grace.[3]

The unregenerate man has a *man* (heart, mind, soul) that is erratic and leads him into worldly attachments. It is controlled by *haumai*, the source of pride and the epitome of self-centredness. The outward expression of a man dominated by *haumai* are evil passions which mark the *manmukh*. Because of these evil passions the unregenerate man remains sunk in *māyā*, seeking fulfilment in attachment to worldly things. For Guru Nanak the world is real but impermanent, or 'false'. *Māyā* is basically untruth as opposed to Truth. So long as man remains entangled in *māyā* it is impossible for him to appreciate Truth. He remains chained to the wheel of death and rebirth, in perpetual separation from God.[4]

When we proceed to inquire 'precisely *how* God communicates with man', we encounter the specific contribution of Guru Nanak's theology, 'a contribution which offers the most significant example of his positive originality'. The reference here is to the concept of divine self-expression in the compositions of Guru Nanak. The first key term is the Word (*shabad*). It is the vehicle of revelation. The Word embraces all that is Truth, all that expresses the nature of God and the means of attaining Him. It may be perceived in the divine laws governing the universe as well in the ineffable mystical experience. If the Word distinctly is the medium of communication, the Name (*nām*) is the object of communication. The communicator of divine Truth is the Divine Preceptor (*gurū*), equated with God, the voice of God within man, and with the Word. In the thought of Guru Nanak, Divine Order (*hukam*) signifies the divinely instituted and maintained principle governing the existence and movement of the universe, and expressed in the moral world. It is an all-embracing principle, 'the sum total of all divinely instituted laws; and it is a revelation of the nature of God'. The fifth key idea is Truth (*sachch*). Its appropriation leads to liberation which, in the last analysis depends on God's grace (*nadar*). There is nothing man can do to 'earn' grace.[5]

To appropriate salvation offered to man by the Guru in the Word, the individual has to strive to cleanse himself of all evil. Inward devotion paves the way to salvation. True religion is to be found not in external practices, but in the inward disciplines of love, faith, mercy, and humility, expressed in righteous and compassionate deeds and in the upholding of all that is true. Loving devotion to God is to be expressed through *nām simran* and fear of God. Meditation on the nature and qualities of God is the core of Guru Nanak's religious discipline, a meditation which must overflow in words and deeds. This meditation has a corporate as well as individual application. From this meditation results the experience of *vismād* which, in turn, becomes a stimulus to more exalted meditation. This experience involves wonder and ecstasy. With the ever-widening *vismād* goes a developing sense of joy and peace. It is a path leading onward and upward. The accent is strongly upon ascent to higher and yet higher levels of understanding and experience. This ascent is particularly evident in Guru Nanak's famous figure of the five *khands*. The fifth and the final state is Sachch Khand, the realm of Truth, the goal and the ultimate end of human existence, the final consummation of man's ascent to God. The blending of light with the Light brings about a condition of peace, of consummate joy and perfect tranquility, a condition transcending all human telling.[6]

McLeod looks upon Sikhism as 'a religion of refined and noble quality'.[7] Like all religious systems, however, it has antecedents which defy ultimate scrutiny. Guru Nanak did receive an inheritance, but to regard him as the mere mediator of other men's ideas would be 'altogether mistaken'. In his hands the inheritance was transformed. Moreover, the pattern which was produced by this transformation has endured. There have been subsequent developments of considerable significance, but this same pattern has remained the core and essence of the continuing Sikh faith. McLeod equates Kabir and Guru Nanak in so far as they both offer syntheses, but in each case 'the nature of the synthesis reflects the personality of its author'. In imparting endurance to Sikhism, the clarity and coherence of Guru Nanak's thought as much as the designation of a successor 'have been factors of fundamental significance'. Nevertheless, his thought is closely related to that of the Sant tradition of Northern India.[8]

In the traditional religions of India, according to McLeod, external authority and conventional ceremony constituted the essence, except in three dissenting movements: Bhaktī in Vaishnavism, the Naths in Shaivism, and the Sūfīs in Islam. 'The Sant tradition was essentially a synthesis of the three principal dissenting movements, a compound of elements drawn mainly from Vaishnava Bhakti and the Hathyoga of the Nath Yogis, with a marginal contribution from Sufism'. The Sants expressed their beliefs in a language that was closely related to that of the common people, as in the case of Namdev, Ravidas and Kabir, who all came from the low caste groups. This Sant tradition was by far the most important element which Guru Nanak inherited from his past or absorbed from contemporary patterns. However, like Kabir, he reinterpreted this tradition in the light of his own experience and in accordance with his own personality.[9] McLeod argues in some detail that Islamic influence on Guru Nanak was not of fundamental significance. Indeed, it was mediated to him through the Sant synthesis. Conventional Hindu beliefs and Islam were 'not regarded as fundamentally right but as fundamentally wrong'.[10]

It is accordingly incorrect to interpret the religion of Gurū Nānak as a synthesis of Hindu belief and Islam. It is indeed a synthesis, but one in which Islamic elements are relatively unimportant. The pattern evolved by Gurū Nānak is a reworking of the Sant synthesis, one which does not depart far from Sant source as far as its fundamental components are concerned. The categories employed by Gurū Nānak are the categories of the Sants, the terminology he uses is their terminology, and the doctrines he affirms are their doctrines. This is not to suggest, however, that Gurū Nānak's thought was a precise copy of what earlier Sants had developed. He inherited the components of his thought from the Sants, but he did not transmit his inheritance unchanged. He received a synthesis and he passed it on, but he did so in a form which was in some measure amplified, and in considerable measure clarified and integrated. This applies in particular to his understanding of the manner of divine communication with man. Gurū Nānak's concepts of the *Sabad*, the *Nām*, the *Gurū*, and the *Hukam* carry us beyond anything that the works of earlier Sants offer in any explicit form. It is Sant thought which we find in his works, but it is Sant thought expanded and reinterpreted. The result is a new synthesis, a synthesis which is cast within the pattern of Sant belief but which nevertheless possesses a significant originality and, in contrast with its Sant background, a unique clarity. It possesses, moreover, the quality of survival, for it remains today the substance of a living faith.[11]

McLeod restates his position on the issue of 'origins' in *The Evolution of the Sikh Community*. In a certain sense Guru Nanak can be regarded as a founder. The following which gathered around him was 'certainly the original nucleus of the Sikh Panth and if we are to follow organizational lines on our movement back through history we shall be able to proceed no further than this nucleus. In another sense, however, the term founder can be misleading. It suggests that Guru Nanak originated not merely a group of followers but also 'a school of thought, or set of teachings'. This can be accepted in a highly qualified sense, he suggests. 'If we place Gurū Nānak within his own historical context, if we compare his teachings with those of other contemporary or earlier religious figures, we shall at once see that he stands firmly within a well-defined tradition.

What Gurū Nānak offers us is the clearest and most highly articulated expression of the *nirguna sampradāya,* the so-called Sant tradition of Northern India'.[12]

In a recent publication, McLeod observes that his treatment of the teachings of Guru Nanak seems to have been accepted. He knows, however, that this acceptance is not extended to his view of Guru Nanak's relationship with the Sant tradition. He reiterates his view that Guru Nanak can be regarded as the founder of the Sikh Panth, and that 'in a certain sense the Panth can be construed as coterminus with the Sikh faith'. But this, in his view, does not imply that Guru Nanak cannot be placed within the Sant tradition.[13]

Must we conclude that Guru Nanak was a Sant? According to McLeod, if it is a strictly neutral question of antecedent and influence the answer must be in the affirmative. 'If, however, the question implies a lack of originality on the part of Nanak the answer must be an emphatic negative. Plainly there is much that is profoundly original in the hymns which we find recorded under his distinctive symbol in the Adi Granth. There is in them an integrated and coherent system which no other Sant has produced; there is a clarity which no other Sant has equalled; and there is a beauty which no other Sant has matched. There is, moreover, the question of permanence. The fact that Nanak appointed a successor to follow him is scarcely unique, but nothing in the Sant experience can compare to the Panth which was eventually to emerge from that decision'.[14] McLeod seems to clarify but not to change his position. The Sikh Panth originated with Guru Nanak but not all the important ideas woven into his religious thought.

McLeod's analysis does not end there. The *Janamsākhīs* provide a few details concerning the life of Guru Nanak and his works provide an 'integrated theology'. McLeod seeks a synthesis between the glimpses provided by the *sākhīs* and the personality of the Guru that emerges from his works. He infers that Guru Nanak gave 'practical expression to his own ideals' during the last three decades of his life. These were the years when he was surrounded by disciples who received instruction from him. This was also the period of his definitive utterances which presumably were recorded by his disciples. He combined a life of disciplined devotion with worldly activities set in the context of normal family life and a regular *satsang*. *Kīrtan* was presumably held in the early morning after individual meditation and in the evening after the day's work. The instruction delivered in the regular gathering of disciples would have the same emphasis upon the greatness of God, His gracious self-revelation, the perils of human condition, and the paramount necessity of meditation on the divine Name as we find in his compositions. Those who placed their confidence in status conferred by caste, or by wealth, would be sternly admonished. Nath Yogīs would be the natural opponents, 'both because of the manner in which their theories and practices conflicted with those of Gurū Nānak, and because of the considerable influence which they still exercised over the popular mind of the Punjab'. Like his disciples, the Guru probably performed daily labours. He maintained an essentially practical participation in the everyday affairs of his community and of the world beyond.[15]

The combination of piety and practical activity which Guru Nanak manifested in his own life was bequeathed to his followers and it remains characteristic of many who own him as the Guru today. At its best it is a piety devoid of superstition and a practical activity compounded with determination and an immense generosity. It explains much that has happened in the Punjab during the last four centuries and it explains much that can be witnessed there today.[16]

II

Justice Gurdev Singh refers to the revelatory status of Guru Nanak's utterances and emphasizes the universality of his doctrine, the originality of his thought, and the social orientation of his egalitarian ideas, citing the views of scholars like Muhammad Mujeeb, Harbans Singh and Attar Singh, and quoting the well known passage of J.D. Cunningham in which he underlines the uniqueness of Guru Nanak in laying the foundations of 'a new nationality'. Sikhism stands by itself as a faith. It rejects idol worship and the caste system. A Sikh accepts the house-holder's life and responsibilities 'to carry out the Attributive Will of God' and to solve the problems of man through 'a continuous virtuous endeavour'; he works not only for his own emancipation but also for 'the good of the society'.[17] This summing up reflects the views expressed by Sardar Daljeet Singh in his 'comparative study' of Nathism, Vaishnavism and Sikhism in the *Perspectives*.

Daljeet Singh's comparative study is formally divided into five parts. It is only in the last two pages of this study of about a hundred pages that he brings in McLeod apparently as a kind of interpolation. The cursory way in which he treats McLeod's work indicates that he does not take it seriously. The hasty manner in which he dismisses McLeod indicates that he is convinced of the correctness of his own understanding.

According to Daljeet Singh, the two most popular religious systems in Northern India in the time of Guru Nanak were Nathism and Vaishnavism. Therefore, the relevant question to ask is whether or not these systems contributed anything to the fundamentals of Sikhism. For a proper answer to this question it is necessary to identify the essentials of each of the three systems and then to compare them in terms of similarities and dissimilarities. The basic questions to ask of each system relate to its metaphysical view, its view of the world as real or illusory, its spiritual goal, the discipline or methods to be followed to achieve the goal, the role of the person who has achieved the goal, and the overall world-view of the system. Ideology is important because it is intimately linked to both perception and activity. For a proper study of religion it is necessary to adhere to the principle of the unity of experience, ideology and activity, and never to ignore the activities of the author of a religious system: 'Deeds alone are the true index of the ideology of the author'. This emphasis is needed because scholars trained in 'a behaviouristic, or mechanical methodology' have the tendency to trace one religious development from a preceding one. Such a chain of ratiocination becomes 'a virtual denial of the validity, the very novelty, and the free character of the religious experience'. Daljeet Singh's own view is that a revelatory religion is 'by its very nature new'.[18]

However, neither Nathism nor Vaishnavism was authored by a single person. The origins of these systems were so remote that nothing directly and certainly was known of the views and actions of those persons who may be looked upon as their protagonists. Significantly, Daljeet Singh's exposition of Nathism and Vaishnavism is based entirely on secondary works which relate mostly to pre-Turkish centuries. His exposition of Sikhism is based entirely on the *Ādi Granth*. Consequently, his interpretation of Nathism or Vaishnavism is not of the same order as that of Sikhism.

Nathism was a Shaiva cult. Though Shaivism could be traced to the Indus culture and the combination of Yoga with Shaivism was nearly as old, Nathism appeared on the scene much later. The followers of Gorakh Nath were moderate in their Yogic practices than their precursors, the Kapalikas. The final goal of Nathism was 'complete dissociation' from the world, involving a 'wholly passive and blissful union' with Shiva. The primary object of Nathism was 'to gain powers' and liberation from 'the oppression of the world'. Being ascetical, the Nath system was monastic. There were twelve sects, each founded by a disciple of Gorakh Nath. A person entering any of these sects was to remain celebate; he was not to engage himself in any gainful activity, sustaining himself by begging for his food; and he was to observe *ahimsa*. His appearance was marked, among other things, by rings in his split ears, ashes on his almost naked body, and a necklace of Rudraksha beads. The Shudras were not admitted to a Gorakh Nathi order. Women generally were not initiated, but exception could be made for widows. The prominent elements of discipline in Nathism were Yogic practices, and the raising of Kundalani with a view to union with Lord Shiva. Both before and after liberation, the Yogi had no social responsibilities. In its approach to the world, its ethics and its discipline, Nathism embodied a world-view of 'life-negation'.[19]

Four streams of thought joined in the Vaishnava system of the pre-Christian centuries. The mystic system of love was not there even in the *Gitā*, not even as an idea or a base for future development. The Bhakti movement started with Ramanuja. Daljeet Singh gives a brief account of Madhava, Ramananda, Tulsidas, Vallabha and Chaitanya as well. The chief features of Vaishnava Bhakti were a pantheistic or dualistic world-view, belief in the Vedas and their ritualistic mysticism, adherence to caste system and its social prohibitions, the other-worldly attitude (though the world was deemed to be real), and merger of the human soul in Brahmaṇ as the goal. There was no involvement in the world of man, no stress on the moral life except for personal purity and aid to meditation, and no social role for the *jīvan-muktā*. The Vaishnavas believed in Avtarhood and practised idol-worship. The basic scriptures of the Vaishnava system were the Vedas and the Upanishads, to which the *Gītā* was added later. The caste system was wholly accepted. The theory of Avtarhood absorbed all kinds of divergent and heterodox systems. The ritualism of the Vedic religion remained a part of Vaishnavism. Any transformation of the love of God into the service of man was obviated by all these features. 'Moral life, at best, meant only a sense of ritualistic or formal piety without the least reaction to any social evil, injustice or cruelty much less to any political oppression or tyranny'.[20]

The Sikh Gurus were uncompromising monotheists. Their conception of God enables us to understand the origin and course of the Sikh tradition, and the significance of Sikh institutions and practices. God is both transcendent and immanent, not in two parts, stages or phases. The transcedent God is everywhere, in each heart, place and particle. God is the creator and the 'ocean of attributes, values and virtues'. He is inextricably linked with the universe through his attributive or immanent aspect. God's virtues and attributes indicate his perpetual interest in man and the universe. They give validity and spiritual sanctity to the moral life 'which in many other systems is deemed to be an entanglement'. Everything is governed by God's will but it is not deterministic because God is creative and 'all movement in life is towards a creative freedom'. God never takes birth or form. The God of will is also a God of grace. His activity is incomprehensible except in terms of His grace or freedom. Sikhism is often described as the way of Nām (*nām mārga*) because Nām is the Reality supporting and directing the created world. Nām may be called 'the creative and dynamic' immanence of God which directs the manifest world of force and form.[21]

The world is real. It is the place of righteous activity. Creative work and virtuous deeds are of fundamental importance. Living in this world is not a bondage but a rare opportunity. The world is a place of beauty. Man's struggle provides an opportunity for his progress. Man in his normal state is dominated by self-will and animal propensities. His main limitations and problems arise from his *haumai*, the self-centred human individuality created by God for man's survival and progress. *Haumai* is opposed to Nām: 'the two cannot be at the same place'. This means that egoism, not the worldly life as such, is opposed to the spiritual life. 'The way to God is through life, not through its renunciation'. Self-centredness must be substituted by God-centredness. The way to higher achievement lies in being altruistic or moral instead of being self-centred. God-centredness and inactivity are a contradiction in terms. Because of the presence of God in man it is possible for man to become conscious of him and to develop a new state of consciousness. Ultimately, it is God's grace that unites man with Nām. For that, however, it is necessary to turn to God and to carry out His will. The mission of the Sikh Gurus was to turn every self-centred individual (*manmukh*) into a God-centred person (*gurmukh*).[22]

The Sikh Gurus made a radical departure from the Indian tradition in their conception of the goal of human life. The dictum that states this goal is well known: 'Everything is lower than Truth, but higher still is truthful living'. Not only to know the truth but also to live the active life of truth is the ideal. To carry out God's will through creative activity in the universe as God's instrument is the ideal of life. Blissful union is not an end in itself, but 'union with a view both to knowing His Will and carrying it out'. The spiritual and moral life are virtually synonymous and coextensive; creative and moral life is the goal in Sikhism. The Sikh of the Guru is described as Gurmukh. He has no *haumai*, he is godly and virtuous, he carries out God's will, taking part in all fields of life, and his aim in life is to make all others God-centred. In Daljeet Singh's view, moral life or service of man and the company of God-centred persons constitute two of the principal modes of discipline in Sikhism.[23]

The third mode of discipline is prayer and remembering God. There is a considerable emphasis on contemplation in the *Ādi Granth*. This contemplation does not mean yogic practices or any mechanical means of worship. Meditation involves the fear of God while embarking on any activity or making any decision. Prayer in Sikhism expresses the humility of the devotee, reminds him of the need of continuous search for God, represents perpetual seeking for God's grace, and is a humble attempt at communion with Him so as to draw upon His light and energy in the fight against evil and for the positive expression of love. 'The very fact that the Gurus started no monastic system shows conclusively that they never advocated prayer as an independent mode of spiritual training'. One is emancipated 'while laughing and playing in life'; the God-centred lives truth 'while a householder'.[24]

Daljeet Singh underlines the great importance of ethical life in Sikhism. The ethical principles in Sikhism are inter-connected and represent differnt facets of a single concept. The basis of human equality and brotherhood is the conception of God as the creator of all. The goal of a truly moral or spiritual living is closely linked with the idea that the world is real. The movement from comparative imperfection to comparative perfection, from comparative necessity to freedom is an outcome of the idea that God is 'the ocean of attributes and values'. God-consciousness is the greatest social virtue since it directs every activity towards the good of all and not towards self-interest alone. Denunciation of caste prejudices, oppression of the rulers, tyranny of the invaders, and corruption of the officials springs from Sikh ethics. Creation of alternative moral institutions was the obverse of this criticism of evil institutions. So long as the end was moral and spiritual the use of force was also justified. Equally radical was the Gurus' attitude towards women. They were never considered to be evil. No human life was possible without them. They were to be equal partners with men. The social, moral and religious implications of this change were enormous. Economic inequality too was criticized by the Gurus. They commended honest work and the production of goods as the moral and spiritual duty of man. To react against social and political wrongs, to face and reshape life boldly, was a corollary of the Sikh ethical ideals.[25]

It is not surprising that the Gurus denounced the ways and the ideals of the Naths and rejected their methods, and their other-worldly approach. The two systems present opposite world-views.

Nathism rejects the world and life as misery, but Sikhism accepts them as spiritually meaningful. Nathism was characterized by withdrawal from the world, asceticism, *ahimsa*, celibacy, the downgrading of women, solitude and Yogic practices. But in Sikhism, virtuous participation in the world, the house-holder's life and responsibilities, the consequent raising of the status of women, and the love and service of man in all spheres of his life become logically necessary because God in Sikhism is attributive. Sikhism and Nathism take the world to be real, but the two systems have entirely different methodologies, goals and world-views. There is hardly a meeting ground between the two systems.[26]

Vaishnavism was a part and parcel of the Brahmanical complex. Its scriptures were the Vedas and the Upanishads. Bhakti in Vaishnavism was basically formal and ritualistic, and marked by devotional idol-worship in temples. It did not lead to virtuous deeds in the social field. Sikhism denies the authority of the Vedas and the Upanishads, discards belief in *avtars*, and rejects the Vedic conception of caste. Once the fundamentals of Vaishnavism are rejected, the question of any similarity between the two systems does not arise. While Sikhism is strictly theistic, Vaishnavism is broadly pantheistic. Unlike the Vaishnava saints, the Sikh Gurus insist on virtuous deeds to seek the grace of God. Vaishnavism accepts 'the sensual path' as an alternative spiritual approach, but Sikhism rejects it. The 'non-participation' of the Vaishnava saints was an inevitable consequence of their ideology and objectives. By contrast, the Sikh Gurus always espoused causes in defence and aid of righteousness. On the whole, whereas Nathism and Vaishnavism are 'quietist', Sikhism is 'activist'. The contrast between the two is 'too glaring to be glossed over'. Daljeet Singh comes to the conclusion that 'far from being connected, Nathism and Vaishnavism on the one hand and Sikhism on the other hand are completely contrasted in their fundamentals, ideologies, goals, methodologies and world-views'. An 'activist amalgam' had never emerged in the history of Nathism and Vaishnavism for two thousand years when they existed side by side. There was little possibility of a Nath-Vaishnava synthesis emerging in the medieval centuries. There was no possibility of such a synthesis resulting in the 'activist' Sikh faith.[27]

Daljeet Singh dismisses McLeod rather brusquely. His views about Sikhism, Nathism and Vaishnavism are 'not only without any basis but also betray an ignorance of the history and the essentials of the three systems'. About half a dozen quotations from the works of McLeod given in one paragraph are meant to make the following points: McLeod places Guru Nanak within the Sant tradition which in McLeod's view is a synthesis of elements from Vaishnava Bhakti, Hathyoga and Sūfism; Guru Nanak did not originate a school of thought, or a set of teachings, and he cannot be regarded as the 'founder' of Sikhism; simply because Guru Nanak used Nath terminology in his works, McLeod talks of 'influence'. Furthermore, he ignores the role of Sikh ideology in Sikh history and looks for other 'influences' on later Sikhism. All these views implicitly stand refuted by Daljeet Singh's own exposition of the Sikh movement.[28]

III

The basic differences between McLeod and Daljeet Singh relate to (a) interpretation of Guru Nanak's ideology and (b) his status as the originator of the Sikh movement. The differences on the first arise essentially out of the degree of importance they give to the socio-political implications of Guru Nanak's ideas. McLeod does not ignore the importance of Guru Nanak's ideas for 'practical activity'. In his view, Guru Nanak discarded the idea of renunciation in favour of the life of a house-holder, and he disapproved of status based on caste or wealth. However, McLeod is silent about the implication of the idea of equality for the position of women, and he does not see any political implications of the verses known as *Bābur-vāṇī*. Clearly, thus, McLeod does not look upon 'practical activity' as central to his interpretation of Guru Nanak's ideology. In fact he lays much greater emphasis on 'interiority' and the ideal of emancipation. Daljeet Singh interprets Guru Nanak's 'ideology' essentially in terms of practical activity, underlining all its socio-political dimensions. For him, *jīvan-muktī* is a prelude to altruistic social action on a higher plane of consciousness. He has little to say about loving devotion (*bhakti*). The differences between McLeod and Daljeet Singh on the issue of ideology are extremely important but they are differences of degree.

On the issue of the status of Guru Nanak as the founder of Sikhism, Daljeet Singh looks upon his utterances as 'revelation', with the implication that he founded a totally new system which had nothing to do with the religious systems prevalent in India. McLeod too refers to Guru Nanak's spiritual experience resulting in his conviction of a divine call to lead men to emancipation, but he does not attach much importance to the verses which are generally quoted in support of the revelatory status of his utterances. Daljeet Singh underlines the uniqueness of Guru Nanak's ideology; McLeod attaches importance to antecedents for his ideas in the context of his times. The *nirguṇa sampradāya* of McLeod's conception differentiates Guru Nanak from all his contemporaries except those who belonged to this *sampradāya*. Even with them Guru Nanak does not share every idea, attitude or practice. What was common to all the Sant figures was, for instance, rejection of the idea of incarnation, belief in a God who is neither Rama nor Allah (but both), and the concepts of Nām, Shabad and Guru.

Not in the *Perspectives* but elsewhere Daljeet Singh has addressed himself to the question of relationship between Sikhism and the 'radical bhagats' like Kabir and Ravidas. They represented a distinct school of Bhakti. Kabir, for instance, rejected Vaishnavism as well as the Vedas. Daljeet Singh does not deny that the concepts of the Guru and the Shabad are common to Kabir and Guru Nanak. Both of them denounced the caste system too. However, the differences between them were more important. The goal of life for Kabir is a blissful union with God in which human personality is dissolved. Kabir believes in self-surrender, recommends ceaseless singing of God's praises, and virtually suggests withdrawal from the world. He is a firm advocate of *ahimsa*. With his ascetical bias, Kabir does not think well of women. In fact he tends to bracket woman with *māyā*. Consequently the world for him becomes a snare. Above all, Kabir 'never took any interest in the social or temporal affairs of his times'. Thus, though theism was common to both Sikhism and the Bhagats and both rejected the fundamentals of Hinduism and denounced the caste ideology, the views of the Bhagats about the reality of the world were 'somewhat ambivalent' and they led a life of withdrawal. The world-views of the two systems contrasted in terms of goals, methodologies and the social role of the liberated-in-life. On the whole, therefore, Daljeet Singh brackets McLeod's 'Sant tradition' with Vaishnavism and Shaivism rather than with Sikhism.[29]

McLeod gives primacy to what Guru Nanak shares with 'the Sants'. Daljeet Singh gives primacy to what he does not share. McLeod looks upon ideas as important in themselves. Daljeet Singh looks for their bearing on social action. McLeod seeks an understanding of Guru Nanak primarily in his environment and secondarily in his personality. Daljeet Singh sees his whole system as underpinned by his spiritual experience and moral vision. McLeod virtually excludes God from his view of the universe. Daljeet Singh places God at the centre of the universe. It is not surprising that they hold opposing views on the role of ideas in human affairs. This is the terrain over which they fight. McLeod approaches religion as a historian. Daljeet Singh approaches history as a theologian. Paradoxically, their contrast forbids a choice in favour of one to the exclusion of the other because their positions are complementary.

NOTES

1. *Perspectives on the Sikh Tradition*, p. 5.
2. Ibid., p. 9.
3. McLeod (1968), pp. 163-77.
4. Ibid., pp. 177-89.
5. Ibid., pp. 189-207.
6. Ibid., pp. 207-26.
7. Ibid., p. 1.
8. Ibid., pp. 149-51.
9. Ibid., pp. 151-57.
10. Ibid., pp. 158-61.
11. Ibid., p. 161.

12. McLeod (1975), p. 5.
13. McLeod (1989b), pp. 18-19 and 22-31.
14. Ibid., p. 31.
15. McLeod (1968), pp. 227-30.
16. Ibid., pp. 231-32.
17. *Perspectives on the Sikh Tradition*, pp. 15-21.
18. Ibid., pp. 55-58.
19. Ibid., pp. 59-75.
20. Ibid., pp. 76-99.
21. Ibid., pp. 100-07.
22. Ibid., pp. 107-15.
23. Ibid., pp. 116-24.
24. Ibid., pp. 125-30.
25. Ibid., pp. 131-39.
26. Ibid., pp. 131-35.
27. Ibid., pp. 135-36.
28. Ibid., pp. 139-40.
29. Daljeet Singh (1990), pp. 112-13.

7. Guru Nanak of Faith

The distinction between Guru Nanak of history and Guru Nanak of faith has arisen gradually in the history of Sikh studies. Even the earliest writers were interested in the life of Guru Nanak but they had no substantial evidence to use. The 'discovery' of *Janamsākhīs* proved to be of great importance. The sceptical attitude of the European writers towards the supranatural and mythical elements in any kind of evidence predisposed them to give a short shrift to the *Janamsākhīs*. Ernest Trumpp provided the first notable example. The early Sikh writers too were critical of the *Janamsākhīs*. J.C. Archer was the first scholar to suggest that the *Janamsākhīs* presented 'the Nanak of faith' and not Guru Nanak of history. This was the background for W.H. McLeod's analysis of the *Janamsākhīs* in search of the historical Nanak.

I

Justice Gurdev Singh thinks that Professor W.H. McLeod in his *Gurū Nānak and the Sikh Religion* made 'an assiduous effort to destroy or distort the prevailing image of this great prophet asserting that the incidents of his life narrated in his numerous biographies have no historical basis but are the brainchild of his devotees who sought to glorify him by attributing super-natural power to him'.[1] Undoubtedly, there is a great difference between McLeod and the biographers of Guru Nanak on this point. However, to say that McLeod looks upon the *Janamsākhīs* as 'the brainchild' of Guru Nanak's followers who wanted to glorify his supranatural powers appears to be a caricature of McLeod's treatment of the *Janamsākhīs*.

Justice Gurdev Singh goes on to state that even the *Ādi Granth* which treasures the hymns of Guru Nanak and his successors is ignored by McLeod, despite specific references in some of the hymns to contemporary events like the invasion of Babur. McLeod doubts the context of the *Bābur-vāṇī* and other suggestive verses, because he refuses to believe that Guru Nanak was present at Saidpur when that town was sacked. The *Janamsākhīs* narrating the events of Guru Nanak's life are discarded as 'hagiographic accounts with a very substantial portion of legend and of very little historical value'. In Justice Gurdev Singh's opinion, the *Early Sikh Tradition* presents only a more detailed examination of the various *Janamsākhīs* and the incidents narrated therein.[2] McLeod summarily rejects all that as smacks of miracle or wonder in his examination of the various incidents in the *Janamsākhīs*. Out of 124 *sākhīs* analysed, as many as 87 are classified as impossible or improbable and only 37 are classed as probable. Summing up his conclusions McLeod says:

> The *Janam-sakhis* have served as the vehicle of a powerful myth, one which still commands acceptance within the society which developed it. The myth which they express may be briefly stated as follows. Baba Nanak was the divinely commissioned giver of salvation. To all who would seek salvation the way lies open. The means of salvation consists in loyalty to the person of Baba Nanak and acceptance of his teachings. This is the myth. The form which was developed to give it expression was the narrative anecdote which, in relating some incidents concerning the life of Nanak, sought to authenticate the claims made on his behalf. These anecdotes collected into anthologies or structured biographies, constitute the *Janam-sakhis*.[3]

This view does not surprise Justice Gurdev Singh because McLeod starts with the assumption that *Janamsākhīs*, like the Gospels, are mainly collections of 'myths' developed during the first two centuries of Sikh history by the imagination of the followers of Guru Nanak. This treatment is wholly untenable in the eyes of Justice Gurdev Singh, especially in view of the authentic hymns of Guru Nanak treasured in the *Ādi Granth* and other contemporary and almost contemporary evidence.

Justice Gurdev Singh believes that the following passage in the *The Evolution of the Sikh Community* indicates McLeod's 'negative attitude':

The basic point which needs to be made as far as the authentic Nanak material is concerned is that the *Janam-sakhi* tradition can provide no more than pointers to possibilities. Each of these possibilities must be subjected to rigorous scrutiny and only when it is actually established can it be accepted. Unlike the person in a court of law *Janam-sakhis* must be held guilty unless proved innocent. Given the hagiographic nature of the *Janam-sakhis* and their general lack of reliability as far as the historical Nanak is concerned, material which cannot be positively established should only rarely be given the benefit of doubt.[4]

With this attitude, asks Justice Gurdev Singh, is it any wonder that McLeod finds next to nothing in the various *Janamsākhīs* and other source material, including the *Ādi Granth* and the *Vārs* of Bhai Gurdas, as positive evidence of historical Nanak?

Finally, Justice Gurdev Singh quotes a long passage from Dr. James A. Veitch to stress the importance of the works like the *Janamsākhīs* in dealing with the lives of great religious teachers:

Of course it is difficult to distinguish between what happened in the life of the historical person Nanak, and how later traditions interpreted the impact he made upon the contemporary religious scene. Later generations, in recapturing the founding vision of Guru Nanak tend to fill out the record with stories which are more interpretative. This should not surprise the European reader: thinking and writing in historical terms is a phenomenon which has had a relatively short history in the West. Stories which are part and parcel of all religious traditions provide the media through which truths are expressed. The question to be asked of stories illustrating difficult incidents in the life of founders of the great religious traditions (such as Guru Nanak, Gotama, Muhammed, and Jesus) is not did it really happen in the way described? but what religious truth is being expressed in this story? However, this sort of comment should not obscure the originality and fresh insight into the nature of the Divine, injected by this remarkable person Guru Nanak into the religious life of North India.[5]

II

With the professed intention of applying rigorous historical methodology to the sources of Guru Nanak's life, McLeod turns to the *Ādi Granth* and the first *Vār* of Bhai Gurdas, the four *Janamsākhī* traditions and the two versions of the eighteenth- century *Mahimā Prakāsh* and concludes that the *Janamsākhīs* appear to provide the most promising source. On this assumption he takes up for critical analysis 124 *sākhīs* from the *Vār* of Bhai Gurdas and the *Purātan* and *Miharbān Janamsākhīs*. This list in his view is comprehensive enough to include all important incidents of Guru Nanak's life mentioned in all the known sources of his life.

McLeod keeps in mind a number of considerations for classifying these *sākhīs* as 'the established, the probable, the possible, the improbable, and the impossible'. His first consideration is 'the incidence of the miraculous or plainly fantastic'. A *sākhī* that is far removed from the realities as they are known today becomes immediately suspect. McLeod points out, however, that the inclusion of a miracle 'does not necessarily mean that the whole *sākhī* must be rejected. In most cases this may be required, but in others the possibility of a substratum of truth must be borne in mind'.[6] He does find a few instances in which the kernel appears to be acceptable despite the shell of miracle. His second consideration is the testimony of external sources, as in the case of Daulat Khan Lodi, Babur, and an inscription in Baghdad. The evidence of Guru Nanak's own compositions is the third consideration. The fourth is the measure of agreement or disagreement in the various *Janamsākhīs* themselves. The relative reliability of the different *Janamsākhīs* is the fifth consideration. Genealogical references are treated as more reliable than others. Finally, there is the consideration of geography: a greater degree of confidence is placed in detail relating to Guru Nanak's life in the Punjab than what concerns his life outside the Punjab.

On these criteria, 39 *sākhīs* out of 124 are discarded as impossible. Among these are *sākhīs* which involve a strong element of the supranatural or infringement of known historical chronology: the field restored, the stationary shadow of a tree, food from God's court, the *bhagats* revealed in stars, a girl turned into a boy, meeting with Kaliyug, the struggle with *Kāl*, meeting with Khwajah Khizr, stopping of the rock at Panja Sahib, the cannibal's cauldron, meetings with Shaikh Farid and Shaikh Bahauddin Zakariya, discourse with figures like Namdev, Kabir, Ravidas and Beni, or with Shaikh Sharaf of Panipat. There are 18 other *sākhīs* which according to McLeod are improbable. These include *sākhīs* like *kharā saudā*, discourse with Abdul Rahman of Iran, or with Raja Harinath, Raja Mitr Sain and Raja Jagannath, the food of Lalo and Bhago, and a visit to Nanakmata. Thirty of the *sākhīs* belong to the category of possible, like 'the watering of the fields' at Hardwar, discourse with the *pandits* at Banaras, visit to Rameshwaram, or Hinglaj, or to Mathura and Kurukshetra. Of the remaining thirty-seven *sākhīs*, some are assigned to the probable category, and others are discussed individually for classification.

McLeod's method can be illustrated with reference to some concrete points. The *Janamsākhīs* agree about the year of Guru Nanak's birth but not about the month. Between Kattak and Baisakh, McLeod is inclined to accept the latter as more probable because of the 'weight of evidence and scholarly opinion' in its favour. Similarly, about the place of Guru Nanak' birth, McLeod is inclined to prefer Chahal, his mother's village near Baraki in Lahore District, over Rai Bhoi di Talvandi (the present Nankana Sahib) where his father lived, because of the weight of the evidence of the *Miharbān Janamsākhī* and the significance of the name Nānak. Of the three conflicting dates for the death of Guru Nanak, McLeod looks upon 7 September 1539 as the most likely on the basis of the entries made in the Kartarpur manuscript of the *Granth Sahib*. Since all *Janamsākhīs* agree that Kalu, a Bedi Khatri of Rai Bhoi di Talvandi, was Guru Nanak's father, this is accepted by McLeod without reservation. In the same manner, Tripta is accepted as his mother. His sister was probably named Nānaki whose husband, Jai Ram, was employed as the steward (*modī*) of Daulat Khan Lodi. The evidence on the other close relations of Guru Nanak also appears to be acceptable, like the one on his close companion, Mardana. That oral evidence on these matters can be regarded as rather strong finds support in the *Janamsākhīs*.

The evidence on the Sultanpur interlude, shorn of its supranatural details, may point to an authentic tradition, including the name of the administrator of Sultanpur, Daulat Khan. A personal meeting with Babur at Saidpur, on the other hand, is most unlikely though not impossible. McLeod agrues in fact that the *Bābur-vāṇī* verses were composed with a general reference to the battles between the Mughals and the Afghans rather than with reference to any specific incident. This suggestion is based on the character and contents of these verses. There is strong proof for the foundation of Kartarpur by Guru Nanak, though we are not sure about the exact year of its foundation. Guru Nanak's visits to Pakpattan and Multan are very probable, but not so his visit to Mecca and Medina or even Baghdad, for which independent evidence is also considered and rejected. The discourse on Mount Sumeru is also improbable. 'This is not to say that Guru Nanak never visited the Himalayas, nor indeed can we maintain with assurance that he did not penetrate as far as Mount Kailash and Lake Manasa'.[7] But there is no 'acceptable evidence' for such a visit in the *Vār* of Bhai Gurdas and the *Janamsākhīs*. Similarly, Guru Nanak's visit to Assam, Dacca, or Ceylon and his meeting with Sajjan, the robber, remain within the realm of possibility but without any credible proof.

McLeod comes to the general conclusion that the *Janamsākhīs* provide us only an outline for the concrete events of Guru Nanak's life, leaving lengthy periods covered by no more than a general comment, or a single detail. The *Janamsākhīs* do remain the most important source, but they cannot be taken at their face value. What we find in the *Janamsākhīs* is 'the Gurū Nānak of legend and of faith, the image of the Gurū seen through the eyes of popular piety seventy-five or hundred years after his death'.[8] It is an important image. But it is not the image of the actual life of Guru Nanak, the Nanak of history.

In his *Evolution of the Sikh Community*, McLeod covers three aspects of the *Janamsākhī* literature. Besides the usefulness of *Janamsākhīs* as sources for the life of Guru Nanak, he takes up the question of their value as sources for the later history of the Sikhs, and the question of their development, purpose, and function. The *Janamsākhīs* can serve a useful purpose with regard to our knowledge of the historical Nanak if they are subjected to rigorous scrutiny. Unlike the prisoner in a court of law, the *Janamsākhīs* must be 'held guilty until proved innocent'.[9] Nevertheless, they are indispensable for understanding how the myth of Guru Nanak was evolved and transmitted. The term myth is used in 'a strictly technical sense' and not as a synonym for 'legend'. McLeod visualizes a stage of oral transmission before the first recordings which were followed by the introduction of chronological sequence, and the addition of exegetical materials. Most of the extant *Janamsākhīs* represent the third or the fourth stage, or more commonly a combination of the two. He illustrates the usefulness of this literature for the historian of the seventeenth-century Sikh Panth and the historian of the seventeenth-century Punjab. McLeod's essay, thus, is not an elaboration of what he had done in *Gurū Nānak and the Sikh Religion* but a positive advance upon it.

A much more comprehensive analysis of the *Janamsākhīs* was the object of McLeod's *Early Sikh Tradition*, published five years later. Its purpose was to examine four aspects of the *Janamsākhī* literature: 'as examples of hagiographic growth-processes, as sources of Punjab history for the post-Nanak period within which they developed, as a cohesive factor in subsquent Sikh history, and as the earliest works of Panjabi prose'.[10] As hagiographic accounts of Guru Nanak's life, the *Janamsākhīs* provide an interpretation of his life, a myth. McLeod underlines that myth is not synonymous with legend. In fact the distinction between legend and myth is of 'much greater importance than the difference between legend and the authenticated historical event'. The myth uses both history and legend for its own purpose. It is 'a construct of human imagination, developing out of an actural situation and seeking to give meaning to that situation'. It is an interpretation of a given array of circumstances, evolved in response to particular needs to fulfil its distinctive function for the society within which it takes shape. When a myth ceases to fulfil its function, 'it must either change or make way for a more effective substitute.'[11] It is in this sense that the *Janamsākhīs* have served as 'the vehicle of a powerful myth': the myth that Guru Nanak was 'the divinely commissioned giver of salvation. To all who would seek salvation that way lies open. The means of salvation consists in loyalty to the person of Baba Nanak and acceptance of his teaching'.[12]

McLeod takes notice of the manuscripts and printed versions of the principal *Janamsākhīs*: the *Bālā,* the *Purātan*, the *Miharbān*, the *Gyān-Ratnāvalī*, the *Mahimā Prakāsh* and the *Janamsākhīs* known as LDP 194 and B40, besides miscellaneous works closely related to *Janamsākhīs*. They were written in Gurmukhi script, and in varying blends of Punjabi dialects, with the exception of the *Miharbān Janamsākhī* which is mostly in Sadhukkari containing elements of Punjabi and Braj. Having introduced the entire range of *Janamsākhī* literature to the reader, McLeod takes up its analysis in the second section of the *Early Sikh Tradition*, which constitutes about two-thirds of the book.

A broad outline of the *Early Sikh Tradition* would make it absolutely clear that McLeod is no longer concerned primarily with the question how much the *Janamsākhīs* do or do not tell us about the actual events of Guru Nanak's life. He wants to understand their nature and character in terms of their genesis and growth with reference to their constituents and forms, and the sources which their compilers used. Furthermore, he wants to know their purpose, function and value, which are taken up in the third section of the book.[13]

The objective of the *Janamsākhī* compilers was avowedly religious. 'Salvation is the issue which concerns them and the promulgation of a particular way of salvation constitutes their conscious intention'. He who accepts Guru Nanak as his guide will attain to salvation. He must heed the words enshrined in the Guru's sacred utterances; he must listen to the exemplary narratives of the Master's life; and he must join the community of the Master's followers. The compilers of the *Janamsākhīs* equate the sacred utterances of Guru Nanak with *shabad* which in his compositions is 'the inner voice of God'. Remembrance of 'the Name' was to be practised individually as well as in congregation (*satsang*). 'The singing of *kīrtan* within the regular *satsang* was accepted as normative by the *Janam-sakhi* narrators and one of their purposes was to encourage the practice'. Faith was due not to a theory but to a particular person who had propounded the doctrine of salvation 'with a unique clarity and beauty'. The status thus attributed to Guru Nanak is declared to be 'the result of a divine commission received direct from God'. To have the Guru's *darshan* in person should be the first preference of a follower. Short of that, he should listen to the Guru's words and to what he did in his lifetime. The *Janamsākhīs*, thus, were meant to provide a 'satisfactory substitute'. They were meant to set forth 'a soteriological interpretation of the life of Nanak'. This interpretation, or 'myth', was conveyed through anecdote, discourse and an occasional declaration of faith. Besides the primary purpose of confirming and strengthening the Sikhs in their faith, the intention of the narrators was also 'the conversion of others to the same interpretation'. The popularity of the *Janamsākhīs* is closely bound up with their purpose. They will continue to serve a viable function 'as long as religious interests retain a primacy within the Panth'.[14]

The function of the *Janamsākhīs* is quite distinct from their avowed purpose: it concerns the role which they have played in the history of the Panth. 'The primary function which they served from the late sixteenth century to the early eighteenth century must be construed in terms of Panthic cohesion, a role which the narrators and compilers would never have suspected'. The personality of the first Guru was projected not merely through the line of successors but also though the *Janamsākhīs*. In McLeod's view, loyalty to a person is far more effective in maintaining cohesion in a community than loyalty to a doctrine. The replacement of the historical Nanak by the Nanak of myth made him all the more prominent. Amidst all the changes which the Sikh community has experienced and witnessed in the course of its history, loyalty to the person of Guru Nanak has remained the *sine qua non* of faith. Without faith in Guru Nanak, a person cannot be a Sikh.[15]

The *Janamsākhīs* bear witness to the faith of the followers of Guru Nanak primarily in the seventeenth century. Above all else, Baba Nanak is 'the giver of salvation'. Through the multitude of the *Janamsākhī* anecdotes emerges 'the uniqueness of the figure' of Guru Nanak. The surviving memories of his authentic personality get blended with traditional symbols, which in a particular tradition may produce the image of a great ascetic. But this is not the dominant image of most *Janamsākhī* traditions. As time passes, Baba Nanak becomes Guru Nanak, the transition symbolizing his status as the Supreme Teacher. He was much more than a *bhalā faqīr* or a *badā bhagat*; he was a *mahāpurakh*, an *avtār* of Raja Janak and, in fact, God (*paramesar*). 'Whatever he does is true and whatever he says is true. The Guru is God not a man'. In the *Janamsākhī* image of Guru Nanak there are two other allied themes: Nanak the unifier, the one to whom both Hindu and Muslim must owe allegiance, and the theme of 'triumph over Islam' in which the faith promulgated by Guru Nanak transcends all other dispensations, including Islam. The third theme, which is close to Guru Nanak's own attitude, is that of encounters with the Naths resulting in their discomfiture.[16]

According to McLeod, the settings provided by the *Janamsākhī* narrators for the incidents of Guru Nanak's life were derived in form and in detail from 'their own contemporary experience', and hence their value for the historian. A lengthy account of Guru Nanak's wedding, for instance, may be taken as a description of seventeenth-century wedding. This would be true also of the *Janamsākhī* descriptions of Guru Nanak's funeral. The general background against which the *Janamsākhīs* set their tales is that of the rural Punjab. McLeod argues in fact that 'the Sikh Panth of this period must have been almost exclusively a rural community'. Within this general context, three social groups appear to constitute the seventeenth-century Sikh community: the Khatris, the Jats, and the artisans, in that order of standing. An awareness of a distinct identity is emerging in the *Janamsākhīs*: the followers of Guru Nanak (Nanak-Panthīs) have a distinct form of salutation, distinct place and modes of worship, and the distinctive ideas of *nām-simran, ashnān* and *sevā*.[17]

The historical evidence of the *Janamsākhīs* is not confined to the Sikh community. The rural Punjab speaks through them 'with an authentic voice'. The existence of substantial wealth among some Khatris and the use they made of surplus wealth is one example. The existence of landlless labourers is another. It is generally in a circumstantial manner that the *Janamsākhīs* yield their significant information concerning the wider life of the seventeenth-century rural Punjab. There is virtually nothing in the *Janamsākhīs* on dates, chronologies and mighty events but there is enough on 'the unspectacular life of the people' to make the *Janamsākhīs* a unique source of historical information on the Punjab.[18] The locale and specific ideas of the compilers are reflected in the *Janamsākhīs*. Thus, the *Janamsākhīs* can yield information on the sub-regions of the Punjab as well as on what may be called sectarian interests within the Sikh community.

The *Janamsākhīs* are the first examples of sustained Punjabi prose. In fact they have continued to exercise perceptible influence upon the style and imagery of later generations of Punjabi writers. Together with the *Ādi Granth*, the works of the Sūfīs, and eventually the western models, they rank as a major influence in the development of Punjabi literature. McLeod does not hesitate to prophesy that when Punjabi eventually receives the attention it deserves the *Janamsākhīs* will receive a significant share of this recognition.

III

McLeod goes into the 'constituents' of the *Janamsākhīs* rather systematically. Their first constituent in terms of temporal priority but not quantity is authentic memory and actual observation. The major constituents are the works of Guru Nanak and the received tradition, especially the ascetic ideal. The received tradition consisted of an amalgam of Puranic lore, tales from the *Ramāyana*, the *Mahābhārata*, the *Yoga-Vasishtha*, Nath legends, Sūfī hagiography and, occasionally, the Buddhist *Jātakas*. Though it is possible to identify the dominant elements as Puranic, Epic, Nath or Sūfī, a single tradition could incorporate all of them. This hypothesis is illustrated with reference to the Epics, the Puranas, and the Nath and Sūfī traditions.

For the use of the compositions of Guru Nanak, the standard procedure is outlined by McLeod with the caution that it is by no means invariable. Guru Nanak's own words in a *shabad* or a *shalok* give answers to an interlocutor's question and serve as a nucleus for the discourse.'The interlocutor's question or comment is followed by a *shalok* or by the first stanza of a *shabad*. Another question or comment is followed by the second stanza or another *shalok*, and so the discourse proceeds until the *shabad* has been completed or the supply of suitable *shaloks* is exhausted. A setting is provided in order to introduce the discourse and in a brief conclusion the interlocutor submits to the Guru'. This point is illustrated with a few examples. McLeod points out that this procedure was not a conscious attempt to construct historical situations. Therefore the question of deliberate fabrication does not arise. All the quotations used are not from the compositions of Guru Nanak, and they are not necessarily authentic. Here, again, it cannot be maintained that there was an attempt at deceit. The number of Guru Nanak's compositions which served the purpose of 'generating' *sākhīs* was not very large.[19]

The ascetic ideal can be regarded as a part of the received tradition, but it has a peculiar significance in being opposed to Guru Nanak's own emphatically stated beliefs against renunciation. 'It is a measure of the power exercised by the ascetic tradition that it could so effectively reassert itself against Nanak's explict opposition'. This emphasis on an old ideal, according to McLeod, seems to have been the work of an ascetically inclined group within the Sikh community. This group was influential because of the appeal of the deeply rooted ideals of asceticism in the Indian tradition. In any case, there are several *sākhīs* which represent Guru Nanak as the performer of austerities, and as a person who sought complete withdrawal from the world.[20]

Most *sākhīs*, according to McLeod, were products of a blending of all the four constituents, a single constituent rarely found in complete isolation. The Sikh tradition can be seen as drawing much of the material from earlier traditions. Nevertheless, it possesses 'a freshness and novelty of its own'. This was because of its new focus and also 'a result of the function it served in giving expression to the distinctive needs of the new community'.[21]

The purpose of the *Janamsākhīs* dictated appropriate forms. The patterns familiar to the audiences could be adapted to serve the specific needs of the new community. Perhaps the most engaging form used by the narrators of the *sākhīs* was that of the 'narrative anecdote'. These anecdotes are divided by McLeod into four categories: moralistic anecdotes, chimeric fairy-tales, devotional legends, and aetiological legends. Each in its distinctive way served to express the same myth. McLeod gives examples of *sākhīs* falling within each category before moving on to the next form, the narrative discourse. Based on the *shabads* and *shaloks* of Guru Nanak, the narrative discourse turned into 'didactic discourse' when a lengthy exegetical supplement was added. This form is a characteristic of the *Miharbān Janamsākhī*. When it appears in some other tradition, it may be treated as a borrowing from the *Miharbān*. The didactic discourse offered a convenient vehicle for the ascetic ideal. Apart from this rather 'unorthodox' intrusion, there were some deviant traditions which in tone and content ranged from mild heterodoxy to virulent polemic. McLeod gives examples of such 'heterodox discourses'. Lastly, there are *sākhīs* which embody the norms of Sikh conduct. These, in McLeod's view, can be seen as the seeds from which the later *Rahitnāmas* were to grow.[22]

The *sākhī* tradition in diverse forms expanded with speed because of the great role that oral tradition played in their growth, evolution and transmission. Written collections began to be made within a hundred years of Guru Nanak's death, embodying the various phases of development. The oral tradition remained supreme, without any restraint other than the requirements of the myth which they were intended to express. The narrator who addressed the local congregations (*sangats*) possessed considerable freedom to bring his points home to the audience. At the second stage of written recording, much greater concern was shown for chronology and an effort was made to order the assortment of *sākhīs* into a coherent sequence. Expository material was also added to the narrative anecdotes and discourses, accounting for a notional third stage in the development of the written collections.

The fourth phase, according to McLeod, began only with the introduction of the printing press. The first lithographed edition of a *Janamsākhī* appeared in 1871. It was a *Bālā Janamsākhī*. More elaborate editions appeared subsequently. McLeod believes that the *Bālā* tradition had become more popular than the others already in the eighteenth century. Macauliffe brought the *Purātan* tradition to the fore in his *Sikh Religion*, and, a few years later, Karam

Singh, 'the historian', sealed the fate of the *Bālā* tradition with his *Katik kih Visākh*, but only for the scholars. The *Bālā* tradition has not yet lost popularity in the Punjab.[23]

The evolution of individual *sākhīs* is discussed by McLeod with a number of examples: Guru Nanak's visit to Multan, Mula the Khatri, Sajjan the robber, the rich man's pennants, Guru Nanak's return to Talvandi, his discourse with Shaikh Brahm, his visit to Mecca, discourses with Naths, Raja Shivnabh, Guru Angad, and Mardana and Bala. These are 'representative' *sākhīs*, according to McLeod, and each represents a certain characteristic. The first one, for instance, is a narrative anecdote in a simple form with borrowings from current tradition. The third is a variant narrative anecdote in a simple form, evolved from a common quotation. The fifth is a narrative discourse combined with a narrative anecdote. The seventh is a combination of narrative ancedotes with subsidiary discourses and exegetical supplements, producing a complex composite *sākhī*. In the eighth, narrative anecdotes are added to narrative discourses to produce complex composite *sākhīs* with a common theme.[24]

Last of all in this section, McLeod takes up the question of 'sources' used by the compilers of the *Janamsākhīs* with particular attention to the B40 *Janamsākhī* and the *Ādi Sākhīs*. He postulates the existence of *Narrative I* as initially an oral tradition. It was a small selection of anecdotes grouped in a simple connected sequence. McLeod himself points out that this is 'a hypothesis'. He further postulates two components of *Narrative I*, which he chooses to designate as Ia and Ib. Written collections also began to appear, and the manuscript embodying *Narrative I* is designated by McLeod as QI. A manuscript Q2 is similarly postulated, embodying Narrrative II. It is distinguished by the presence in it of the ascetic ideal. A composite tradition, *Narrative II* also is divided into IIa and IIb. Then there are *sākhīs* derived from neither *Narrative I* nor *Narrative II*. This source is designated as *Narrative III*. It is a distinct tradition but not necessarily a completely independent one. The three *Narratives* do not exhaust all the sources of the compilers of the *Janamsākhīs*. There is the distinct *Miharbān* tradition as a source. The B40 *Janamsākhī* is analysed by McLeod in terms of all these sources. The pattern that emerges is not simple. The intricacy of the pattern reflects the complexity of the process.[25]

A close look at McLeod's treatment of the *Janamsākhīs* has revealed, first, that his analysis of this genre of Punjabi literature is comprehensive. It has also revealed that, whereas an important concern in *Gurū Nānak and the Sikh Religion* was to find out what the *Janamsākhīs* tell us about the concrete events of Guru Nanak's life, the objective of his essay in *The Evolution of the Sikh Community* and the *Early Sikh Tradition* is to discover what they tell us about the seventeenth century Sikh Panth and the Punjab. Thirdly, whatever the limitations of his analysis, it is difficult not to see the honesty of purpose in this arduous research conducted over the years.

In the light of this analysis three safe conclusions can be drawn about the criticism made by Justice Gurdev Singh. First, he has failed to grasp the meaning of the term 'myth' as used by McLeod. For Justice Gurdev Singh this term is synonymous with legend and clearly derogatory, but for McLeod it is a technical and neutral concept. Second, Justice Gurdev Singh fails to notice that McLeod's aim in the *Early Sikh Tradition*, or in the *Evolution of the Sikh Community*, is quite different from that in *Gurū Nānak and the Sikh Religion*. The scope of the discussion in the former work is far wider than the limited purpose of knowing what the *Janamsākhīs* tell us about the concrete incidents of Guru Nanak's life. Third, by characterizing McLeod's approach as 'negative', Justice Gurdev Singh assumes that he has reinstated the *Janamsākhīs* as 'biographies' of Guru Nanak. This amounts to evading the issue.

Justice Gurdev Singh's failure to see the real nature of the challenge is evident from the fact that the quotation from James A. Veitch does not support his view of the *Janamsākhīs*. Ironically, it reinforces the view put forth by W.H. McLeod.

IV

In a recent publication, McLeod states that the first response to the biographical portion of *Gurū Nānak and the Sikh Religion* was 'a brief flurry of activity intended to probe its findings and to test them rigorously'. Scholars were dispatched to places which figure prominently in the traditional records and which have received special attention in his analysis: Assam, Sri Lanka and Baghdad. However, when the information collected from Sri Lanka in support of Guru Nanak's visit was shown to be 'wholly inaccurate', the effort to refute him lost its drive. Nevertheless, the biographical part of *Gurū Nānak and the Sikh Religion* has been generally ignored, and most publications from whitin the Panth continue to treat the *Janamsākhīs* as acceptable sources for the life of Guru Nanak, though a rationalizing process is now at work by which 'the grosser elements' are eliminated. In the process, the *Purātan* rather than the *Bālā* tradition has come to occupy the more prominent position as the source for the life of Guru Nanak. On the whole, McLeod's scholarly challenge has been ignored. In short, no historical biography of Guru Nanak has been attempted.[26]

We may agree with McLeod that no fresh evidence of any significance for the concrete incidents of Guru Nanak's life has been brought to light in support of the tradition embodied in the *Janamsākhīs*. It is also true that no biography of Guru Nanak in the modern sense of the term has been written to demonstrate how the *Janamsākhīs* can be used in a rationally convincing manner, particularly in terms of concrete incidents. However, McLeod's approach to the *Janamsākhīs* appears to have one limitation. He remains occupied with the question 'what do the *Janamsākhīs* tell us about the concrete incidents of Guru Nanak's life'? In the process, he comes to attach too much value to 'certainties' and too little to 'probabilities'. Furthermore, this approach obliges him to leave out a whole host of relevant questions which can be asked by a biographer of Guru Nanak.

Guru Nanak lived for seventy years: for about twenty years in a village of the Rachna Doab, for about ten years in the town of Sultanpur in the Jalandhar Doab, for about a quarter of a century on visits to places of pilgrimage at least in the Indian subcontinent, and for about fifteen years leading a more or less settled life at Kartarpur in the upper Rachna Doab. He preached a message that became acceptable to a considerable number of persons, and thereby founded the nucleus of a new community of his followers. Obviously, his was not an ordinary life. According to McLeod himself, Guru Nanak wrote a large volume of powerful poetry of great beauty. We know that there is hardly any important aspect of the contemporary society–political, religious, social or cultural– which is not commented upon in Guru Nanak's compositions. [27] Undoubtedly, he kept his eyes and ears open when, as he says in his own poetic expression, he visited numerous towns and cities in all the nine regions of the earth. In McLeod's own analysis, all the *Janamsākhīs* put together leave much out of the crowded life of Guru Nanak. To capture something of his crowded life we need a three-pronged but integrated approach which combines the evidence of the *Janamsākhīs* and the compositions of Guru Nanak with information which is not directly related to his life.

This point can be clarified with reference to Guru Nanak's stay in Sultanpur. We do not need the evidence of *Janamsākhīs* or of the compositions of Guru Nanak to know that Sultanpur was the seat of an influential *shiqdār*, Daulat Khan Lodi, who was later to become the governor of Lahore. It was a flourishing town on the route from Delhi to Lahore. Its populace consisted of Hindus and Muslims, following diverse professions. It is difficult to imagine that there was no one in Sultanpur to expound or to administer Islamic law, or that there was no Sūfī to represent Islamic mysticism. It is safe to assume that there were Khatri shopkeepers and traders, Brahman priests and astrologers. There were many who served Daulat Khan in the administration of the territory under his jurisdiction. There were *qānūngos* to assist the administrator in the assessment of land revenue. There were others to assist him in the collection of revenue. Indeed, there was an official storehouse (*modīkhāna*) for the revenues collected in kind. This information, combined with the evidence of the *Janamsākhīs*, may convince us that Jai Ram, an Uppal Khatri, who was married to Guru Nanak's sister, was an employee of Daulat Khan. On his request and surety, Guru Nanak was given employment in the *modīkhāna* of Daulat Khan. For about a decade Guru Nanak performed his duties well, living as a house-holder in Sultanpur. His two sons, Sri Chand and Lakhmi Chand, were born there. But neither his service to Daulat Khan Lodi nor his attention to his family was the most notable aspect of his life at Sultanpur. He was in search of something more important, the purpose of human life. Possibly, he had met wandering ascetics (*sādhs*) in or near Rai Bhoi di Talvandi. In Sultanpur he could meet the representatives of both 'Hinduism' and Islam. Religious discussions between Hindus and Muslims were not uncommon in the fifteenth-century Punjab. Guru Nanak meditated on the mysteries of life and reflected on views expressed by others on some of the fundamental questions of life. His search for truth ended in a sense of divine calling. This marked the end of his stay in Sultanpur around 1500.

Now, in the compositions of Guru Nanak, we have proof of his intimate knowledge of both orthodox Islam and the Sūfīs. Where did it come from? His stay at Sultanpur opens up a great probability. In the absence of a better explanation, this probability would acquire the status of an 'almost certainty'. This is one situation in which the evidence of the *Janamsākhīs* and the *Ādi Granth*, seen in conjunction with secular evidence, makes a lot of sense. Our immediate purpose is to suggest that the broad outline of Guru Nanak's life delineated by McLeod can be meaningfully filled up with reasonable certainty or high probability.

We may draw the general conclusion that McLeod has presented the most comprehensive analysis of the *Janamsākhīs*, going into the question of their origin, growth and development, their purpose and function, their significance for the historian of the Sikhs and of the Punjab, and their relevance for the development of Punjabi language and literature. He has also demonstrated their limitation as well as their usefulness for reconstructing the life of Guru Nanak. McLeod's critics have little to say about the merit of his scholarly venture. They merely denounce his critical attitude towards the *Janamsākhīs* as sources for the concrete events of Guru Nanak's life. Justice Gurdev Singh laments the 'negative' attitude of McLeod, but he cannot go beyond reiterating his faith in the *Janamsākhīs*. It may be added, however, that a search for the concrete events of Guru Nanak's life imposes a limitation which tends to become unproductive. A more positive and meaningful interest in the life of Guru Nanak can enable a historian to make better sense of the available sources in rational terms. McLeod's work does not close but paves the way for a sound biography.

NOTES

1. *Perspectives on the Sikh Tradition*, Introduction.
2. Ibid., p. 6.
3. Ibid., pp. 6-7.
4. Ibid., p. 7.
5. Ibid., p. 8.
6. McLeod (1968), p. 68.
7. Ibid., pp. 121-22.
8. Ibid., p. 147.
9. McLeod (1975), p. 26.
10. McLeod (1980), p. 7.
11. Ibid., p. 9.
12. Ibid., p. 10.
13. Ibid., pp. 240-43.
14. Ibid., pp. 244-47.
15. Ibid., pp. 248-56.
16. Ibid., pp. 256-65.
17. Ibid., pp. 266-67.
18. Ibid., pp. 268-69.
19. Ibid., pp. 64-73.
20. Ibid., p. 74.
21. Ibid., p. 79.
22. Ibid., p. 81.
23. Ibid., pp. 82-105.
24. Ibid., pp. 117-73.
25. Ibid., pp. 174-234.
26. McLeod (1989b), pp. 19-20.
27. Grewal (1969).

8. Religious Ideology and Social Environment

How do changes in history take place? has been an important question in modern historical writing. Interest in the development of the Sikh Panth involved the issue of causation from the very beginning of Sikh studies. The early European writers tried to account for the change in 'Sikhism' (equating the term with the Sikh Panth) in terms of external environment in the form of repression and persecution by the Mughal state. J.D. Cunningham introduced the factor of ideology with great emphasis on the relevance of the faith of Guru Nanak for the development of the Sikh Panth. He also extended the scope of social environment by adding 'ethnicity' to the political factor generally invoked by his predecessors. That the historians of the Sikhs have been conscious of the role of ideas and the role of environment in the history of the Sikh Panth is evident from the key terms they have used. G.C. Narang talks of the transformation of 'Sikhism', carrying the implication that Sikh ideology did not remain the same. Banerjee talks of the evolution of 'the Khalsa', taking into account the ideas of Guru Nanak and his successors but emphasizing the crucial role of social environment, including ethnicity. Teja Singh and Ganda Singh talk of 'transfiguration' deliberately to hammer the point that developments in Sikh history were inspired by one and the same ideology expounded by Guru Nanak and his successors. W.H. McLeod, in theory, does not deny the role of ideas but, in practice, he concentrates on the social environment in his exposition of institutionalization, militarization, the Khalsa *rahit* and the doctrines of Guruship. The criticism of McLeod's presentation as much as his presentation itself can be appreciated in this broad context of views on causation in Sikh history.

I

Quite a few of the salient propositions which, according to Justice Gurdev Singh, have been put forth by W.H. McLeod to 'belittle the Sikh faith in the eyes of the English speaking people' and to 'shake the faith of the younger generation of the Sikhs in their religion' relate to what is generally referred to as the development, evolution or the transformation of the Sikh Panth. One of these is that the ten Gurus never preached 'one set of religious doctrines or system'. Guru Amar Das created new institutions 'on the old Hindu lines, the very thing Guru Nanak had spurned'. Then, from the time of the sixth Guru onwards 'the teachings of Guru Nanak were completely given up in favour of a militant pose in response to socio-political situation'. The arming of the Panth was not the result of any decision by Guru Hargobind; it was due to Jat influx in the Panth. The growth of militancy was due primarily to 'the impact of Jat cultural patterns and to economic problems which prompted a militant response'.[1]

For W.H. McLeod, Sikh history offers 'an unusually coherent example of how a cultural group develops in direct response to the pressure of historical circumstances'.[2] The historians like Harbans Singh, Khushwant Singh and Gokul Chand Narang think of the development of Sikh community as marked by 'three major stages'. The first of these was the work of Guru Nanak who founded Sikhism and the Sikh Panth. The second stage came in the time of Guru Hargobind in the early seventeenth century. His father, Guru Arjan, had incurred the displeasure of the Mughal authorities and suffered the death of a martyr. Guru Hargobind responded to the manifest intention of the state to put down the developing Panth by arming his followers and inculcating martial instincts. The religious teachings of Guru Nanak were retained but those who practised them were now prepared to defend their right to do so by 'military means'. The third stage began when Guru Gobind Singh fused the military aspect with the religious by promulgating the Order of the Khalsa on the Baisakhi of 1699 in view of the growing hostility of the hill *rājās* and the Mughal authorities and the weakness of his followers. In McLeod's view, the importance of these three stages cannot be disputed, but this interpretation of evolution can be 'considerably modified'. In this interpretation, the process starts too late and ends too soon. It over-simplifies the events and over-emphasizes their importance and significance. What is needed is 'a more radical concept of development' so that it can take into consideration 'a much wider range of historical and sociological phenomena' and it can express 'a much more intricate synthesis'.[3]

McLeod's essay on the evolution of the Sikh community tends to become a critique of 'the generally accepted understanding' of the subject rather than an exposition of the subject. He does not know whether or not any important development took place in the time of Guru Nanak's first successor, Guru Angad, from the viewpoint of evolution. In the time of Guru Amar Das, however, a large well with eighty-four steps was dug at Goindwal and, according to the Sikh tradition, it was meant to serve as a *tīrath*, or centre of pilgrimage for the Sikhs. This should not be interpreted as a doctrinal change because the compositions of Guru Amar Das are 'in accord with those of the first Guru'. However, Guru Amar Das may be seen as forging bonds 'other than those based upon religious belief'. The second generation of Sikhs was coming up, needing new bonds. Besides the pilgrimage centre, Guru Amar Das provided 'distinctive festival-days, distinctive rituals, and a collection of sacred writings'. McLeod thinks that Guru Nanak had 'rejected all of these'. His successor was compelled to return to them 'in different and more difficult circumstances'. His 'innovations' must be seen as 'concessions to social needs, not as a conscious shift in doctrine'. In fact they were no innovations because Guru Amar Das did little more than 'reintroduce traditional Hindu customs'. McLeod qualifies this statement by pointing out that the 'pilgrimage-centre is in Goindval. It is not at Hardwar, nor at Kurukshetra, nor at any of the other places which his followers might have visited'. Furthermore, the Sikh Panth was developing a consciousness of 'its own separate nature'. Its links with Hindu tradition are very clear but so too is the intention 'to draw lines which will imply distinction'.[4]

Another development which appears to have started in the time of Guru Amar Das was an increase in the number of Jats in greater proportion than before. McLeod is prepared to 'allow a measure of doubt' on this point. He feels sure, however, that this development was taking place by the time of Guru Arjan (1581-1606). This inference is drawn from the founding of Tarn Taran, Sri Hargobindpur and Kartarpur, all of them in Jat territory. It is reinforced with reference to Jat influence in the Sikh Panth during the time of Guru Hargobind on the basis of the *Dabistān-i Mazāhib*. Since the Sikh Gurus rejected the theory of caste and raised Jats to positions of high authority in the new Panth, the Jats felt attracted to it. They had improved their economic position by abandoning pastoralism in favour of agriculture and they could improve their social position by joining the Sikh Panth. Their egalitarian background also attracted them to a *panth* that was more egalitarian than the society around. Their entry was presumably facilitated by the fact that Khatris commonly served as teachers of the Jats. It is significant that Mughal hostility was developing during this period. It should not be attributed solely to Jahangir's orthodoxy, or to the promptings of his Naqshbandi courtiers. 'The increasing influence of the Jats within the Sikh Panth suggests that Jahangir and his subordinates may well have had good reason for their fears, and that these fears would not have related exclusively, nor even primarily, to the *religious* influence of the Guru'.[5]

The Jats constituted the elite of the Punjab villages as peasants and landlords because of their martial traditions, their normally impressive physique, and their considerable energy.[6] They did not enter the Panth empty-handed. They would have been bearing arms many years before the death of Guru Arjan. Their mere presence would impart to the Panth a militant appearance. In any case, 'the arming of the Panth would not have been the result of any decision by Guru Hargobind'. However, the death of Guru Arjan may have persuaded his son and successor of 'the need for tighter organization'. The influence which the Jats enjoyed in the time of Guru Hargobind increased with the passage of time. Therefore, the growth of militancy within the Panth 'must be traced primarily to the impact of Jat cultural patterns'. To this cause were added others later. A militant response could be due to 'economic problems'. McLeod does not elaborate this point. Another factor mentioned is the Shakti cult of the hill culture. It penetrated the Jat culture of the plains and 'produced yet another stage in the evolution of the Panth'. For Guru Gobind Singh the characteristic name of God was All-Steel (*sarabloh*), and he used a two-edged sword for stirring baptismal water. In his writings and in those which were produced at his court there are constant references to the mighty exploits of the Mother Goddess, one of the most notable being his own *Chandī kī Vār*. It is in the works of Guru Gobind Singh and 'in the developments which followed his death' that McLeod can observe the influence of the hill culture most plainly.[7]

Furthermore, in his discussion of the Khalsa *rahit*, McLeod maintains that the Jat cultural patterns provided the most important Khalsa symbols, known as *panj kakke* or 'Five Ks' because of the letter *kakkā* or 'k' with which they all begin: *kesh* (uncut hair), *kanghā* (comb), *kirpān* (dagger), *kaṛā* (steel bangle), and *kachh* (a pair of breeches which must not reach below the knees). There can be 'no doubt that the Five Ks reflect the complex of Jat cultural patterns and contemporary historical events which produced so many features now associated exclusively with the Khalsa brotherhood'. Uncut hair was a Jat custom observed during the seventeenth-eighteenth centuries, as earlier, by all Jats whether Hindu, Muslim or Sikh. The bearing of arms was a Jat practice that received ample encouragement from the events of the eighteenth century. With these two symbols may be paired the comb and the bangle respectively. The breeches are harder to understand in this context but it seems safe to assume that this symbol 'must also relate in some way to the same situation'.[8]

Justice Gurdev Singh maintains that Professor Jagjit Singh has refuted McLeod successfully on the question of militarization in the *Perspectives on the Sikh Tradition*. His essay on the militarization of the Sikh movement relies on the work he had done already. Its first part deals with 'some specific points raised by McLeod'. The proposition that 'the arming of the Panth could not have been the result of any decision of Guru Hargobind' and that 'the growth of militancy within the Panth must be traced primarily to the impact of Jat cultural patterns and to economic problems which prompted a militant response'. raises three issues: the question of leadership and initiative, the impact of Jat cultural patterns, and the relevance of economic problems which prompted a militant response.[9]

To underline that the Sikh Gurus were the real leaders of the community, Jagjit Singh makes the general proposition that there were three turning points in Sikh history during the times of the Gurus: a break with the ascetic tradition, rejection of the caste structure, and militarization of the Panth. All the three changes represented departures from the prevailing tradition. 'Only a purposeful and determined leadership could have brought about the said departure'.[10] If Jahangir felt concerned about the growing Jat following of Guru Arjan, why does he say in his *Memoirs* that he ordered the Guru's execution because of his blessings to the rebel Prince Khusrau? If the mere entry of Jat elements into the Sikh ranks could arouse the fear of the authorities, a similar action should have been taken against the Miṇas and the Handālīs whose following also included Jats. But this was not done, because they did not challenge the political authorities of the day: they did not have the socio-political concerns which the Sikh Gurus had. Moreover, there is no basis for McLeod's assumption that the Jats were armed and the Khatris were not. Among the Cherished-Five, who were willing to lay down their lives for the Guru, there was only one Jat. When the Khalsa were divided into five fighting units in the early eighteenth century, two of them were headed by Khatris (and one by a Ranghreta). This does not suggest Jat dominance. In any case, Jagjit Singh feels convinced that 'the initiative and determination for carrying on the armed struggle against the established state was invariably that of the Guru and not that of his followers'.[11]

Jagjit Singh does not accept the proposition that the Jats who came to pay homage to the Guru came armed. When the Sikhs complained to Guru Gobind Singh that they were harassed on their way to Anandpur, they were advised to come armed. The bearing of arms could not have been a Jat peculiarity; no exception could be made in their case if the policy of the state was to keep the populace disarmed. Jagjit Singh argues, further, that the Jats started joining the Sikh movement in large numbers only after the decision of Guru Hargobind and Guru Gobind Singh to militarize the Panth. Therefore it was a case of Sikh ideology influencing the Jats and not of the Jat character moulding the Sikh movement. The inspiration from Sikh ideology turned even the castes lower than the Jats into a fighting class. McLeod's hypothesis that the Khalsa adopted the 5Ks under the influence of Jat cultural patterns is no more than a conjecture. There is no reason to suggest that the 5Ks were characteristic Jat features. Moreover, how would one explain the total disappearance of these cultural symbols, supposed to have been borrowed by the Sikhs from Jats, from amongst the non-Sikh Jats of the Punjab and the neighbouring states? In any case, symbols by themselves do not lead to anything, much less to militancy. Revolutionary movements are not made by symbols; it is such movements that give meaningful significance to them. Obviously, 'the Sikh movement needed no goading from the Jats for its militarization'.[12]

About the impact of economic conditions on militarization, Jagjit Singh states that the responses of the Jat peasantry and the lower castes to economic problems were not uniform. Nor did they produce the same or similar results. The Sikh political struggle lasted for three generations and it was waged by the lower castes as much as by the Jat peasantry. What sustained their struggle was a distinct ideology with clearcut revolutionary aims. 'It is, therefore, idle to trace the source of a revolutionary movement, divorced from its ideology and leadership, to sheer economic causes'.[13] Equally pointless is the conjecture that the synthesis of the Devi cult with the Jat culture had much to do with the evolution of militancy in the Sikh Panth. The cult of the Goddess was not dominant in the countryside inhabited by the Sikhs. If the Devi cult inspired the Jats who visited Anandpur, why did that inspiration disappear afterwards?[14]

In the second part of his essay, Jagjit Singh takes up the question of militarization in a wider context. He can see no signs of any shared motivation in the Jat organization 'which could urge the

Jats for sustained action, much less for a political adventure'. The Jats of the Sikh tract 'lacked even the *gotra* solidarity beyond the village level'.[15] There was a spirit of equality among the Jats, and it was reinforced by the *bhāichārā* system of land tenure. However, this egalitarianism was confined to their clans. They conformed to 'the hierarchical pattern of the caste system', having no qualms about submitting to the higher castes or dominating the lower ones. Like the peasantry in general, they lacked political aspiration and initiative.[16]

By contrast, what bound the Sikhs together in the Sikh Panth was 'the primacy of the Sikh ideals rather than any caste, clan or regional interests and sentiments'. The creation of the Khalsa provided the 'real organizational base'. Recruitment to this order was strictly on an individual and voluntary basis. 'No caste or clan loyalties were involved, because no one could become a member of the Khalsa brotherhood without being baptized, and no one could be baptized without taking the five vows'. The *misls* were not formed 'on the basis of caste or clan affiliation'. The spirit of equality among the Sikhs was altogether differnt from that of the Jats. A product of Sikh ideology, the Sikh egalitarian approach was not marked by dichotomy towards the higher or lower castes. The Sikh movement was an egalitarian revolution in social as well as political terms. If its objectives were not fully realized, its actual achievement was so considerable that it can be looked upon as more significant than the French Revolution. It enabled the individuals belonging to the lowest castes in the traditional Indian society to come into political power which gave them a new social status. The genesis of the Sikh revolutionary spirit lay essentially in the religion of the Sikhs which 'stands for social and political equality'.[17]

Jagjit Singh concludes that McLeod's hypothesis about the militarization of the Sikh movement is untenable on more than one count. There is no reason to infer that Jats were the predominant element in the Sikh Panth when Guru Hargobind decided to militarize the movement; they were not predominant in the battles of Guru Gobind Singh, or those of Banda Bahadur. There is nothing to suggest that the Jats used to come armed when they came to pay homage to the Gurus. The keeping of sword and hair was not a speciality of Jat culture and, therefore, the Sikh movement could not have borrowed these features from the Jats. Nor did the Sikh movement need the inspiration of the Devi cult for its militancy. The Sikh militancy must by viewed in relation to the Sikh egalitarian revolution: it was geared to achieve the essential purpose of capturing political power.[18]

That McLeod holds a different view of the role of ideology in history is evident from a recent work in which he talks of the various attitudes and theories in relation to the issue of transformation in Sikh history. The theory which has long dominated Sikh historiography on this point was first put forth by J.D. Cunningham in a rather stirring statement:

> It was reserved for *Nanak* to perceive the true principles of reform, and to lay those broad foundations which enabled his successor *Gobind* to fire the minds of his countrymen with a new nationality, and to give practical effect to the doctrine that the lowest is equal with the highest in race as in creed, in political rights as in religious hopes.[19]

As a recent example McLeod quotes Jagjit Singh:

> The Sikh movement was an organic growth of the Sikh religion or the Sikh view of life. The founding of the Sikh *Panth* outside the caste society in order to use it as the base for combating the hierarchical set-up of the caste order, and the creation of the Khalsa for capturing state power in the interests of the poor and the suppressed, were only a projection, on the military and political plane, of the egalitarian approach of the Sikh religious thesis.[20]

For McLeod, this view of the Sikh movement implies that the Gurus envisaged a particular pattern for the Panth and the actual form which it assumed corresponded to their intentions. It gives too much credence to conscious intention and to the role of ideas in history to leave any scope for the operation of other factors. McLeod's own view is that the progressive development of the Panth 'must be explained not merely in terms of purposeful intention but also (and in significant measure) by the influence of social, economic and historical environment'.[21]

The opposition posed between ideology and environment is not easy to resolve. On the question of numbers, Jat predominance in the Panth is firmly established in the census of 1881. The general statements on the composition of the Sikh Panth during the late eighteenth century indicate Jat preponderance. Among the Sikh chiefs of this period, there was one from a family of carpenters and another from a family of vintners; there were two Khatri Sikh chiefs too who failed to found a dynasty; but more than ninety per cent of the Sikh chiefs were Jat. The presence of Sikhs with low caste background in the Panth during the early eighteenth century is beyond any doubt, but unless they were present in the Sikh Panth in great disproportion to their total numbers in the Punjab, and the Jats were in much smaller proportion to their total numbers, Jat dominance in the early eighteenth-century Panth is a certainty. Jat representation among the *masands* is mentioned by the author of the *Dabistān-i Mazāhib* in the early seventeenth century, and Jats are mentioned by Bhai Gurdas also among the eminent Sikhs of the Gurus. Coming after an overwhelming presence of Khatris among the prominent Sikhs, this evidence can be taken as an indication of the increasing number of Jats. What exactly was their proportion in the Sikh Panth in the early seventeenth or the late sixteenth century cannot be estimated from the evidence available at present. It leaves much scope for hunches and conjectures. It is interesting to note that whereas McLeod attaches importance to their presence in the Sikh Panth before the martyrdom of Guru Arjan, Jagjit Singh looks upon the measures of Guru Hargobind as a factor responsible for their increased number in the Panth. This apparently small difference regarding what came first acquires great significance because of the decided preference of McLeod for ethnicity and of Jagjit Singh for ideology as the primary operative factor.

On the question of the Khalsa *rahit*, McLeod does not explain the adoption of *kachh*. He looks upon the *kaṛā* and the *kanghā* as paired respectively with the *kirpān* (actually arms) and the *kesh*. The whole argument hinges essentially on the bearing of arms and the wearing of uncut hair. McLeod asserts that both these customs were prevalent among Jats, whether Hindu or Muslim, or Sikh. But there is no credible evidence for this. The point is so crucial to his hypothesis that it demands more reliable and more acceptable evidence. His view that the Shakti cult of the hills blended with the Jat culture of the plains to produce one more synthesis to accentuate militancy is based essentially on the evidence of the *Dasam Granth*, consisting of a few works attributed to Guru Gobind Singh and the largest bulk to others. The Mother Goddess figures much less prominently in the *Dasam Granth* than the other *avtārs*, notably Krishna and Rama. They symbolize legitimacy of the use of physical force in the cause of righteousness. In this respect, the *Dasam Granth* elaborates and reinforces the idea present in the compositions of Guru Nanak that God protects his saints and destroys the wicked. However, during the late eighteenth and the early nineteenth century, the *Dasam Granth* came to influence the beliefs and attitudes of Sikhs in a manner that suggests considerable importance of the Goddess and of Rama and Krishna. But the evidence is merely suggestive. Finally, the historian who has underlined the importance of the economic factor for the Sikh revolt against the Mughals has also emphasized that religious ideology provided the source of cohesion for the oppressed Sikh peasantry. The evidence advanced by McLeod in support of his hypothesis is too weak to sustain it. It must be added, however, that Jagjit Singh does not account for Jat predominance in the Sikh Panth: he simply ignores it.

II

An important proposition attributed to W.H. McLeod by Justice Gurdev Singh relates to the Khalsa *rahit*. McLeod does not accept the traditional account of the founding of the Khalsa on the Baisakhi day of 1699. He has 'compulsive reasons for scepticism'. He goes to the length of saying that 'the traditions relating to the period of Guru Gobind Singh must be, in some considerable measure, set aside. The slate must be wiped clean and must not be reinscribed until we have ascertained just what did take place during the eighteenth century'. The Sikh code of discipline (*rahit maryādā*) and symbols were evolved during the eighteenth century 'as a result of gradual growth' and not of any pronouncement by Guru Gobind Singh on the Baisakhi day of 1699.[22]

McLeod refers to the year 1699 as the high point of Sikh tradition which presents the institution of the Khalsa on the Baisakhi of that year as the climax of all that had preceded and the fount of all that followed. According to the Sikh tradition, Guru Gobind Singh reflected on the perils of his situation and the weakness of his timid followers, and he devised a plan to infuse a spirit of strength and unity. He summoned his followers from far and wide on that day and they came in thousands. When the Baisakhi fair was in full swing the Guru suddenly appeared before his followers and, with his sword raised aloft, demanded the head of any of his Sikhs. A hush fell upon the concourse and he had to repeat the demand. A loyal Sikh came forward and he was conducted into a tent. The thud of a descending sword was heard outside and the Guru reappeared with his bloodstained weapon to demand a second head. Another Sikh came forward and the process was repeated till the number reached five. Then the Guru drew back the side of the tent, and horror turned into amazement when the gathering observed corpses of five decapitated goats beside the five alive volunteers.[23]

Guru Gobind Singh is believed to have delivered a sermon on this occasion in which he declared the five volunteers to constitute the nucleus of a new brotherhood, the Khalsa. Those who chose to join this brotherhood were to abandon pride of caste, the old scriptures and places of pilgrimage and the worship of minor gods and goddesses as well as *avtārs*. They were to follow only God and the Guru. A new baptismal ceremony was adopted by mingling sweets with water, stirring it with a two-edged sword in an iron bowl. This *amrit* was administered to the five foundation members. They administered the same baptism to the Guru himself. All others who were willing to join the brotherhood and to accept its discipline were invited to take baptism, and many thousands of all castes came forward to take it. The discipline promulgated at this time included dissociation with five groups of people consisting of all those who had at different times disputed succession to Guruship, together with their successors and followers, and all those who cut their hair. Various other prohibitions were enjoined, notably tobacco, meat from animals slaughtered in the Muslim fashion, and sexual intercourse with Muslim women. Members of the new brotherhood were to wear the 5Ks as symbols and to add the name 'Singh' to their given name. All women were to add 'Kaur'. Thus was established a powerful brotherhood which in unity, loyalty, and courage was to struggle against overwhelming odds, survive the cruelest of persecution, and ultimately rise to political supremacy in less than a century on the ruins of the Mughal power and Afghan pretensions.[24]

At the end of the eighteenth century 'we find a clearly defined Khalsa Panth with formulated religious doctrines, a coherent code of discipline, and the strong conviction that it has been born to rule'. But was this the position immediately after the creation of the Khalsa, or even in the second decade of the eighteenth century? McLeod is extremely sceptical. The eighteenth century on the whole was a critical period, marked by warfare, disaster and eventual triumph. To its distinctive problems the Khalsa responded by finding distinctive solutions. In both tribulation and success the expanding Khalsa was ever seeking a self-understanding and a self-definition. Therefore, the traditional explanation must be evaluated in the light of what we find in the period extending from the institution of the Khalsa in 1699 to the capture of Lahore by Ranjit Singh in 1799. Our knowledge of this period is rather limited. 'Traditions abound but so too do compulsive reasons for scepticism. What we do know, however, indicates that the traditions relating to the period of Guru Gobind Singh must be, in some considerable measure, set aside. The slate must be wiped clean and must not be reinscribed until we have ascertained just what did take place during the eighteenth century'. In other words, there are features of the received tradition relating to the Baisakhi of 1699 which were actually incorporated later. It does not mean that the entire tradition stands rejected. 'We may be sure that something certainly did happen on the Baisakhi day of 1699, and that some of the traditions will eventually turn out to be substantially accurate'. The fact that the Khalsa did eventually establish an effectual claim to represent the orthodox form of the Sikh Panth lends considerable support to the traditional hypothesis. However, it does not follow that every feature of the tradition has to be literally and uncritically accepted.[25]

In McLeod's view, the Khalsa *rahit* or the code of discipline crystallized during the eighteenth century. The whole of this code was not promulgated on the Baisakhi day of 1699 and it did not continue unchanged. If we examine the written codes or the *Rahitnāmas* of the eighteenth century we find that 'the conventions of the Khalsa were in the process of evolution during this period'. The question of 5Ks, for instance, was not 'finally settled until well into the eighteenth century'. As we noticed earlier, McLeod sees the influence of Jat cultural patterns in the evolution of the five symbols. The same complex of Jat culture and contemporary circumstances accounts for the explicit prohibitions which find a place in the Khalsa discipline. The prohibitions directed against the consumption of *halāl* meat and intercourse with Muslim women do not reflect the 1699 situation. In fact they accord well with the eighteenth-century struggle against the Mughals and, more particularly, against the Afghans. Presumably, the same situation accounts for the ban on the use of tobacco. More examples could be cited to support the view that the discipline evolved gradually during the course of the eighteenth century in respone to inherited patterns and the impact of contemporary events. The *Rahitnāmas* invoke the authority of Guru Gobind Singh in order to acquire the sanction needed to enforce the code. Their contents cannot be treated as a record of the actual instructions of Guru Gobind Singh.[26]

Justice Gurdev Singh invokes the authority of Hari Ram Gupta to refute McLeod. As we pointed out earlier, Gupta's contribution to the *Perspectives on the Sikh Tradition* was not written as a critique of McLeod. There is only one reference to McLeod in a footnote which is worth quoting:

> The word Wah Guru is used in *Puratan Janam Sakhi* on p. 23. It says Guru Nanak used it. McLeod, op. cit., 41.

Since this is the only reference to McLeod, it is not clear to which of his works 'op.cit.' refers.[27] Justice Gurdev Singh appears to have used a chapter from Gupta's *History of the Sikh Gurus* without bothering to modify the footnotes.[28]

Justice Gurdev Singh states that Gupta has written authoritative books on the history of the Punjab, and that his detailed account of the founding of the Khalsa is based on 'authentic contemporary and near contemporary evidence'. But there is no such evidence in his essay. Gupta draws largely upon 'secondary' works. More than half of the references are to a single secondary work. Gupta himself is rather modest about his linguistic competence: 'In the translation from *Bachitra Natak*, *Chandi Charitra* and *Akal Ustat*, my friend and colleague Nirbhai Singh has given me great help'.[29] These are the major contemporary sources cited by Gupta. But, having been written before the event, these sources have nothing to say about the 'founding of the Khalsa'.

For the founding of the Khalsa, Hari Ram Gupta relies heavily on M.A. Macauliffe, supplemented indiscriminately by the secondary works of M'Gregor, Bhai Vir Singh, Bhagat Lakshman Singh, Kartar Singh, and Indubhushan Banerjee. The authority of Sainapat is invoked but only to make the point that Guru Gobind Singh 'invited the entire audience' at Naina Devi to attend 'the grand function' at Anandpur later.[30] The early nineteenth century authority of Bhai Santokh Singh is cited by Gupta on the point that 'the tobacco leaf resembles the ear of a cow, and so the Guru prohibited its use'.[31] Bhai Nand Lal's authority, which is believed to be contemporary, is invoked on the point that the Sikhs should not worship tombs, graves and relics of cremation.[32] Thus, the evidence cited by Gupta relates to points which have no bearing on Justice Gurdev Singh's criticism of McLeod.

Gupta gives a fanciful interpretation of 'the meaning of the Khalsa' without citing any evidence whatever. The salutation 'Wah Guru ji ka Khalsa, Wah Guru ji ki Fateh', according to him, was given by Guru Gobind Singh to the Khalsa with a view to 'giving to the Singhs an optimistic view of life in the midst of trials and tribulations which lay ahead of them'. The Guru was in search of a word that should have 'the sanctity of five and the presence of God'. This word was '*Khālsā*'. It consists of five letters: *khe*, *alif*, *lām*, *swād* and *alif* or *hāe*. The first stands for *khud* or oneself; the second for both Akal Purakh and Allah; the third for *labbaik*; the fourth for Sahib or Master; and the fifth for *āzādī* or freedom (if it is taken to be *alif*) and for *humā* (if it is taken to be *hāe*), the legendary bird about which it was believed that 'every head it overshadows, in time bears a crown'. Gupta takes his fanciful interpretation to a breaking point when he explains *labbaik*: the Singhs enter into pleasant conversation with the Lord; God himself asks the Singhs 'What do you want from me? Here am I. What would you have?' and the Singhs reply, 'Lord ! give us liberty and sovereignty'.[33]

After this, it should not come to us as a surprise that, according to Gupta, Guru Gobind Singh evolved the 'formula of five' for the guidance of the Khalsa: five beliefs, five symbols, five vows, five deliverances, and five rules of conduct. The five beliefs are: belief in Akāl Purakh, Guru Granth, the greetings *Wāh Gurū jī kā Khālsā Wāh Gurū jī kī Fateh*, and Guru Nanak's *Japjī*. Gupta does not realize that these 'beliefs' amount only to four. The five symbols are easier to count and remember: *kesh*, *kanghā*, *kirpān*, *kaṛā* and *kachhā*. It must be underlined that Gupta cites no evidence on this point. The five vows are: not to cut hair, not to smoke, not to eat *halāl* meat, not to wear a cap, and not to worship tombs, graves and relics of cremation. The five deliverances are: *dharam nāsh*, *karam nāsh*, *janam nāsh*, *sharam nāsh* and *bharam nāsh*. Only for the first of these, Gupta provides an 'authority' but only that of Bhagat Lakshman Singh's biography of Guru Gobind Singh in English. The five rules of conduct are: starting every enterprise after a prayer, helping one another and the Panth, practising riding and using arms, not coveting another's property, and not having sexual intercourse with another's wife. Only for the last of these Gupta cites an authority, that of M.A. Macauliffe.[34] His account of the birth of the Khalsa, thus, is not based on contemporary or near contemporary sources. Justice Gurdev Singh's reliance on H.R. Gupta is totally misplaced.

It does not follow, however, that McLeod's own hypothesis is valid. He tends to suggest that all the 5Ks came from the Jat cultural patterns in combination with the developments of the eighteenth century. But the evidence for wearing *kesh* is quite early, and McLeod himself pairs *kanghā* with the *kesh*. Similarly there is early evidence for bearing arms, and we know that Guru Gobind Singh attached great importance to the sword. McLeod pairs *kaṛā* with the sword. Thus, on the point of 5Ks McLeod's hypothesis, essentially, does not hold good. There is early evidence also for ban on the use of tobacco. Much of McLeod's interpretation springs from the view that the *Gursobha* was not necessarily written in 1711. He also visualizes the possibility that Guru Gobind Singh added *rahit* injunctions between 1699 and his death in 1708. McLeod appears to be right in suggesting that the ban on sexual intercourse with 'Muslim' women came later. The ban suggests not merely a state of armed struggle but also a situation in which the Khalsa could be victorious (because the possibilities of such 'intercourse' were there normally for the victors). This situation definitely emerged for the first time in the time of Banda Bahadur. However, this ban was merely an extension of the general injunction against extra-marital intercourse. It is interesting to observe in this connection that Qazi Nur Muhammad in the third quarter of the eighteenth century admires the Singhs specifically for their restraint: they never molested the women of the vanquished. McLeod mentions the ban on *halāl* meat as a later introduction. It must be remembered, however, that *jhatkā* was the customary Indian method of decapitating goats for meat. It may not be unreasonable to conclude that all the items cited by McLeod were not necessarily later additions, but his general hypothesis of 'an evolving code' is not demolished.

III

Justice Gurdev Singh criticizes McLeod for suggesting that the doctrines of Guru-Panth and Guru-Granth arose out of the need for cohesion during the eighteenth century, and not because of Guru Gobind Singh's explicit injunction.[35] McLeod's treatment of 'the Khalsa theory of authority', like his treatment of the Khalsa code of discipline, is avowedly an 'informed conjecture'.[36] According to the Sikh tradition, the functions of the Guru after the death of Guru Gobind Singh were vested jointly in the body of the believers (the Khalsa Panth) and the scripture (the Granth Sahib). McLeod suggests that tradition may 'perhaps be a retrospective interpretation, a tradition which owes its origin not to an actual pronouncement of the Guru but to an insistent need for maintaining the Panth's cohesion during a later period'.[37] There were several cohesive ideals and institutions at work during the eighteenth century, like Amritsar as a religious centre, a distinctive Sikh historiography, and the conviction that 'the Khalsa shall rule' (*rāj karegā khālsā*).[38] More important, however, was the Khalsa code of discipline. But the most important was the doctrine of Guruship.

The personality of Guru Nanak had been a cohesive factor of continuing importance in two distinct ways. There was a line of successors deemed to be one person in ten manifestations in different bodies, a torch lit from another torch giving the same flame. There can be no doubt that the function of this doctrine was 'a simple extension of the first Guru's authority' and it continued to serve a cohesive role until the death of Guru Gobind Singh. The other cohesive factor was provided by the *Janamsākhīs*, especially during the pre-Khalsa period. They provided a single focus of common loyalty for all members of the Panth. 'Everything clusters around a single centre. If a person owns allegiance to this single centre he is *Nanak-panthi*, a Sikh of Guru Nanak'. Distinctive ceremonies for birth, marriage and death tended to reinforce cohesion. The appointment of *masands* to various *manjīs* created a network which served the same purpose. Nevertheless there were disputes about succession to Guruship. These disputes made the presence of the Jats in the Panth a factor of considerable importance. The Miṇas or the followers of Prithi Chand, for example, appear to have limited their concerns to the religious aspects of Guru Nanak's teachings, thereby opposing the wider concerns which increasingly occupied the Panth's interest. They failed to accommodate Jat aspirations. However, a truly radical break came with the death of Guru Gobind Singh, raising the question of authority and, therefore, of the Panth's cohesion in an exceedingly acute form.[39]

It is relevant in this context that in the literature of the early seventeenth century there are indications of 'a developing doctrine of the *Guru Panth*, a doctrine which affirms that in the absence of the personal Guru the local sangat, or congregation, within any area possesses the mystical power to make decisions on his behalf'. After the death of Guru Gobind Singh, especially after the failure of the personal leadership of Banda Bahadur, 'a new theory of leadership was needed'. Three things were necessary for a new theory to be effective. It should permit ample freedom to small scattered groups; it should preserve the ideal of a unified authority; and it should possess a powerful sanction. An answer to this need was provided by the doctrine of the corporate and scriptural Guru. During the eighteenth century it was the corporate aspect of the doctrine which possessed the greater importance and which served to impart a measure of cohesion to the community. Later, however, the doctrine of the corporate Guru 'effectively lapsed and an undisputed primacy was given to the scriptural Guru theory, a primacy which continues to this day'.[40]

Dispersion of the Sikhs during the eighteenth century was relevant for the emergence and crystallization of the doctrine of Guru-Panth. Like the Sikh *sangats*, or congregations, the Khalsa *jathās* were widely scattered and within both of them the instrument of authority increasingly came to be identified with the group itself. 'The Guru was present in the sangat and the corporate voice of the sangat was accordingly the voice of the Guru'. The *sangat* provided a religious context and the *jathā* was 'a military extension of the same idea'. It assumed a position of primacy within the Panth during the middle years of the eighteenth century. 'The Guru, though absent in the body, is very much present in spirit wherever his words are devoutly sung'. They who participate in this *kīrtan* (communal singing) with genuine devotion manifest the Guru's own presence in their assembly and when they speak as an assembly 'they speak as the Guru'. For any particular purpose, five representatives (*panj piāre* or the 'five beloved') could be chosen temporarily to exercise the authority of the *sangat*. However, the military needs and the extension of the Khalsa influence shifted the Panth's primary interest from the *sangat* towards the *jathā*, and later towards the *misl*. This shift carried with it the belief in the presence of the Guru in the *jathā*. 'As military and eventually political issues began to command an increasing attention, the doctrine was extended to cover the quasi-parliamentary sessions of the Sarbat Khalsa'. The need of cohesion did not end with the local *sangat*. The *misl sardārs* also had their problems to solve and the doctrine of Guru-Panth proved to be well suited to their needs. This doctrine found explicit expression in the institution of the *gurmata*, rooted in the theory 'that corporate decisions of the Sarbat Khalsa were to be regarded as the word of the Guru with the full force of his authority to back it'. But for the respect accorded to this institution, the disunity of the *misls* would have been much more serious. The *gurmata* expressed a continuing sense of unity and did much more to sustain it during a disintegrative phase. Although essentially a response to military need, the doctrine expressed in an unusually coherent form the more general religious doctrine of the Guru's continuing presence within any congregation of his disciples.[41]

When Ranjit Singh extinguished 'the misl sytem' and replaced it with a strong and relatively centralized monarchy, the need of the doctrine of Guru-Panth was no longer there. The monarchy itself now assumed the cohesive role as the *Sarkār Khālsā*, or the rule of the Khalsa. In this situation the *gurmata* could only be regarded as a positive hindrance. As a result, the theory of the Guru-Panth quickly lapsed into disuse, leaving the issue of religious authority to the doctrine of scriptural Guru, the Guru-Granth. 'All other questions previously determined by reference to the corporate Guru were meanwhile appropriated by Ranjit Singh and later by his British successors'. The way was being prepared for the ascendancy of the doctrine of Guru-Granth by the custom of deciding all *gurmatas* in the presence of the scripture during the eighteenth century itself. In fact, it was due to this reason that the *gurmata* held a special sanctity. In the time of Ranjit Singh, the scripture assumed a primary religious authority. 'This authority it has never relinquished and to this day it serves as the focus not merely of Sikh devotion but also of Sikh loyalty to the Panth. It still survives in situations which permit a growing neglect of the Khalsa discipline'.[42]

Justice Gurdev Singh does not say anything about the doctrine of Guru-Panth in McLeod's 'informed conjecture'. He objects only to McLeod's treatment of the doctrine of Guru-Granth. He thinks it is unfair on McLeod's part to suggest that *Granth Sahib* was installed as Guru to serve as cohesive force for the leaderless community after the execution of Banda Bahadur and not because of an injunction of Guru Gobind Singh. Justice Gurdev Singh believes that there is an unbroken tradition that Guru Gobind Singh vested Guruship in the *Granth Sahib* in perpetuity, deliberately putting an end to the line of personal Gurus. There is another reason for rejecting McLeod's suggestion. The martial Khalsa could have chosen the *Dasam Granth* as a more suitable instrument of cohesion, if cohesion was their concern. They owned and revered the *Granth Sahib* because of the Guru's injunction and 'never entertained the idea of any individual succeeding the Tenth Guru, nor of a successor other than Guru Granth Sahib'.[43]

According to Justice Gurdev Singh, Ganda Singh has examined the question of succession to Guru Gobind Singh in all its details, and has 'unreservedly rejected the suggestion that an individual has succeeded the Tenth Master as the Guru of the Sikhs'. Ganda Singh's assertion is 'unequivocal' that before his death Guru Gobind Singh had 'installed Granth Sahib as the perpetual Guru of the Sikhs'. Harbans Singh has examined the issue from another angle as well. The Word was to take the place of the Guru sooner or later. When Guru Gobind Singh declared the Guru Granth Sahib to be his successor, the 'inevitable came to pass'. The Guruship could be made lasting 'only through the Word'. Like Ganda Singh, Harbans Singh has based his conclusions on ample historical evidence.[44]

Ganda Singh's essay in the *Perspectives on the Sikh Tradition* was not written with reference to the work of W.H. McLeod. Ganda Singh was keen to establish all along that Guru Gobind Singh really died on 6-7 October 1708 and he was actually cremated at Nander. This could demolish the myth created by Sewa Das, an Udāsī Sadhu, in his *Parchiān* written in 1741, that Guru Gobind Singh had gone to heaven bodily. This was reinforced by Koer Singh who wrote his *Gurbilās* in 1751.[45] Ganda Singh's second concern was more important: to authenticate beyond doubt that Guru Gobind Singh did not appoint anyone of his followers to succeed him and commanded his followers to look upon the Word of the great Masters 'embodied in their holy book, the *Granth Sahib*, as their Guru, thenceforward known as the *Guru Granth Sahib*'.[46]

At the end of his essay Ganda Singh refers to a contemporary *Bhatt Vahī* quoted by Guninder Kaur in her *Guru Granth Sahib, Its Physics and Metaphysics*, which contains an entry regarding the Guru Granth Sahib as the future Guru of the Sikhs. The earliest literary work cited by Ganda Singh himself is the *Sri Gur Sobhā*, written by Sainapat in 1711. A day before his death, Guru Gobind Singh responded to a question of his followers by announcing that he had 'bestowed his physical form upon the Khalsa' (*bakhsh diò khālis ko jāmā*) and that 'the Limitless and the Eternal Word was the True Guru' (*satgurū hamārā apar apārā shabad bichārā ajar-jaran*). The Guru's last message and his final commandment in unmistakable terms and clear words was that he did not appoint any particular individual as his successor and that 'the Khalsa under the guidance of the Divine Word – the *gurbani* – was to be the future physical and spiritual representative of the Guru'. That the Sikhs accepted this creed is evident from the *Rahitnāma* of Bhai Nand Lal in which it is stated by the Guru himself that his two forms were the Granth and the Khalsa. In the *Gurbilās Chhevīn Pātshāhī*, assumed by Ganda Singh to have been written in 1718, the author invariably uses the epithet 'Guru Granth'. In another manuscript in Ganda Singh's possession, relating to the death of Guru Gobind Singh, the Sikhs are entrusted to *Sri Sāhib* and the *Sabda* 'the great Word, as given in the *Granth Sahib*'.[47]

From the second half of the eighteenth century comes the evidence of Koer Singh, Kesar Singh Chhibber and Sarup Das Bhalla. The statements quoted from Koer Singh are to the effect that Guru Gobind Singh did not appoint anyone as his successor; the entire Khalsa had been entrusted to the protection of 'the Wielder of the Sword' (*asiketu*); they should accept 'the embodiment of the Word' (*shabad kā rūp*) as their sheet; and they should recognize *Sri Granth* as the ever-present *darshan* of the Guru. Koer Singh also mentions how the *Ādi Sat-Gurū* was accepted by Guru Gobind Singh as the Guru. The phrase 'Guru Granth' occurs in Koer Singh's work at several places. Kesar Singh Chhibber refers to the last commandment of Guru Gobind Singh: 'The *Granth* is the Guru; you hold the garment (seek the protection) of the Timeless God' (*bachan kītā Granth hai Gurū laṛ pakṛo Akāl*). Sarup Das Bhalla states that the body of Guru Gobind Singh was cremated and 'the *Sṛi Guru Granth Sahib* was recognized in place of the Guru'.[48]

Ganda Singh refers to a large number of works in Persian and English, written by Indians and Europeans during the eighteenth and nineteenth centuries. The eighteenth century Persian and English writers cited by Ganda Singh refer to the end of personal Guruship after the death of Guru Gobind Singh. Sohan Lal Suri, the author of the *Umdat ut-Tawārīkh* which was written in the reign of Ranjit Singh, mentions only the *Granth Sahib* as the Guru. Guru Gobind Singh himself had declared that 'the Guru is *Granthji*'. Ghulam Muhiyuddin refers to the last commandment of Guru Gobind Singh as 'there is no difference between the Guru and the *Granth*'. This is repeated by Ernest Trumpp in his *Ādi Granth* and by Bhai Kanh Singh Nabha towards the end of the nineteenth century. However, some other writers mention the Khalsa as well as the Granth Sahib as the Guru after the death of Guru Gobind Singh. Among them are J.D. Cunningham, Syed Muhammad Latif, Munshi Sant Singh (the author of the *Bayān-i Khāndān-i Karāmat Nishān-i Bediān*) and M.A. Macauliffe.[49]

Harbans Singh's contribution to the *Perspectives on the Sikh Tradition* also was not written with reference to McLeod's work. He goes into the process by which the Granth Sahib was prepared by Guru Arjan who, in Harbans Singh's view, enjoined the Sikhs to regard the Granth as equal with the Guru and to make no distinction between the two. Indeed, the Word enshrined in the Holy Book was always revered by the Gurus as well as by their disciples as of divine origin. The Guru was the revealer of the Word. One day the Word was to take the place of the Guru. The line of personal Gurus could not have continued for ever. 'The inevitable came to pass when Guru Gobind Singh declared the Guru Granth Sahib to be his successor'. Ever since the passing away of Guru Gobind Singh, the understanding and conviction of the Sikh community has been that 'the Guru Granth is Guru Eternal'.

Harbans Singh labours this point because, among other things, certain cults among the Sikhs still owning personal Gurus ask for authentic evidence to the effect that Guru Gobind Singh had named the Guru Granth Sahib his successor.[50]

Apart from the evidence of Bhai Nand Lal, Sainapat and Koer Singh, which is cited by Ganda Singh also, Harbans Singh cites three sources which are supposed to be contemporary or very close to the time of Guru Gobind Singh. One of these is the *Bhatt Vahī* to which Ganda Singh made only a reference. This evidence is a part of the collection of *vahīs* or scrolls made by 'a dogged researcher', Giani Garja Singh, which has not yet been published. We are told that Bhatts used to record events of the lives of the Gurus and their records have been preserved by their descendants. These *vahīs* were written in a script called *bhatakshri*, 'a kind of family code like *lande* and *mahajani*'. The only scholar to have worked on these materials is Giani Garja Singh. The entry quoted by Harbans Singh, with translation in English, comes from the *Bhatt Vahī Talaudā Pargana Jīnd.* In this entry, Guru Gobind Singh places five pice and a coconut before Sri Granth Sahib, bows before it, and then tells the *sangat*: 'It is my commandment: Own Sri Granthji in my place. He who so acknowledges it will obtain his reward. The Guru will rescue him. Know this as true'. Another document cited is a letter of Mata Sundariji, which is now in the village of Bhai Rupa. In this document the Sikhs are told to believe only in ten Gurus and not in Banda Bahadur and Ajit Singh, to believe only in the Timeless One, and to go only to the ten Gurus 'in search of the Word'. In fact the original says 'upto the tenth king'. It is emphasized that the Guru 'resides in *sabda*'. Harbans Singh infers that the *sabda* refers only to the *Ādi Granth.* The third piece of evidence cited by him is that of a Sanskrit manuscript in which Guru Gobind Singh declares that the Granth, 'which itself is the doctrine of the Guru, shall be your teacher. This is what you should see; this is what you should honour; this is what should be the object of your discourses'. On the evidence of Sainapat, Harbans Singh adds that, along with the Guru Granth Sahib, 'the Khalsa was now the person visible of the Guru'.[51]

The essential difference between the early evidence used by

Ganda Singh and Harbans Singh lies in the latter's use of the *Bhatt Vahī* which makes explicit reference to 'Sri Granthji' in connection with succession to Guru Gobind Singh. They both accept the authenticity of this source. However, the nature and character of *Bhatt Vahīs* has not yet been examined critically to evaluate their authenticity. The use of the phrase 'Sri Granthji' itself is rather exceptional. In all the other evidence cited by Ganda Singh and Harbans Singh, explicit reference to the *Granth Sahib* appears much later. In the earliest known evidence the term used is Shabad and not Granth. Ganda Singh and Harbans Singh themselves draw the inference that it refers to the *Granth Sahib* compiled by Guru Arjan. The earliest known evidence also refers to the Khalsa in connection with succession after Guru Gobind Singh. Thus, the idea of Guru-Panth as well as the idea of Guru-Granth may be said to have been there in early evidence. In neither case, however, has the form crystallized, except in the *Rahitnāmas* and the *Gurbilās Chhevīn Pātshāhī*. The time of their composition is a matter of debate.

It is nonetheless important to realize that the doctrines of Guru-Panth and Guru-Granth do not appear to have crystallized in the earliest known evidence. That the former crystallized earlier than the latter is indicated by the evidence used by Ganda Singh and Harbans Singh. The use of the word Shabad in the earliest known evidence is not without significance. It is true that the *bāṇī* of the predecessors of Guru Gobind Singh was embodied in the *Granth Sahib*, and the use of the word Shabad would refer primarily to the *Granth Sahib*. However, Guru Gobind Singh had also composed *bāṇī*. Was it to be treated as Shabad or no ?

To a writer like Kesar Singh Chhibber, the existence of the *Dasam Granth* presented a problem. He does declare the *Ādi Granth* to be the Guru, but he does not reject the other *Granth*. That too was entitled to respect and veneration, though a little less. And then there was also the doctrine of Guru-Panth which appears to have been more important than the doctrine of Guru-Granth till the establishment of Sikh rule in the third quarter of the eighteenth century. It is clear, however, that both these doctrines owed their distant origin to the days of Guru Nanak, and their immediate origin to an injunction of Guru Gobind Singh. The eighteenth-century situation was conducive to their crystallization.

NOTES

1. *Perspectives on the Sikh Tradition*, p. 9.
2. McLeod (1975), p. 2.
3. Ibid., pp. 3-5.
4. Ibid., pp. 7-9.
5. Ibid., pp. 9-10 and 12.
6. Ibid., pp. 10-11.
7. Ibid., pp. 12-14.
8. Ibid., pp. 51-52.
9. *Perspectives on the Sikh Tradition*, pp. 325-26.
10. Ibid., p. 327.
11. Ibid., pp. 328-31.
12. Ibid., pp. 331-39.
13. Ibid., pp. 339-41.
14. Ibid., pp. 341-42.
15. Ibid., pp. 342-47.
16. Ibid., pp. 347-54.
17. Ibid., pp. 378-79.
18. Ibid., p. 380.
19. McLeod (1989b), pp. 35-38.
20. Ibid., pp. 39-40.
21. Ibid., p. 40.
22. *Perspectives on the Sikh Tradition*, p. 9.
23. McLeod (1975), pp. 14-15.
24. Ibid., pp. 15-16.
25. Ibid., pp. 16 and 19.
26. Ibid., pp. 50-53.
27. *Perspectives on the Sikh Tradition*, pp. 178-79.
28. Justice Gurdev Singh does not mention that Professor Gupta's contribution is actually a chapter in his book. The episode of the Goddess given by Professor Gupta is excised by Justice Gurdev Singh.
29. Ibid., p. 178 and n 45.
30. Ibid., pp. 161-62.
31. Ibid., pp. 170 and 178 n 80.
32. Ibid., pp.170 and 178 n 81.
33. Ibid., pp. 168-69.
34. Ibid., pp. 169-72.

35. McLeod (1975), p. 18.
36. Ibid., p. 17.
37. Ibid., pp. 53-54.
38. Ibid., pp. 38-44.
39. Ibid., p. 45.
40. Ibid., pp. 46-47.
41. Ibid., pp. 47-49.
42. Ibid., p. 50.
43. *Perspectives on the Sikh Tradition*, pp. 9, 10 and 28-29.
44. Ibid., p. 30.
45. Ibid., pp. 183, 193-94 and 196.
46. Ibid., p. 183.
47. Ibid., pp. 186-87 and 191-92.
48. Ibid., pp. 194-98.
49. Ibid., pp. 198-210.
50. Ibid., pp. 211-17 and 223-24.
51. Ibid., pp. 217-23.

9. Character of the Sikh Social Order

Comments on the egalitarian character of the Khalsa began to appear in the late eighteenth century in the notices of the Sikhs taken by European writers. They refer particularly to the rejection of caste distinctions for initiation into the Sikh Panth. They refer also to Sikh practices in commensality and connubium. The Sikh writers of the twentieth century have laid great emphasis on the norm of equality in relation to caste and gender. However, there were no studies of gender relations and there were only cursory remarks on the prevalence or absence of caste in the Sikh social order. C.H. Loehlin can be seen as a scholar who showed some interest in the question of caste. Like the earlier writers, he saw the character of the Sikh social order as relevant for the issue of Sikh identity. The first writer to give a general exposition of caste in the Sikh Panth was Professor Jagjit Singh. He saw in the Sikh Panth an egalitarian social order springing from ideology. W.H. McLeod's essay on caste in the Sikh Panth was not written with reference to Jagjit Singh's work. Nevertheless, he showed greater concern for empirical realities and gave more importance to social environment. None of them talks of gender relations, but both of them look at caste in the larger context of the character of the Sikh social order.

One of the propositions attributed to W.H. McLeod by Justice Gurdev Singh is that, though the Gurus denounced caste system and preached against it, 'yet they did not seem sincere or serious in removing caste differences'.[1] Justice Gurdev Singh explains at another place that, while conceding that the Sikh Gurus were beyond all doubt vigorous and practical denunciators of caste, McLeod has accused them of insincerity by gleefully introducing the 'fib' that the Jats bewail that there was never a single Jat Guru, and the

Gurus did not marry outside the Khatri fold. Calling this a violation of their own injunction against the caste system, McLeod tells us that some critics accuse them of insincerity, and asks: 'How one can respect a commandment when its promulgators ignore it?' This question is not posed by McLeod, but by the critics of the Gurus. Justice Gurdev Singh believes that there were no such critics, and that is why it is a 'fib'. He gives the impression as if the statement attributed to the critics of the Gurus, namely that the Gurus married their sons and daughters within Khatri families and that no Jat was nominated as a successor, is factually incorrect. He asserts that Jagjit Singh, 'himself a Jat', has examined the Sikh attitude towards caste in all its aspects and has demonstrated 'how untenable and unfair is McLeod's criticism and charge of insincerity against the Gurus.[2] Ironically, Justice Gurdev Singh's own charge against McLeod is imaginary.

I

McLeod introduces the issue of caste in the Sikh Panth with reference to the comments of British observers of the Sikh society during the last two decades of the eighteenth century. One such comment is that the Sikhs consisted 'mostly' of the Jat 'tribe'. Another comment is that the acceptance of the Sikh doctrine 'causes an essential deviation' from the Hindu system. The wonderful barriers 'constructed and affixed' for the 'different ranks and professions' among the people were overthrown by the Sikh doctrine. In other words, caste distinctions stood obliterated within the eighteenth-century Sikh Panth.[3] McLeod thinks that the statement on the obliteration of caste within the Sikh Panth has to be substantially qualified. A British writer of the first decade of the nineteenth century observed that the Sikhs allowed 'foreigners of every description' to join their standard, to sit in their company, and to shave their beards but, except in the case of the Jats, they did not consent to intermarriages. Furthermore, they did not eat or drink from the hands of 'an alien' unless he was a Brahman. Indeed, the Sikhs professed 'the highest veneration' for Brahmans. McLeod draws the inference that there were restrictions on intermarriage and commensality within the Sikh Panth. In support of this inference he refers to 'Punjabi sources' of the eighteenth century as well as to nineteenth and twentieth century observations, which reveal an insistent regard for marriage alliances along conventional lines, qualified only by a limited measure of freedom in the case of the Jats. Entry into the Panth was open to all, and caste was certainly 'discounted'. But it was by no means 'obliterated'. It survived 'in terms of commensality and marriage patterns'.[4] Thus, besides the caste constituency of the Panth, there arises the question of the survival of caste observances within the Panth. Though separate, the issues of constituency and observances are intimately related, and McLeod decides to treat them 'concurrently'.

Guru Nanak declared his attitude in a famous and oft-repeated couplet:

> Worthless is caste and worthless an exalted name.
> For all mankind there is but a single refuge.

This is only one of his numerous pronouncements on caste, and many more could be added. McLeod adds two more to the effect that the divine light in a man and not his caste is important 'for there is no caste in the hereafter'. 'In the hereafter name and caste count for nothing'. Caste status provided no help to an individual in his quest for salvation. In fact it was a positive hindrance because it nurtured a detrimental pride. This message is repeated by Guru Nanak's successors. Guru Amar Das, for instance, emphasizes that your deeds and not your caste determines your fate because when you die 'you do not carry your caste with you'. The message is carried forward by Guru Ram Das when he says that there are four castes but 'he who meditates on God he it is who is supreme'. The message is repeated by Guru Arjan who included in the *Granth Sahib* the works of 'low-caste' poets, two of whom had denounced caste in strong terms.[5]

The expression of what may be called egalitarian ideas was accompanied by certain actions which reinforce the impression that the Sikh Gurus were 'vigorous and practical denunciators of caste'. Guru Amar Das, for instance, introduced the practice of 'compulsory commensality' which was meant to strike at the very heart of an important aspect of caste. A reference in the works of Bhai Gurdas suggests that *kaṛāh prasād* deposited in a common dish by the low caste or even the outcaste Sikh as an offering was consumed by high caste Sikhs. This custom was observed by the Khalsa of Guru Gobind Singh who, moreover, drank from a common bowl at the time of initiation. In the first five Sikhs initiated into the Khalsa Order, the Cherished Five, was witnessed a representative range from the high caste Khatri through middle caste Jat to low caste barber and washerman. If the utterances of the Gurus suggest that salvation was open to all regardless of caste, the institution of *langar*, distribution of *kaṛāh prasād* in the *gurdwaras*, and bapitsm from a common bowl indicate that their denunciation of caste was meant to be 'carried significantly further'.[6] In other words, whereas there is no ambiguity about the ideal of equality, the relevant question to ask is in what ways and to what extent this egalitarian ideal was actualized in the Sikh Panth.

McLeod poses this question in a manner that has misled Justice Gurdev Singh. As we noticed earlier, McLeod refers to comments by others underlining the fact that all the nominated successors of Guru Nanak were Khatri and that all the Gurus had matrimonial alliances with Khatris. Far from levelling the charge of insincerity against the Gurus, McLeod replies to the 'suggestion of inconsistency' on their part by concluding that they were vigorously opposed to 'the *vertical* distinctions of caste' though they were content to accept caste 'in terms of its *horizontal* linkages'. McLeod goes on to elaborate this statement. He sets aside the 'classical model' or the *varna* model commonly understood as a uniform hierarchical system with the Brahman at the apex of the pyramid, followed by the Kshatriya, the Vaishya, and the Shudra. McLeod adds that below the pyramid were the outcastes like the sweepers and leather-workers. This model can provide only a misleading starting point. Therefore, McLeod prefers to start with two of its components which were most meaningful to the individuals concerned: the *zāt* and the *got*. The former is an endogamous grouping consisting of several smaller groups known as *gots*. In contradistinction to the *zāt*, the *got* is exogamous.[7]

Notwithstanding the importance of horizontal *got* and *zāt* relationship Indian society was strongly hierarchical, and one could expect to find the society of a particular area ordered within a distinct pattern of rank and status. While the Sikh Gurus continued to accept the beneficial patterns of horizontal connection, they denied the justice of privilege or deprivation based upon notion of status and hierarchy. In other words, they were opposed to the discriminatory aspects of vertical relationships. McLeod looks upon the issues of caste constituency and attitudes within the Sikh Panth in the dual context of horizontal and vertical relationships. He finds it significant in this context that Bhai Gurdas does not conceal the caste affiliation of the important Sikhs of the Gurus in the early seventeenth century. It is also significant that the number of castes represented in the Sikh Panth was quite large. Nevertheless, the largest number of his eminent Sikhs came from the Khatri caste, indicating that Khatri leadership within the early Panth extended much beyond the actual line of Gurus.[8]

The evidence of the *Dabistān-i Mazāhib* coupled with that of Bhai Gurdas shows that in the early seventeenth century, though the Khatris enjoyed a particular prominence within the diverse following which constituted the Panth, a share in leadership was entrusted to individual Jat members. This presumably reflected the numerical importance of Jats within the Panth. This numerical importance greatly increased during the course of the seventeenth and eighteenth centuries, producing the strong Jat predominance noted by the early European observers towards the end of the eighteenth century. Jat preponderance was matched by an increase in Jat authority. McLeod mentions two processes to account for this situation: the accession of Jats to the Khalsa, and the failure of other castes, notably the Khatris, to join the Khalsa in numbers corresponding to their position within the earlier Nanak-Panth. The continuance of the non-Khalsa Sikhs after the institution of the Khalsa is borne out by the B40 *Janamsākhī* and the early British censuses. Significantly, Khatris are prominent among these Nanak-Panthi Sikhs but the Jats are absent. The levelling implications of the Khalsa initiation rite, which would present a serious deterrent to Brahmans as well as Khatris, partly explain this development. Brahman Sikhs in fact became a rare phenomenon after the institution of the Khalsa.[9]

The caste constituency of the Khalsa Sikhs becomes much clearer in the census returns of 1881. The largest constituent, 66 per cent, came from Jats. There was a spectacular drop to the second-largest constituent, the Tarkhans (carpenters), who formed 6.5 per cent of the total Khalsa Sikh population of over 1,700,000. Next came two outcaste groups, the Chamars with 5.6 per cent and the Chuhras with 2.6 per cent. The Khatris, with a mere 2.2 per cent, were a little behind the Aroras with 2.3 per cent. They were followed by twenty other castes but only five of them were more than 1 per cent: the Kambos with 1.7 per cent, the Lohars with 1.4 per cent, the Jhiwars and Nais with 1.2 per cent each, and the Rajputs with 1.1 per cent. The Brahmans and Kalāls (Ahluwalias) were among those who formed less than 1 per cent of the Khalsa Sikh population. By far the largest bulk of Sikh population consisted of agrarian castes, followed at a great distance by artisan castes and outcastes. They lived mostly in the countryside. The mercantile castes, with less than 5 per cent of the total, lived mostly in towns and cities.[10]

The over-all Sikh population increased after 1881, affecting the number and proportion of various castes within the Panth but without any appreciable change in the basic pattern. By 1931 the total Sikh population was over 4,000,000. It included the non-Khalsa Sikhs, but their number was less than 300,000. A switch from Hindu to Sikh explained the great increment in excess of natural increase. This was observed chiefly among the agrarian, artisan and the outcaste groups, in response to a belief that the change would result in enhanced status. That the Sikh Panth retained its egalitarian appeal is indicated by the caste return of half a century from 1881 to 1931. This process was promoted by the reforming zeal of the Singh Sabha protagonists and the political concerns of the Akali Dal. Insistence on equality was a fundamental aspect of Singh Sabha policy, reinforced by the threat of conversion of Sikh outcastes to Christianity. The Singh Sabha movement was also responsible for an increase in the proportion of Khalsa Sikhs within the Panth.[11]

For further light on the subject, McLeod turns to particular castes in the Sikh Panth. The civil administrators looked upon the Jats as the finest peasantry in India and the military authorities regarded them as one of the finest 'martial races'. However, careers and professions among Jat Sikhs were not confined to agriculture and the army. More significant from the present viewpoint was 'the pronounced rise in status which marks the history of the Sikh Jats over recent centuries'. In terms of status no Jat feels 'inferior or downtrodden'. The experience of Sikh Jats as rulers and their dominance in the countryside have enabled them to rise above the low status traditionally assigned to Jats. The same factors may account for their political skills. Two other features mark the Sikh Jat society. The absence of formalized social stratification within the endogamous *zāt* is one: no Sikh Jat *got* is regarded as above another in status. The other is that the Sikh Jats follow the customary rules of propinquity in marriage: a matrimonial alliance within the same *got* is as a rule forbidden. In his own eyes a Sikh Jat remains a Sikh even if he cuts his beard or smokes tobacco. But if a Khatri shaves he is regarded as Hindu by others and soon comes to regard himself as one.[12]

In spite of their small numbers, the Khatris retain their prominence in commerce and industry, government service, higher education and the professions. They claim an elevated position in Punjabi society. However, the difference between them and the Jats has shrunk as the Jats have moved upwards. Unlike the Jats, the Khatris are divided into at least a few endogamous groups, consisting of four, twelve or fifty-two *gots*. A fourth endogamous group has arisen, consisting of the four Khatri *gots* of the Sikh Gurus – Bedi, Trehan, Bhalla and Sodhi. Confessional differences are comparatively less important among the Khatris and marriages between Hindu and Sikh Khatri families have always been very common. Since the Khatris have not looked upon Sikh identity as a means of enhancing social or ritual status, their number and proportion in the Panth have actually declined during the twentieth century. This does not mean that they regard their membership of the Panth with indifference. If anything, they take it more seriously than the Jats. The Khatris have played an important role in the affairs of the Sikh Panth, a role that is out of all proportion to their small numbers. The Aroras appear to have entered the Panth later than the Khatris, but they have caught up with them since the early nineteenth century. However, though their role in the Panth has been somewhat similar to that of the Khatris, it has been a little inferior.[13]

The artisan and outcaste groups regard membership of the Sikh Panth as a means of improving status. The Tarkhans present an unusually interesting case. They must have entered the Panth in imitation of the Jat landowners whom they traditionally served in a client relationship. The most famous of all Tarkhan Sikhs was Jassa Singh Ramgarhia, a *misl* leader who established his own principality. The name Ramgarhia has been taken up by an increasing number of Sikh Tarkhans since the end of the nineteenth century, with the obvious intention of replacing a lowly title with one of acknowledged repute. A few other castes have joined the Ramgarhias to form a new, composite, and distinctively Sikh *zāt*. They have taken up new professions in a bid for upward mobility. The Ranghreta or Mazhabi and Ramdasia Sikhs, the erstwhile Chuhras and Chamars, increased their numbers in the Panth during the early twentieth century in a desire to purge the traditional taint of the outcaste status. Their hope of achieving this end through the egalitarian traditions of the Khalsa has been partially fulfilled.[14]

According to McLeod, two general hierarchies can be discerned in Punjabi society, one urban and the other rural. Within Sikh society the two intersect without losing their essential clarity. The Sikh component of the urban hierarchy is very small and very distinct, with Khaṭris occupying a superior ranking and with Aroras close behind. At the base are the Mazhabis and Ramdasias. The Ramgarhias are clearly above them, but equally clearly they are below Khatris and Aroras. The position of the erstwhile outcaste and artisan groups in the countryside is similar to their position in towns and cities, but their numbers in the countryside are much larger. Indeed, the rural hierarchy is numerically much larger and the massive Jat constituency commands the heights. In terms of order, the rural hierarchy is less clear than the urban hierarchy. Many of the features commonly regarded as typically Sikh are characteristically the features of the predominant constituent, the Jats.[15]

McLeod is aware that he has placed a good deal of stress upon 'the caste diversity' in the Sikh Panth, and on the fact that notions of status based on caste are by no means extinct within it. He is therefore keen to point out that this should not conceal 'the significant degree to which the Panth has succeeded in eliminating many of the discriminatory aspects of caste'. He goes on to add that the Sikh insistence on equality is far from being a pious myth. 'Freedom within the Panth may not be a total freedom but it represents an impressive achievement nevertheless and an endeavour which is still proceeding. Sikhs are above all else loyal to the Guru. The question of equality within the Panth offers no exception to this inflexible rule'.[16]

II

Jagjit Singh has not written on 'caste system and Sikhs' with reference to McLeod's essay on the subject. Therefore there is no criticism of McLeod in Jagjit Singh's essay. His objective is to show how the Sikh Gurus steered away from the shackles of the 'constitutive elements' of 'the caste system' to create a new society.[17] In order to bring their achievement into high relief Jagjit Singh gives an exposition of the Indian caste system. One could find elements of caste in other countries too: antipathies based on the differences of race or colour, taboos regarding human beings and animals or even callings, notions of purity and impurity, restrictions on marriages, differences of status based on heredity, social disabilities or segregation. But in India alone could one find all such elements woven into an organic whole. In the Indian system over 3,000 subcastes were meticulously arranged in an hierarchical social pyramid in which each subcaste was fixed irrespective of its political and economic position. Practically all aspects of the social behaviour of each subcaste were regulated by fixed rules and codes. These subcastes were, by and large, endogamous groups, and they worked sedulously to isolate themselves from each other in other social matters too. Nothing could change this hierarchical pattern.

Marginal exceptions were made, but only to preserve the over-all structure. There was practically no upward social mobility. The Indian caste system was thus a continuously downgrading process.[18] Restrictions on connubium and commensality were the most outstanding features of caste hierarchy. All the constituents of the caste system were inter-dependent and interlocked both horizontally and vertically in the social fabric.

Three main factors accounted for this unique social formation in India. First, the 'caste ideology' based on the principle of human inequality by birth gave pre-eminence to caste status. Wealth and power could serve only as the adjuncts of this status. The authority for caste ideology was provided by religious scriptures and it was reinforced by the concept of *varnashrama* Dharma. The system was further cemented by custom, ritual and ceremonies, the notion of pollution and purity, and the theory of Karma.[19] The second factor was the support provided to the system by the Brahmans who served as its ministers and ideologues.[20] The third factor mentioned by Jagjit Singh is the caste society itself as the primary institution based on caste ideology.[21]

Jagjit Singh underlines the achievement of the Sikh movement during the period of 'ideological ascendancy' from the beginning of the movement till the beginning of Sikh rule. The Sikh movement in this period broke away from the caste ideology and the caste society. Guru Nanak did away with the consciousness of caste-status and obliterated the gap between the rich and the poor in terms of status-consciousness. By repudiating the Brahmanical scriptures, Sikhism and the Sikh Panth cut themselves away from the perennial source of caste ideology. Cutting itself away from Hinduism, Sikhism delinked itself from the daily operation of the Hindu Dharma. The Sikh Gurus had no veneration for the cow and they discarded the notion of ritual purity and pollution. There was no priestly class among the Sikhs, and Brahmans remained insignificant within the Sikh Panth. By eliminating the influence of Brahmans, the Sikh society eliminated the kingpin of the caste system from within its ranks.[22]

The achievement of the Sikh Gurus was not restricted to the ideological plane. By founding the Sikh Panth, Guru Nanak started the process of founding a separate society. His successors worked consistently to establish a separate identity of the Sikh Panth as of the Sikh Church. The creation of the Khalsa by Guru Gobind Singh was the acme of the Sikh movement. The Sikhs were militarized not only to fight religious and political oppression but also to capture political power for an egalitarian cause. The Khalsa made a clean break with the caste society as much as with the caste ideology. The *raison d'etre* of the Khalsa and the proof of its separate identity was its success in giving an egalitarian socio-political orientation to the Sikh society. The Khalsa had a plebian base. If anything, the spirit of equality, brotherhood and fraternization was reinforced by the Khalsa. The leaders of the Khalsa included members of the erstwhile lower castes and even outcastes. Caste prejudices and caste priorities were abolished in matters of commensality. The Sikh revolution raised the social and political status of a large section of the commoners *en bloc*. The taste of political power made the Sikh Jat feel prouder than the Rajput, and made the Ranghretas feel equals of the Sikh Jats.[23]

Jagjit Singh's exposition of the subject is looked upon by Justice Gurdev Singh as radically different from McLeod's. Therefore we may go into a little more detail. On the theme of caste ideology, Jagjit Singh quotes Guru Nanak to the effect that the Hindus who looked down upon the Chāndāls as foul and vain were themselves perverse and their acts produced strife. The Vedas created myths and illusions regarding what is good and what is evil. Guru Nanak identified himself with the lowliest of the low, and denounced the pride of caste as the source of errors. Guru Gobind Singh writes that he does not accept the Vedas, Shāstras, Smritis and the Purānas. This presumably is the evidence for Jagjit Singh's view that Guru Nanak and his successors discarded caste ideology. He goes on to say that according to Bhai Gurdas, Guru Nanak made the *dharma* perfect by blending the four castes into one; the king and the pauper were treated on equal footing and even the outcaste were regarded as noble. The grammatical construction of Bhai Gurdas's language indicates that he was not repeating a precept of the Gurus but referring to actual practice. This evidence enables Jagjit Singh to infer that all distinctions of caste stood obliterated within the Sikh

Panth. The evidence for the rejection of all notions of purity and impurity is the well known verse of Guru Nanak to the effect that if the ideas of impurity are admitted there is impurity in everything–cowdung, wood, grain and even water. According to the *Mahimā Prakāsh*, all castes were treated as equal in the congregation and *langar* of Guru Angad, and Guru Amar Das made it compulsory for all visitors to eat in the *langar*. According to Koer Singh, Sikhs of all castes, including the Shudras, ate together. According to Ratan Singh Bhangu, even the Ranghretas were included in inter-dining.[24] This evidence is meant to show that there were no restrictions on commensality in the Sikh Panth.

On the question of Brahmans and their influence within the Sikh Panth, Jagjit Singh refers to their insignificant numbers within the Panth rather than to any statement of a Guru or a Sikh writer.[25] On the question of 'a separate Sikh society', Jagjit Singh gives quotations in support of the distinct identity of the Sikhs in religious and social terms. The quotations which have a bearing on caste within the Sikh Panth are to the effect that all four castes were blended in the Khalsa and they ate together. Thus, the discussion of this point does not carry the argument any further. On the question of a new socio-political order, Jagjit Singh emphasizes the presence of lower castes and outcastes in the Khalsa Panth, the spirit of equality among the Khalsa, the spirit of service among the Sikhs, and the emergence of lower caste leaders (including outcaste leaders). Their success in capturing political power raised the status of individuals and groups coming into power. The basic point made here relates to upward social mobility through the mediacy of the Sikh movement. On the whole it appears that Jagjit Singh does not address himself seriously to those features of the caste system which he regards as 'the most outstanding': connubium and commensality.[26] The picture of an egalitarian Panth which he conjures up remains idealized. It is the result of broad generalizations based on highly selective and partial evidence.

Jagjit Singh's assumption of a more or less egalitarian Sikh Panth before the establishment of Sikh rule has interesting implications for his treatment of caste in the Sikh Panth after the establishment of Sikh rule. He thinks in terms of 'aberrations in Sikh society' due to the large influx of proselytes from the caste society who retained some of their caste prejudices and usages. But even so the Brahmans did not become a point of reference with regard to social status or hierarchy, and Sikhs have never owed allegiance to a scripture other than the *Guru Granth Sahib*, or to any *dharma* other than the Sikh Dharma. Therefore, notions and practices regarding connubium and commensality, or the survival of hierarchy in villages, must be seen as a heritage from previous connections with the caste society. Their survival must not be connected with any of the three facets of the caste system, namely the caste ideology, the dominance of Brahmans and the caste society as an institution. The only relevant question, therefore, can be the extent to which some of the prejudices and practices inherited from the caste society have been shed off or modified at various levels of the Sikh society.[27]

Jagjit Singh takes up this point at what he calls 'the Panthic level' first. The large scale conversions to the Panth during the late eighteenth century, and the continuation of this process in the nineteenth and twentieth centuries, indicates that the Panth remained open to all castes, including in fact the outcastes. This in itself should be seen as a radical departure from the caste ideology which admits 'no change of caste'. The institution of *langar* has been kept alive as an anti-caste heritage. People from all castes, including the Mazhabi Sikhs, take part in preparing the food and in serving it to others. Commensal restrictions did creep into the Sikh society, but it is not clear when. Evidence for the late eighteenth century is contradictory. Even when such restrictions crept in, only the outcaste Sikhs were not allowed to eat with others. The Jat Sikhs, Khatri Sikhs, Arora Sikhs and Ramgarhia Sikhs interdined. In fact they were not castes in the Brahmanical sense as they did not constitute an hierarchy. There was no question of superiority or inferiority between the Jat Singhs on the one hand and the Khatri and Arora Sikhs on the other. The Ramgarhias were not a subcaste among the Tarkhans. In any case the Ramgarhias do not accept the Jat Sikhs as superior to them and there was no outside pressure on them to do so. Like the Ramgarhias, the Kalāl Sikhs (the Ahluwalias) raised their social status after capturing power during the eighteenth century. The other artisan groups among the Sikhs face no social pressure, except that the Jat, Khatri, Arora and Ramgarhia Sikhs are reluctant to intermarry with them.[28]

At the village level, since hierarchy is a heritage from the remotest past, it would be too much to expect drastic changes in the hierarchy of Sikh villages, or in the social status of the artisans and menials who embraced Sikhism so late as the post-Khalsa period. Nevertheless, they do not have the same degree of social stigma attached to them as their counterparts in the caste society. The Sikh Chhimbas are not treated as outcaste. The Jhiwar and Labana Sikhs have hypergamous relations with their Hindu counterparts. Sikhs of all *jātīs*, except the Mazhabis, inter-dine in the villages. The Mazhabis sit with others in *gurdwaras*. On the whole, the position of artisan and menial groups in the Sikh society is better than the position of their counterparts amony the Hindus, or even the Muslims. Nonetheless, the Chuhras and Chamars present a really tough problem.[29]

Jagjit Singh insists that the achievement of the Sikh movement should be judged in the context of the Indian caste system and not in comparison with some other societies. No other movement in India enabled the Shudra Jat to regard his status as higher than that of the Rajput; raised Jats, carpenters and Kalāls to be the rulers of the land; and made the Khatris, Aroras, Jats, artisans, village menials and outcastes forget their caste biases to merge into a genuine brotherhood on equal terms.[30]

The success of the Sikh movement in matters of marriage on caste lines was negligible even in relative terms. Jagjit Singh's explanation is rather significant. In his view, the role of endogamy in the caste complex has been over-emphasized. Even in those societies which have no castes, individual and group prejudices regarding marriage exist on the basis of various kinds of considerations. Few societies have tended to lay down positive laws governing marriages between different social groups and classes. What makes endogamy obnoxious in the caste society is that inter-caste marriage is prevented by 'hard and fast' rules of the caste ideology. The stand of the Sikh Gurus is clear: they did not object to inter-caste marriages. There was a sound reason for this attitude. They did not want to take any steps which might adversely affect the very objectives of their movement. They could not risk the future of the movement by insisting on inter-caste marriages. To fight the religious and political oppression of the rulers of the day was more urgent and more important than the abolition of all caste distinctions. The prejudices of the caste society, which was the recruiting ground of the Sikh movement, coupled with priorities of the Gurus, explain their politic attitude towards caste endogamy within the Sikh Panth. Moreover, they could hope that caste endogamy would disappear with the disappearance of caste-status and the ritualistic barriers between castes.[31] This is Jagjit Singh's way of confessing that the egalitarian ideology of the Sikh movement did not change the traditional patterns of matrimony. Nevertheless, his idea that the Sikh Gurus were not opposed to inter-caste marriage is of crucial importance.

III

W.H. McLeod and Jagjit Singh have written on caste in the Sikh Panth independently of each other. Since McLeod's essay was published earlier he could not have seen Jagjit Singh's *Sikh Revolution* or his articles in the *Perspectives*. Jagjit Singh does refer to the views of others, but there is no indication that he includes McLeod among them. However, there are some important similarities in their views. Both of them look upon commensality and connubium as of crucial importance in a discussion of caste. In their actual analyses, however, McLeod gives much greater importance to this aspect than Jagjit Singh. Both subscribe to the view that restrictions on inter-caste marriage and inter-caste dining were there in the Sikh Panth during the nineteenth century and have survived into the present. For the earlier centuries, McLeod visualizes a much greater operation of these restrictions than Jagjit Singh who sees no restrictions on commensality before the late eighteenth century. Both seem to agree that there was no caste system among the Sikhs in the sense of an accepted order of caste status, but only Jagjit Singh is explicit on this point. Both see the relevance of Sikh ideology for caste relations within the Sikh Panth, but Jagjit Singh attaches far greater importance to it than McLeod.

The differences between McLeod and Jagjit Singh are not

unimportant. Jagjit Singh tends to think that empirical inequalities in the Sikh Panth were there in spite of the Sikh ideology which was totally egalitarian. He does well to highlight the absence of approval for inequalities in the *Granth Sahib*. But he dwells largely on ideas, feelings and sentiments in illustrating the operation of the ideal of equality. McLeod does not appear to assign so comprehensive a scope to Sikh ideology as to make it all-embracing. He appears also to attach greater intractability to social realities already in existence. Consequently, McLeod and Jagjit Singh differ in their understanding of the character of the Sikh social order even before the establishment of Sikh rule. Jagjit Singh does not visualize any restrictions on commensality but recognizes the continuance of the traditional patterns of marriage. McLeod does not visualize any change in the patterns of marriage and looks upon commensality as confined virtually to the ritual distribution of sacred food and the institution of *langar*. Jagjit Singh is right in asserting that there was no formal restriction on inter-dining among the 'caste' groups which joined the Sikh Panth, but he appears to go a little too far when he asserts that even the 'outcastes' were included. He cites only Ratan Singh Bhangu in support of his statement that the Ranghretas (the erstwhile Chuhras) used to inter-dine with the other Sikhs. But he ignores, or perhaps merely fails to notice, Bhangu's observation on the same page that his maternal grandfather, who was among the prominent leaders of the Khalsa during the eighteenth century, made a clear distinction between the 'caste' and 'outcaste' members of the Panth in matters of commensality.[32] The Ranghretas were surely among the latter. It may also be added that Jagjit Singh overlooks the views of writers like Kesar Singh Chhibber whom he quotes with approval in support of the distinctive identity of the Khalsa Panth. Chhibber is quite categorical that the Sikhs were equal only in the realm of faith: in matters of commensality and matrimony they must observe their caste *dharma*.[33]

Three more observations may be made on the treatment of caste in the Sikh Panth by McLeod and Jagjit Singh. It is quite safe to suggest that McLeod is much more rigorous in his methodology than Jagjit Singh. Consequently, they interpret the evidence which is common to their essays in different ways. McLeod seldom sees too much in his evidence and Jagjit Singh seldom sees too little. This difference may be attributed partly to the fact that whereas Jagjit Singh's purpose is to bring the achievement of the Sikh movement into high relief, McLeod's aim is to understand the bearing of ideas on social realities. Secondly, both the authors have offered what may be called a preliminary exposition. They try to cover a long span of time in their surveys. Consequently, their treatment of the relevant evidence is not thorough or exhaustive. Their outlines can serve as the starting point for further study, always keeping the two poles of ideology and empirical realities in mind. Finally, it is impossible to agree with Justice Gurdev Singh that McLeod insinuates insincerity on the part of the Gurus, or that Jagjit Singh has given a better exposition of caste in the Sikh Panth.

NOTES

1. *Perspectives on the Sikh Tradition*, p. 9.
2. Ibid., p. 31.
3. McLeod (1975), p. 83.
4. Ibid., p. 84.
5. Ibid., pp. 85-86.
6. Ibid., pp. 86-87.
7. Ibid., pp. 87-90.
8. Ibid., p. 91.
9. Ibid., p. 92.
10. Ibid., p. 93.
11. Ibid., p. 94.
12. Ibid., pp. 95-97.
13. Ibid, pp. 98-101.
14. Ibid., pp. 101-03.
15. Ibid., p. 103.
16. Ibid., p. 104.
17. *Perspectives on the Sikh Tradition*, p. 231.
18. Ibid., pp. 232-37.
19. Ibid., pp. 238-56.
20. Ibid., pp. 256-58.
21. Ibid., pp. 258-63.
22. Ibid., pp. 263-72.
23. Ibid., pp. 272-86.
24. Ibid., pp. 263, 264, 266, 267, 270 and 272.

25. Ibid., pp. 271-72.
26. Ibid., pp. 277, 278, 279, 280, 281, 282 and 285.
27. Ibid., pp. 280-90.
28. Ibid., pp. 290-97.
29. Ibid., pp. 297-303.
30. Ibid., pp. 303-05.
31. Ibid., pp. 315-20.
32. Ibid., pp. 271 and 310 n 197.
33. Grewal (1989).

Part Three

EXTENSION OF THE CONTROVERSY

10. The Debate Continues

Before we move on to the extended debate we may review the issues raised by the *Perspectives on the Sikh Tradition*. Three of the contributors to this volume have nothing to say against McLeod. Another is critical not so much of McLeod as of 'critical scholarship'. Yet another presents a scholarly disagreement with McLeod in one of his contributions. Only Daljeet Singh is strident in his rejection of McLeod's interpretation of Sikhism. The tone of the volume is sought to be set by the editor. His whole argument is directed against McLeod's work. He presents McLeod's position partially and unfairly, often resorting to caricature. He attributes extra-academic motives to McLeod without any specific evidence. His eristic 'Introduction' and Khushwant Singh's journalistic 'Foreword' give the impression that McLeod is not a genuine or a serious scholar. Their aggressive pronouncements tend to create disrespect for McLeod's scholarship and resentment against his person. Not by a direct attack so much as by implication, the polemical character of the *Perspectives on the Sikh Tradition* devalues the historical approach.

We have seen that Professor King's criticism of McLeod amounts to little more than a critique of historical scholarship in general. His critique is applicable to the best of historians who may have nothing to do with Sikh studies. Daljeet Singh has presented a valuable interpretation of the Sikh tradition, underlining the independent character of the Sikh faith and the social relevance of its ideology. By that token alone, however, he does not become a sound critic of McLeod. Relatively speaking, McLeod's interpretation can be inadequate but not wrong. There is no evidence to doubt his motives or to undervalue his scholarship. There are important differences between him and Daljeet Singh but they share a common ground: the role of ideas in historical processes. This actually is the ground they contest. On Guru Nanak of faith, McLeod's challenge to the biographer of Guru Nanak has not been grasped by his critics. Without a proper understanding of the challenge, there is hardly any possibility of meeting it. The debate about this or that *sākhī* being rejected without justification is marginal to the challenge. Even if everything in the *Janamsākhīs* is accepted, it would give only a partial view of Guru Nanak's life. A historical biography of Guru Nanak should depict his fuller life on the basis of credible evidence.

Justice Gurdev Singh is totally wrong in saying that Professor Gupta produces contemporary or even near contemporary evidence on the 5Ks. This does not mean, however, that McLeod's hypothesis is acceptable. McLeod is off the mark also in maintaining that Guru Gobind Singh made no pronouncement on the vesting of Guruship. What McLeod tries to underline is that the Khalsa *rahit* evolved over time and that the doctrine of Guru-Panth crystallized in the eighteenth century. Justice Gurdev Singh's assertion that Jagjit Singh has refuted McLeod on militarization of the Sikh movement amounts to little more than an expression of his own preference for Jagjit Singh. His views on caste in the Sikh Panth are only slightly different from those of McLeod. Whereas McLeod gives much greater importance to social environment, Jagjit Singh gives all importance to religious ideology. They differ basically in their assumptions about causation in historical processes. On the whole, Justice Gurdev Singh's criticism of McLeod is misplaced. At the same time, we can see that McLeod's interpretation of the Sikh tradition is marked by certain inadequacies.

I

The *Perspectives on the Sikh Tradition* was followed by the *Advanced Studies in Sikhism* in 1989. Half of this volume is covered by eight papers contributed by Noel Q. King, Daljeet Singh and Jagjit Singh. Daljeet Singh criticizes McLeod in two of his five papers. Several other contributors also criticize him, two of them in direct 'critiques'. The editors also echo this concern when they say that it is even contended that Guru Nanak made 'no new contribution to religious thought and life in India'. They also refer to 'the prevailing confusion' in Sikh studies. In fact some of the scholars who held views 'contrary to the traditional versions' were specially invited to defend their views.[1] Thus, several links can be seen between the *Perspectives* and the *Advanced Studies*.

Indeed, all the themes covered in the *Perspectives* are taken up in the *Advanced Studies*. King's paper on 'critical methodology' is followed by Daljeet Singh's paper on 'issues of Sikh studies' which relates to methodology. As in the *Perspectives*, Jagjit Singh has discussed 'caste' and 'militarization' in two papers in the *Advanced Studies*. Similarly, one of Daljeet Singh's papers in the *Advanced Studies* is 'a comparison' of Sikhism with Vaishnavism, Vedanta and Nathism. In two other papers he discusses the doctrines of *nām* and *haumai*. His fifth paper relates to an issue raised by Justice Gurdev Singh but not taken up in the *Perspectives*: the authenticity of the *Ādi Granth*.[2] Among the remaining nine contributors, Raja Mrigendra Singh's critique of McLeod relates to 'the faith of Guru Nanak'. Two papers relate to what we have called 'Guru Nanak of faith': one by Professor Surinder Singh Kohli and the other by Professor Surjit Singh. Three papers deal with 'unity' in the thought of all the Gurus and, therefore, relate to what we call development in terms of 'religious ideology and social environment': one by Professor Kohli, another by Sardar Inderjit Singh, and the third by Professor Avtar Singh. Two papers by Professor Madanjit Kaur and one by Dr. Gobind Singh Mansukhani deal with the institution of the Khalsa in 1699, the Khalsa *rahit,* and Guruship after Guru Gobind Singh. The paper by Professor James R. Lewis, on 'mis-representation of Sikh tradition in world religions text books', gets related broadly to methodology. There is only one paper which deals with a totally new theme: Dr. G.S. Dhillon's paper entitled 'Singh Sabha Movement – A Revival'.

The *Advanced Studies* by and large, supplements the *Perspectives*. Daljeet Singh reinforces his earlier views on the faith of Guru Nanak and his criticism of W.H. McLeod.[3] Raja Mrigendra Singh's long critique of McLeod is reduced by the editors to a few pages in print. It does not make any significant point.[4] S.S. Kohli quotes Justice Gurdev Singh to denounce McLeod's approach to 'Guru Nanak of faith'. Kohli's own account of the various *Janamsākhī* traditions is poor in comparison with McLeod's. Kohli suggests that, besides discovering the kernel of truth in the *sākhīs*, a biographer can turn to external evidence. Furthermore, it is necessary to collect oral traditions, to study contemporary history of the lands visited by Guru Nanak, and to consult old revenue records. In other words, a historical biography of Guru Nanak is a project for the future.[5] Surjit Singh expresses the view that it is unfair and unrealistic to look for actual incidents of Guru Nanak's life in the *Janamsākhīs*. He also maintains that an intuitive truth can be conveyed to 'the peasant mind' in terms of a miracle.[6] Neither for 'the faith of Guru Nanak' nor for 'Guru Nanak of faith', the argument moves any farther than in the *Perspectives*.

Kohli's essay on unity of Sikh thought gets related to the debate on the development of Sikhism from the pacifism of Guru Nanak to the militancy of the Khalsa. In Kohli's view the spiritual unity of the Sikh movement was never impaired because 'the spirit of the founder Guru worked within all the successive Gurus'. This for Kohli is the 'constant unity of Sikh thought'. The Gurus as religious leaders had no political aspirations, but an obstacle in the way of spiritual development was to be removed with 'the sword of Dharma'. McLeod may be following 'the most scientific methodology' but being a 'foreign missionary' he could never understand the 'real spirit of Sikhism'. His view of the *bāolī* at Goindval is seen by Kohli as an example of misconception. McLeod raises the issue of Khatri and Jat culture, which has no relevance for the evolution of the Sikh movement, merely to create a cleavage. 'The missionary zeal lurking in his mind seems to be the cause of raking up the above issue, with the secret design of creating a cleavage among the Sikhs on caste basis'.[7]

Inderjit Singh also refers to the unity of Guruship in Sikhism to emphasize the unity of Sikh thought. They who see differences between the teachings of the ten Gurus do not understand that 'the message was one and the same'; what differed was 'only the social and political environment'. Self-defence in the face of persecution was consistent with the teachings of Guru Nanak and his first four successors. There was absolutely nothing in the teachings of Guru Nanak to support the suggestion that he accepted the doctrine of *ahimsa*. Indeed, Sikhism provided 'guiding principles' which were relevant for all times.[8] Avtar Singh's essay on 'Sikh identity and continuity' is more sophisticated. According to him, the normative ideals and imperatives 'cannot be established in terms of actual conduct or the practical'. Indeed, the normative is 'the critique' in terms of which the actual is evaluated. Explicit preference for ethical living is embodied in the often quoted line of Guru Nanak: 'Truth is higher than everything but higher still is true conduct'. In this respect the Sikh Gurus departed completely from the earlier Indian ethics. Their values provided the impulse for many an ideal of social concern and service. 'In all this lies the strength and identity of the Sikh ethics'.[9]

Madanjit Kaur's essay on the creation of the Khalsa is professedly meant to examine its 'ideological and historical importance'. She goes on to add that she would also examine W.H. McLeod's 'thesis' on the 5Ks which he has borrowed from J.S. Grewal. She is emphatic that the Sikh tradition regarding the institution of the Khalsa is 'so clearly supported by the Sikh sources that it cannot be rationally ignored'. At the same time she makes the following statement: 'We are fully aware of the lack of a sense of historicity among the early Sikh scholars. Moreover, the extraordinary circumstances following the founding of the *Khalsa* left little scope for the preservation of the contemporary historical records'. In other words, the events possibly were not recorded by the early Sikh writers; if they were, the records were lost. This is Madanjit Kaur's way of admitting that no contemporary records are available to the historian today.[10]

Gobind Singh Mansukhani's evidence comes mostly from the *Rahitnāmas*. He refers even to the *Rahit-Nama* of Bhai Chaupa Singh published by McLeod himself, not realizing that there is no reference to 5Ks in this *Rahit-Nama*. The most crucial evidence adduced by Mansukhani is that of a *hukamnāma* attributed to Guru Gobind Singh. It bears the date 23 May 1699, and mentions *kesh*, *kachh, kirpān* and *kaṛā* as the articles of *rahit*. Though the formulation of 5Ks is strictly not there even in this *hukamnāma*, it comes closer to the formulation than any other document of proven authenticity. However, the authenticity of this *hukamnāma* has been rejected by some scholars. That may be the reason why Mansukhani does not give it the importance it deserves.[11]

In the essay on the succession of *Granth Sahib* to Guruship, Mandanjit Kaur covers the ground already covered by Dr. Ganda Singh and Professor Harbans Singh. Her professed purpose in this paper is to examine W.H. McLeod's thesis on the issue of Guruship which he puts forward on the authority of J.S. Grewal. The attribution of this 'thesis' to J.S. Grewal is rather obtuse, because Grewal is talking of 1699 and not of 1708. Despite all the padding, it is easy to see that Madanjit Kaur has presented in this paper a poor rehash of the evidence and arguments put forth by Dr. Ganda Singh and Professor Harbans Singh.[12]

Comparing the *Perspectives* with the *Advanced Studies*, we find that there is greater concern in the latter for methodology, authenticity of the Kartarpuri Bīṛ, and Sikh identity. However, the eristic purpose and the tone of a number of contributions reinforce the polemical protest without carrying the discussion forward. The old contributors mostly repeat themselves. Neither in terms of information nor in terms of interpretation any fresh ground in broken. Some of the writers tend to assume that McLeod's motives are unacademic and that he has been successfully refuted in the *Perspectives on the Sikh Tradition*. There is only one contribution in which there is some positive appreciation for McLeod's work. James R. Lewis places McLeod among those Western writers who do not subscribe to the notion of syncretism in Sikhism and stress the 'originality of Guru Nanak'.[13]

II

Two more publications appeared on the initiative mainly of those who had organized the Los Angeles conference: *Recent Researches in Sikhism* and *Fundamental Issues in Sikh Studies*. The papers in these two volumes are divided into four 'sections': ideology, methodology, Sikh history, and general. Nearly half of these papers relate to themes we have already noticed. There is no paper on 'caste' and there is no paper on 'Guru Nanak of faith'. More than half of these papers relate to 'the faith of Guru Nanak'. Five papers relate to religious ideology and social environment. Three others relate specifically to the institution of the Khalsa, the Khalsa *rahit,* and Guruship.

On the faith of Guru Nanak, Professor King suggests in one of his papers that faith in the principles enunciated by Guru Nanak enabled the Sikhs to respond successfully to all changing historical situations.[14] In another paper, he appreciates the daily prayer of the Sikhs as a liturgy which has common ground with other faiths and yet has 'fundamental differences'.[15] Daljeet Singh gives a clear exposition of Sikhism in one of his papers, underlining its uniqueness and universality in terms which are familiar to us by now.[16] In another paper he gives yet another exposition of the ideology of Guru Nanak in more or less the same terms that we find in his earlier work.[17] Kharak Singh gives a brief outline of Sikh ideology on the basis of his understanding of Daljeet Singh's position on this theme and tries to show how the findings of S.S. Hans in his reconstruction of Sikh history from Sikh literature are indefensible.[18] Professor Gurtej Singh discusses the 'political ideas of Guru Nanak' as an integral part of his ideology.[19] Professor Harnam Singh Shan presents Sikhism as an original, distinct, revealed and complete religion.[20] Dr. Gurnam Kaur discusses the importance of 'revelation and reason' in Sikhism in one of her papers; in another, she gives an exposition of perceptual, rational and intuitive knowledge in Sikhism, providing 'the enduring foundations of human knowledge' in which intuitive knowledge does not contradict but transcends rational knowledge.[21] Baljit Singh Bagga equates the *nām mārg* with the activist mysticism of Sikhism as a new way of life in one of his papers. In another, he gives an exposition of the cherished ideal mood, the high spirit (*charhdī kalā*) which never despairs, never admits defeat, and refuses to be crushed by adversities.[22] With the partial exception of one paper, the faith of Guru Nanak in these papers is presented in positive terms and not in reaction or response to any other writer. Nonetheless, it is possible to see that all these papers supplement or reinforce Daljeet Singh's exposition of Sikhism.

On the theme of development, Daljeet Singh and Jagjit Singh have written on the concept of *mīrī-pīrī*. For Daljeet Singh, *mīrī-pīrī* is an essential doctrine of the Sikh religion. This is his way of underlining that in Sikh ideology there is no dichotomy between the spiritual and the temporal. The two concerns are in reality related to a single ideology which distinguishes Sikhism from all other Indian systems of religious belief and practice. This unity is amply demonstrated in Sikh history and the struggle of the Sikhs for basic human rights to the point of martyrdom. Daljeet Singh emphasizes that the concept of *mīrī-pīrī* originated with Guru Nanak and not at some later stage in the history of the Sikhs.[23] Jagjit Singh reinforces the point that worldly sovereignty and spiritual pursuit are inseparable in Sikhism. Indeed, even the acquisition of political power for a noble cause is 'a legitimate spiritual pursuit'. Jagjit Singh makes the significant statement that it was 'not Guru Arjan's martyrdom which gave a political turn to the Sikh movement; rather it was the political aspect of the movement which contributed to his martyrdom'.[24] Kharak Singh's exposition of *sant sīpāhī* and a paper contributed jointly by Kharak Singh and G.S. Dhillon on '*rāj karegā khālsā*' underline the inseparable link between the temporal and the spiritual in Sikhism.[25] This view is supported by Professor Avtar Singh in his presentation of Sikh ethics in his abstracts on the 'essence of Sikh ethics' and on 'the role of moral philosophy in Sikhism'.[26]

Madanjit Kaur takes up the story of worship of the Goddess by Guru Gobind Singh for instituting the Khalsa. Koer Singh's *Gurbilās Pātshāhī 10*, which according to Madanjit Kaur was composed between 1751 and 1762, is the first known work to give the story. It is a myth, without any factual basis. We may agree with Madanjit Kaur. But this myth has been discarded by the Sikh historians since the first decade of the present century. Why flog this dead horse? Her answer is that McLeod seems to suggest that Guru Gobind Singh 'could bring forth good results' only after he invoked the help of Durga. In this insinuation lies the justification for Madanjit Kaur's thin contribution.[27] Himadri Banerjee discusses 'the Khalsa' in Bengali, Hindi and Oṛiya literature. In the works he analyses Sikhism is assumed to be a part of Hinduism and the Khalsa represents the militant form of Hinduism. The Sikhs do not possess any separate or independent identity of their own, and their struggle against the Mughals is appreciated as Hindu resistance to Muslims.[28] Ironically, for editors of the *Recent Researches*, Banerjee unfolds a healthy and meaningful perspective on how the interest and activities of a minority were viewed in the early part of the century.[29] R.S Wahiwala's paper is meant to show that the *rahit maryādā* approved by the Shiromani Gurdwara Prabandhak Committee has its basis in the past. It retains genuine elements and discards un-Sikh elements from the earliest sources.[30]

Two papers by S.S. Kohli, one on Guru Arjan and the other on Guru Tegh Bahadur, give familiar interpretation of their life and work.[31] G.S. Dhillon's paper on Maharaja Ranjit Singh presents him as a 'Sikh' ruler who treated all religious communities alike.[32] His paper on the Sikhs under the British is meant to show that the colonial rulers did not treat the Sikhs in any favourable way and they had no interest in promoting the identity of the Sikhs.[33] The editors underline that this paper was meant to serve as a corrective to the views held by W.H. McLeod, among others.[34] But the view attributed by Dhillon to McLeod is not really his view: McLeod is talking of a theory put forth by Richard G. Fox.[35] Two papers relate to contemporay problems: one by Daljeet Singh and the other by Kharak Singh. They give clear and convincing exposition of the Punjab problem, especially the river waters issue. The reason for taking up these themes is 'misrepresentation' of these issues by W.H. McLeod and Harjot Oberoi.[36]

The question of Sikh identity, raised and discussed with reference to Oberoi's paper on the nineteenth century, is taken up by Daljeet Singh from the very origins of Sikhism. He explains 'how in the matter of spiritual experience, the concept of God, ideology, class, scripture and its institutions, Sikhism is entirely different from the other religions, and has a personality of its own'. [37] Iqbal Singh Sara rightly points out the inevitability of empirical links of a new religion with the pre-existing systems. But to treat such links as evidence of equation between the new and the old amounts to misrepresentation. The backdrop of Hinduistic environment in the case of Sikhism cannot be used as an argument for denying separate identity to the Sikhs. In fact there was plenty of evidence in Sikh and Muslim sources of the early centuries of Sikh history in support of a distinct Sikh identity. The kind of work done by Harjot Oberoi in the Chair of Sikh Studies, established largely with funds raised by the Sikh community, needed to be reviewed. There was urgent need for 'public accountability'. No research can be supported 'to ring the deathknell of Sikhs and Sikhism'.[38]

Four papers in these two volumes relate broadly to methodology, one each by James R. Lewis and Kharak Singh, and two by G.S. Mansukhani. G.S. Mansukhani's paper on 'integrated methodology' for the appraisal of sources for Sikh studies is directly related to methodology. His account of the 'origin and development' of Sikh studies can also be considered as related to the theme in its wider sense. There are two papers on texts. Madanjit Kaur has argued that S.S. Hans is wrong in placing Koer Singh's *Gurbilās Pātshāhī 10* in the early nineteenth century. She upholds the traditional view against Hans's arguments for placing it after Sukha Singh's *Gurbilās*.[39] The other paper related indirectly to texts is a specially invited paper by Gurtej Singh in which he compares the treatment of the *Dasam Granth* by D.P. Ashta on the one hand and Ratan Singh Jaggi on the other.[40] There is one paper which brings in altogether a new theme, the 'Sikh women', raising the question of gender relations in the Sikh Panth. This issue, like that of 'caste', is linked with the idea of equality in Sikhism.[41]

The atmosphere of controversy and debate induced Dr. Trilochan Singh 'to remove the dark errors and misconceptions created about Sikhs and Sikhism and to create authentic understanding and appreciation of Sikh history and doctrines'.[42] The publication of the *Perspectives on the Sikh Tradition* revealed the enormity of the harm that was being done to the Sikh tradition by McLeod and some scholars in the universities of the Punjab. 'After years of silence', therefore, Trilochan Singh decided 'to give a comprehensive answer to all the clap-trap methods and theories of Dr. McLeod on Sikh religion and history based on scepticism and conjecture'.[43] Trilochan Singh sees some redeeming features in Trumpp but none in McLeod.[44] Twelve chapters of his book deal with McLeod's 'false construction of Sikh history and scriptures' and provide 'authentic factual background' of the themes discussed by him.[45]

Trilochan Singh argues that Guru Nanak was not a Sant but a Prophet. He founded a new religion which is summed up as *Gurmat*. It was the outcome of personal experience. It was 'uniquely distinct' from what McLeod refers to as the *nirguṇ Sant sampradāya*. Trilochan Singh rejects McLeod's 'repulsive theory' about the Jat influx obliging Guru Hargobind 'to fall in line with the Sword-happy savage instincts of the Jats'. There were no castes in the Sikh Panth; there were only different occupations and professions. All Sikhs ate together in the *langar*. The trained missionaries of Sikhism 'included women'.[46] Trilochan Singh expresses the view that 'Guru Nanak of faith is Guru Nanak of history, and Guru Nanak of history is Guru Nanak of faith. The two are inseparable from each other'.[47] McLeod's analysis of the *Janamsākhīs* and the *Rahitnāmas* is 'deceptive and fallacious'.[48] Trilochan Singh fails to see the difference in McLeod's treatment of the *Janamsākhīs* in his three different publications.[49] According to Noel Q. King, Trilochan Singh's mind was 'saturated with traditional Sikh scholarship'.[50] He is a noble knight of the order of the Honourable Khalsa, the lion-hearted.[51] McLeod is 'obedient to the truth' seen from the viewpoint of 'Enlightenment' in which 'everything said about the divine and revelation must be a human artefact and explained in non-supernatural terms'. McLeod's limitations and his strength are not personal but institutional. 'He remains a clear-sighted, hard-working, immensely able devotee to the ideals of the western University'.[52]

Trilochan Singh felt obliged to take notice of two more works: 'Pashaura Singh's thesis on the text and meaning of *Adi Granth* "Guided" by Dr. Hew McLeod' and 'Dr Piar Singh's Book *Gatha Sri Adi Granth*', both bringing the *Ādi Granth* to the centre of the debate in Sikh studies.[53] Professor Piar Singh's book was meant to search for the authentic text of the Granth prepared by Guru Arjan and authenticated by Guru Gobind Singh. This search was based on the assumption that the Kartarpuri Bīṛ was not authentic. In fact Piar Singh argued against Daljeet Singh's view. Within four weeks of its publication, the sale of Piar Singh's book was suspended. The controversy went on for many months in 1993. Piar Singh appeared before the Jathedar of the Akāl Takht. Declared guilty on 1 April 1994, he was asked to do penance for forty days. After its due performance, he was exonerated on 12 May. Ironically, however, he asked for a formal statement of his 'guilt'. Presumably in the absence of any response from the Jathedar of the Akāl Takht, Piar Singh started preparing his response to the criticism of his book. This was published posthumously in 1996 as *Gatha Sri Adi Granth and the Controversy*.

Pashaura Singh had submitted his doctoral thesis to the University of Toronto in1991. Dr. Jasbir Singh Mann managed to get a copy of this thesis, made further photo-copies, and circulated them widely in 1992 for 'spontaneous' response. By the middle of 1993 a whole volume of papers on Pashaura Singh's work was ready for publication. It was brought out in 1994 as *Planned Attack on Aad Sri Guru Granth Sahib: Academics or Blasphemy*. Before the end of June 1994, Pashaura Singh was indicted by the Jathedar of the Akāl Takht and declared guilty of five charges of blasphemy.[54] Pashaura Singh has published his main argument in the *International Journal of Punjab Studies* responding to only two of his critics. Nearly all the arguments in this debate about Pashaura Singh's thesis are based on the internal evidence of MS 1245. They relate to its authenticity which brings in the issue of its date and the idea of a draft. Pashaura Singh is criticized for over-interpreting the evidence because of his preconceived notion. His real purpose was to attack the *Guru Granth Sahib* by proxy. His work treats revelation as ordinary poetry and he goes to the length of arguing that Guru Arjan changed Guru Nanak's *mūlmantar*. Thus, the arguments of Pashaura Singh's critics are both historical and theological.

The publication of Harjot Oberoi's *Construction of Religious Boundaries: Culture, Identity and Diversity in the Sikh Tradition* in 1994 did not come as a surprise but it did call for immediate notice. Three reviews of the book were published in the *Abstracts of Sikh Studies* of July 1994. In an article in the same number Iqbal

Singh Sara raised the question of the U.B.C. Sikh Chair, characterizing Oberoi's work as 'an eminent and impressive exercise in destructive scholarship'. The work produced by Oberoi was 'a planned part' of the promotion of 'Indic culture' and the repression of 'Sikh religion and history'.[55] More reviews of and articles on Oberoi's work appeared in the succeeding numbers of the *Abstracts*.[56] In 1995 appeared a book entitled *Invasion of Religious Boundaries*, containing over thirty contributions as 'a critique of Harjot Oberoi's work'. The gravest charge against Oberoi was his treatment of Sikh identity. His methodology was another 'basic fault'.[57] Oberoi had failed to fulfil 'the objectives of the Sikh Chair'. The editor of the *Abstracts* felt gratified to inform its readers that 'after six long years, the incumbent of the Chair has had to resign his position', hoping that his successor 'will be a genuine scholar who understands Sikhism and Sikh sentiments, and whose bona-fides are above suspicion'.[58]

III

The Sikh intelligentsia have become more sensitive to developments in Sikh studies now than ever before. A considerable number of scholars, both professional and amateur, have joined the original nucleus formed by Sardar Daljeet Singh, Justice Gurdev Singh and Professor Jagjit Singh. The new scholars belong to a number of institutions in India and North America. They represent a number of disciplines, including areas other than historical and religious studies. Among their sympathizers are retired judges, civil servants, army officers, former ministers, chief ministers, and Vice-Chancellors. They have access to the President of the Shiromani Gurdwara Prabandhak Committee. A number of organizations have been established in the Punjab and in North America and U.K. which take interest not only in Sikh studies but also in the Sikh affairs in general. Two organizations have been quite active in holding conferences and bringing out publications: the Institute of Sikh Studies in Chandigarh and the Centre of Sikh Studies in Santa Ana (U.S.A). Since 1991 they have been jointly bringing out the *Abstracts of Sikh Studies* as a bi-annual publication till

1994 and as a quarterly since 1995. Its objective is to bring to the notice of scholars and general readers 'the advances in Sikh studies', to project 'a correct image' of Sikhism and the Sikh community in India and abroad, and 'to watch, report and rebut any distortions or misrepresentations' of Sikh religion and Sikh history.

The number of 'critical scholars' whose work is criticized has also increased. Closely associated with W.H. McLeod are Pashaura Singh and Harjot Oberoi. Another scholar associated with him is Gurinder Singh Mann. These scholars are working in foreign universities. The places where programmes of Sikh studies have been started are Toronto, Vancouver, Ann Arbor and New York. A few other scholars associated with critical scholarship at these places are Joseph T. O'Connell, Mark Juergensmeyer and John Stratton Hawley. But far more important is Piar Singh of Guru Nanak Dev University, who was not connected with 'critical scholars' but who is nonetheless bracketed with them. Two other scholars whose work is marginally criticized are S.S. Hans and J.S. Grewal. Then there are a number of other scholars who have written mostly for encyclopaedias or for books on religions of the world. Two of the scholars who have written on Sikhism and the Sikhs on the basis of their interest in Sikh studies are J.C. Archer and C.H. Loehlin. Then there is Ernest Trumpp. All these scholars are supposed to have misrepresented Sikhism and Sikh history in one way or another. They are not all foreigners, missionaries or unbelievers. What is supposed to be common between them is their lack of sympathy for the Sikh tradition if not an outright hostility towards it.

The credentials of such scholars are suspect, either because of their Euro-centrism, their religious concerns, their political purposes, or their mundane personal interests. The suggestion thrown out by Justice Gurdev Singh about McLeod's evangelical purpose has become an established fact for others. Indeed, Daljeet Singh is credited by his admirers for making the discovery that Christian missionaries had the deliberate design of misrepresenting Sikhism and distorting Sikh history. G.S. Dhillon talks of McLeod's inability to shed the bias 'naturally associated' with a Christian missionary organization in the Punjab, which explains his 'blasphemous and unethical attacks against the Sikhs'. Another critic appeals to McLeod's decency, telling him that 'enough is enough': if he failed to convert the Sikhs of the Punjab to Christianity he should not mislead innocent Sikhs now 'by bringing out (himself as well as through his stooges) ill-conceived and preposterous publications'. Several other writers make reference to McLeod in a manner that suggests that they take his evangelical purpose for granted. Non-academic motivation is attributed to Piar Singh, Pashaura Singh and Harjot Oberoi.[59]

The recent crisis appears to have a direct bearing on the recent debate in Sikh studies. The editors of the *Advanced Studies in Sikhism* explicitly refer to 'the recent political crisis' as one of the reasons for their interest in Sikh studies.[60] One of the reasons why the Sikhs have been pushed into 'the pit of persecution, political slavery and cultural tyranny' is 'lack of social and political freedom after 1947'.[61] Since the Sikhs have no political power to promote their own identity, 'the Punjab crisis in the early 1980s forced the western Sikh communities to take the responsibility on themselves to project the authentic image of Sikhism in the West', an image that was being politically eroded by 'anti-Sikh forces'.[62] Professor Gurtej Singh clearly states that 'Sikh identity' is seen by the most important political parties in India as inconvenient and scholars like Oberoi and McLeod provide subtle support for its dissolution. The 'state inspired academic activity' and formulations tailored to this 'preconceived sinister design' can never be objective.[63] Intellectuals installed in the departments of Sikh studies and Punjabi literature in the universities of the state have been given high positions to 'run down Sikhism'.[64] The 'mischievous propaganda' of a critical scholar is seen as 'a part of some international conspiracy'.[65] That the critics of critical scholars are sincere in their view of the present crisis is evident from those of their publications which have nothing to do with the debate in Sikh studies.[66]

The tone and language used by the critics of critical scholars conveys a feeling of anger and resentment to the reader. The Sikh writers associated with W.H. McLeod are 'pseudo-Sikhs'. They have jumped on his 'band-waggon'. They have joined his 'band'. They belong to his 'pack'. They are 'docile', 'role dancing', 'myopic', and 'instrumental' scholars. They publish 'maliciously vulgar assaults' on Sikhism. Trilochan Singh denounces McLeod's 'absurdities', his 'irrational monstrosity', 'naked antagonism' and 'malicious hostility'. 'McLeod is neither honest nor rational nor reasonable and logical in his analysis of historical events, nor does he anywhere, in any of his books follow the *minimum* rules of academic ethics'. Sikh scholars are 'greedy sycophants and highly paid servile agents' of the Delhi rulers.[67]

Like Justice Gurdev Singh, Trilochan Singh can use quotation marks over his own statements to caricature views attributed to a critical scholar. On McLeod's presentation of the Jats, for example, the following statement is placed within quotation marks: 'For centuries the sword of the Jats could not restrain itself from drinking blood again and again, and the Jat sword found Sikhism a haven for giving vent to its tribal passions. Once they became a dominant majority during the period of Guru Arjan, even Guru Hargobind and Guru Gobind Singh could not control them. Both the Gurus surrendered and sacrificed the best that was in Guru Nanak's faith at the altar of powerful Jat cultural lobby within Sikhism'. The reader does not know that this direct speech is a device used by Trilochan Singh for 'as if '.[68]

The critics of critical scholarship profess to go a long way on freedom of research but not all the way. Professor King is opposed to 'moratorium' on critical scholarship'.[69] Trilochan Singh is against ban on books.[70] The editor of the *Planned Attack* favours 'dialogue and discussion' and disfavours 'caustic observations'.[71] The editor of the *Abstracts* tells its readers that 'Sikhs place a high value on academic research on their religion and history'. But genuine research demands honesty and objectivity. No freedom is absolute. It cannot be allowed to be abused 'to mount subtle attacks on our Gurus and our sacred institutions'.[72] Universities are approached to appoint 'ethics committees'. The S.G.P.C. is approached to 'punish' errant scholars.[73] The collective authority of the community is invoked against those who appear to cater to anti-Sikh forces. In this context the Institute of Sikh Studies takes credit for bringing Piar Singh and Pashaura Singh to the Akāl Takht.[74]

Irritation with critical scholarship can lead at times to erroneous perceptions. The use by Pashaura Singh of an article by C.H. Loehlin is a case in point. Trilochan Singh suggests that the article attributed to Loehlin is actually a distorted version prepared by McLeod's 'clique'. To suit their purpose they changed the title of the article to 'The Need for Textual and Historical Criticism'.[75] S.S. Kohli goes into greater detail, mentioning the original title of the paper in 1965 and its garbled publication under the new title in 1987 and 1990. He quotes the lines which in his view were forged by a 'clique' with which Pashaura Singh was associated as a researcher. Furthermore, the additional matter contains 'blasphemous and obnoxious statements'.[76] Understandably, the editor of the *Planned Attack* dwells long on this 'extremely suspicious' piece.[77] But the article in question is nothing but an exact reproduction of Loehlin's appendix to his book published in 1971.[78]

Impatience with McLeod can at times lead to a total misunderstanding of his position. According to G.S. Dhillon, for instance, McLeod 'holds that there were several Sikh identities during the post-Annexation period, but the Khalsa identity was promoted by the British in order to serve their vested interests. Therefore, according to him, the Singh Sabha version of the Khalsa identity should be regarded as a British creation'.[79] We do find the following statement in McLeod's *Who is a Sikh?*: 'The British selected one of the available identities (the Khalsa identity) and insisted that its army recruits should thereafter observe routine Khalsa standards. This identity was also assumed by those members of the trading castes who sought economic and educational advantage on the basis of their claim to be Sikhs. They in turn communicated it to the petty commodity producers of central Punjab, already well prepared for its adoption by instruction received in the Indian army'.[80] This statement may appear to support Dhillon's contention. But this statement is meant to summarize Richard Fox's view. McLeod's own view is that the Khalsa identity in the early nineteenth century was 'by far the strongest'. McLeod is quite explicit: 'The suggestion that the "Singh identity" was selected by the British and then appropriated by a particular caste group for its own class purposes is unacceptable'.[81] Thus, it is easy to see that Dhillon has attributed Richard Fox's position to that of McLeod. Incidentally, Dhillon says nothing in his review about the basic argument developed by McLeod in *Who is a Sikh*?– that is, Sikh identity.

Daljeet Singh makes the following observation: 'For McLeod to say that in a mood of magnanimity Prime Minister Rajiv Gandhi conceded most of the Akali demands or that these are "unacceptable Sikh demands" is to betray an ignorance of the Punjab problem which though gross enough, is partly understandable from a distant outsider. But what is really not understandable is why a person so unaware as McLeod should rush on to a ground which angels would fear to tread'.[81] The statement made by McLeod is actually meant to represent the view of some other people and not his own. Daljeet Singh has missed the context. One has to read several paragraphs carefully to know this. Having summarized one view of the situation, McLeod says: 'This is one interpretation. The other one claims that the Punjab issue must be set within the context of all-India politics and specifically the electioneering strategy of the ruling Congress government in New Delhi'. A part of this second interpretation is the statement attributed by Daljeet Singh to McLeod. No ambiguity whatever is left for the reader when McLeod repeats at the end the statement: 'That is the other interpretation and time alone will tell which of the two is more accurate'.[82] Daljeet Singh's review of McLeod's *Who is a Sikh*?, like G.S. Dhillon's, makes no reference at all to the basic argument developed in the book, namely Sikh identity.[83]

As it may be expected *a priori*, there is a wide range in the quality of contributions made by the critics. They reveal a wide range in their understanding of the issues. We may give only two examples to make the point clear. Without any reflection on the person we may take up a contribution made by S.S. Sodhi who appears to be a prominent member of the group. He quotes Thoreau about the bad odour of 'tainted goodness' presumably with reference to Christian missionaries. He goes on to talk of the 'pathological functioning' of 'Sikh scholars', their narcissistic arrogance and scholarly ignorance'. In the third paragraph then 'these historians' are named: A.L. Basham, Ernest Trumpp, Huston Smith, Archer,

C.H. Loehlin, J.S. Grewal, S.S. Hans, M. Juergensmeyer, W.H. McLeod, Pashaura Singh, Piar Singh, Harjot Singh Oberoi and O'Connell. We are told further that most of these historians are either non-believers or they are running away from their own religions. 'Most of them start as missionaries'. Then he lists objectionable ideas in single sentences, but almost all the authors cited are new. In this manner, Sodhi goes on from paragraph to paragraph, unmindful of any connections, relevance or coherence. He never 'deviates into sense'. The only point that he succeeds in making is that he is angry with McLeod and his 'pack': A case of too much heat, and no light.[84]

As a total contrast to Sodhi, we may refer to a review of Harjot Oberoi's *Construction of Religious Boundaries* by Dr. Narinder Singh Kapany, which is meaningful as well as dispassionate. For him, Oberoi's book is a classic example of what may be termed the 'hegemony' approach to the study of religious reform in colonial India. Its fundamental weakness is that it is based on the ideological difference between 'popular' and 'elite', and between 'plural' and 'uniform'. Oberoi accepts the nineteenth century view that Indian civilization was characterized by a tolerant spirituality, carrying the implication that different religions in India were manifestations of 'this universal Indian spirituality', which is equated with 'Hinduism'. This illusory device was meant to serve some social and political purposes. If the purpose of Oberoi's book was to show that religious boundaries were absent in the pre-colonial Punjab, it has failed in its purpose. Moreover, Oberoi does not seem to be aware that the historical interpretation of Sikh history is more than an academic discussion of the nature of religious world-view. 'Momentous political issues involving the rights of minorities are obscured by the assertion that Indian religion was uniquely tolerant and willing to absorb other systems into itself'.[85]

IV

We can see that the scope of the controversy has been enlarged since the publication of the *Perspectives on the Sikh Tradition*. For one thing, the number of 'the critics' and the number of the scholars criticized has increased. The polemical purpose of the bulk of the literature produced has become more evident. The assumption about unacademic purposes of the scholars criticized has become more general. Their scholarship is seen as subserving the purposes of those parties and forces which are inimical to the Sikh tradition and hostile to Sikh aspirations. The tone of denunciation has become more strident. Most of the critics favour the idea of bringing 'the culprits' to 'the book' through extra-academic means.

On the themes of the faith of Guru Nanak and Guru Nanak of faith, the debate has not moved forward. Mostly we meet the same old information and the same old arguments. There are fresh assertions but no fresh information or argument on the themes related to religious ideology versus social environment – militarization of the Sikh movement, the Khalsa *rahit*, and the doctrines of Guruship. There is no further debate on the issue of caste. Thus, the debate on all the old issues has added only quantity.

Nevertheless, the extended debate has reinforced and somewhat amplified the interpretation of the Sikh tradition put forth by Daljeet Singh. It is assumed by his admirers that 'the enemy' has been silenced. Their mistrust of the 'outsiders' is matched by their credulity about the 'insiders'. Hyper-critical about the former, they are uncritical about the latter. A certain degree of insularity is visible in their writings. There is a large degree of duplication and repetition. The quality of scholarship is often indifferent.

Perhaps the most important dimension of the extended controversy is its expansion in terms of scope. Methodology has been an old concern of the critics. It has been reinforced by new as well as the old contributors. Another theme that has emerged in the extended controversy rather prominently gets related to textual studies. Historical approach to the compilation and canonization of the Sikh scripture has been pursued by one set of writers and criticized by another. The third major theme to emerge from the extended controversy is that of Sikh identity. This has been treated separately in the *Historical Perspectives on Sikh Identity* in which I have taken into account the relevant writings of W.H. McLeod, Daljeet Singh, Harjot Oberoi and G.S.Dhillon. Here we may take up the other two themes.

NOTES

1. *Advanced Studies in Sikhism*, pp. vii-viii.
2. Ibid., pp. 138-60. Daljeet Singh's article is based on Daljeet Singh (1987).
3. *Advanced Studies in Sikhism*, pp. 33-35, 56-88 and 89-97.
4. Ibid., pp. 326-28.
5. Ibid., pp. 301-16.
6. Ibid., pp. 317-23.
7. Ibid., pp. 98-108.
8. Ibid., pp. 109-18.
9. Ibid., pp. 163-73.
10. Ibid., pp. 195-213.
11. Ibid., pp. 174-91.
12. Ibid., pp. 121-37.
13. Ibid., pp. 265-77.
14. *Recent Researches in Sikhism*, pp. 3-8.
15. Ibid., pp. 9-12.
16. Ibid., pp. 14-41.
17. *Fundamental Issues in Sikh Studies*, pp. 3-20.
18. *Recent Researches in Sikhism*, pp. 72-90.
19. Ibid., pp. 61-71.
20. *Fundamental Issues in Sikh Studies*, pp. 24-59.
21. Ibid., pp. 60-77. *Recent Researches in Sikhism*, pp. 91-105.
22. *Fundamental Issues in Sikh Studies*, pp. 78-88 and 89-95.
23. *Recent Researches in Sikhism*, pp. 42-60.
24. Ibid., pp. 136-51.
25. *Fundamental Issues in Sikh Studies*, pp. 116-26 and 187-95.
26. *Recent Researches in Sikhism*, p. 13. *Fundamental Issues in Sikh Studies*, p. 23.
27. *Fundamental Issues in Sikh Studies*, pp. 170-78.
28. *Recent Researches in Sikhism*, pp. 152-60.
29. Ibid., pp. xx-xxi.
30. *Fundamental Issues in Sikh Studies*, pp. 229-37.
31. *Recent Researches in Sikhism*, pp. 125-35. *Fundamental Issues in Sikh Studies*, pp. 160-69.
32. *Recent Researches in Sikhism*, pp. 247-72.
33. Ibid., pp. 173-225.
34. Ibid., p. xxi.
35. McLeod (1980), p. 37.
36. *Fundamental Issues in Sikh Studies*, pp. 136-59 and 196-228.
37. Ibid., pp. 105-15.
38. *Recent Researches in Sikhism*, pp. 330-34.
39. Ibid., pp. 161-72.

40. *Fundamental Issues in Sikh Studies*, pp. 179-86.
41. Ibid., pp. 96-104.
42. Trilochan Singh (1994), p. 12.
43. Ibid., p. 80.
44. Ibid., pp. 60, 61-62 and 63.
45. Ibid., pp. 81, 83 and 87.
46. Ibid., pp. 92, 93, 101, 105, 109, 117, 119, 130, 131, 137, 147, 148-49, 158, 162, 164, 168, 184, 185, 187, 199, 207, 215 and 220.
47. Ibid., p. 236.
48. Ibid., pp. 264 and 283.
49. Ibid., p. 80.
50. Ibid., pp. 316-33.
51. Ibid., pp. xiv and xxi.
52. Ibid., pp. xix-xxi.
53. Ibid., Appendixes I and II.
54. *Abstracts of Sikh Studies* (July 1994), pp. 133-44.
55. Ibid., pp. 71-80.
56. Ibid. (Jan 1995), pp. 68-76.
57. *Invasion of Religious Boundaries*, p. 316.
58. *Abstracts of Sikh Studies* (Oct-Dec 1996), p. 91.
59. Ibid. (January 1995), p. 4; ibid. (July 1994), pp. 84 n 4, 99 and 115; Trilochan Singh (1994), pp. xxvii, xxxi, 218, 304 and 309; *Planned Attack*, pp. 219, 223 and 254.
60. *Advanced Studies in Sikhism*, p. vii.
61. Trilochan Singh (1994), pp. 125 and 280.
62. *Invasion of Religious Boundaries*, p. 2.
63. *Abstracts of Sikh Studies* (July 1994), pp. 104 and 108.
64. Trilochan Singh (1994), p. 284.
65. *Invasion of Religious Boundaries*, p. 275; *Planned Attack*, p. 386.
66. G.S. Dhillon published his considered view of the contemporary crisis in 1992 in a book carrying the eloquent title, *India Commits Suicide.* Gurtej Singh has brought out his *Tandav of the Centaur* on the grave predicament of the Sikhs in the context of post-1947 India. Their recent articles are also relevant in this connection: *Abstracts of Sikh Studies* (Jan-March 1996), pp. 48-64 and 68-89.
67. *Abstracts of Sikh Studies* (April 1995), p. 233; *Invasion of Religious Boundaries*, p.1; Trilochan Singh (1994), pp. 12, 83 and 87.
68. Trilochan Singh (1994), p. 211. For another quotation ibid., p. 279.
69. *Perspectives on the Sikh Tradition*, p. 52.
70. Trilochan Singh (1994), pp. 14, 19, 21 and 378.
71. *Planned Attack*, pp. 37-38.
72. *Abstracts of Sikh Studies* (April 1995), p. 11. Also, ibid. (July 1994), p. 124; (April 1995), pp. 1-11; *Planned Attack*, pp. 32, 37-38, 179, 298-99 and 400-01.

73. *Abstracts of Sikh Studies* (January 1994), pp. 120-22. Also, Ibid (January 1993), pp. 131-33; (July 1994), pp. 129 and 130-33; (April 1995) pp. 122-23; *Planned Attack*, pp. 180, 225, 377 and 392.
74. *Abstracts of Sikh Studies* (January 1995), p. 5.
75. Trilochan Singh (1994), p. 351.
76. *Planned Attack*, pp. 217-18.
77. Ibid., pp. 10 and 13-15.
78. Loehlin (1971), pp. 96-103.
79. Dhillon (1991), p. 192.
80. McLeod (1989a), p. 77.
81. Daljeet Singh's review of *The Sikhs*, in the *Punjab Past and Present*, Vol XXIII, part 1, p. 256.
82. McLeod (1989a), pp. 12-13.
83. Daljeet Singh's review of *Who is a Sikh*? in the *Abstracts of Sikh Studies* (July 1992), pp. 137-42.
84. *Abstracts of Sikh Studies* (July 1994), pp. 81-83.
    It is not without interest that when Sodhi spoke from the core of his heart at a conference 'sometimes his emotional outbursts took uncontrollable turn for which he did extend his apologies at the end'. Ibid., pp. 128-29.
85. *Abstracts of Sikh Studies* (October 1995), pp. 81-83.

11. Sikh Scriptures and Textual Criticism

The doctrine of *Guru-Granth* gave a unique importance to the Sikh scripture. The question of its authenticity was settled for the majority of the Sikhs when the Damdami recension was printed in the 1860s for wide circulation. It was believed that this recension was the one that had been canonized by Guru Gobind Singh by adding the *bāṇī* of Guru Tegh Bahadur to the Granth compiled originally by Guru Arjan. In the early twentieth century, when scholarly interest in the contents of Guru Granth Sahib was beginning to emerge, the extreme view was advocated by the Panch Khalsa Diwan of Bhasaur that only Gurbāṇī should be regarded as the Sikh scripture. The most objectionable portion for the Diwan was the *Rāgmālā*. By the 1940s, the Shiromani Gurdwara Prabandhak Committee was inclined to excise the *Rāgmālā* from Guru Granth Sahib. This decision was not implemented because of the report of Bhai Jodh Singh on the basis of a personal examination of the Kartarpuri Bīṛ, which was generally believed to be the original Granth compiled by Guru Arjan, that the *Rāgmālā* formed a part of the Kartarpuri Bīṛ. Bhai Jodh Singh also published a rebuttal of G.B. Singh's book on the old Bīṛs in which, among many other things, he had expressed the view that the Kartarpuri Bīṛ was not authentic. Professor Sahib Singh, who looked upon the Kartarpuri Bīṛ as authentic, wrote his hypothesis about how the Kartarpuri Bīṛ was compiled. Two Western scholars, J.C. Archer and C.H. Loehlin, doubted the authenticity of the Kartarpuri Bīṛ and favoured the idea of detailed textual studies. With this background, Bhai Jodh Singh published his *Kartarpuri Bīṛ de Darshan* to place the authenticity of the Kartarpuri Bīṛ beyond any doubt. Expression of doubt about its authenticity, which was equated with the authenticity of

Guru Granth Sahib, was seen by Bhai Jodh Singh and some other Sikh scholars as an act hostile to the Sikh tradition. W.H. McLeod's essay on the Sikh scriptures appeared in this context.

I

Justice Gurdev Singh attributed the following proposition to W.H. McLeod: 'The authenticity of the current version of *Guru Granth Sahib* which is widely accepted and used by the Sikhs, is open to question since there are three manuscripts (Birs) available which are not entirely identical'.[1] Nothing more is said about this subject in the *Perspectives on the Sikh Tradition*. But this proposition could not be ignored for long because of the serious implication of the point it raised. In the *Advanced Studies in Sikhism,* Daljeet Singh argues in favour of the authenticity of the *Granth Sahib* in the possessioṉ of the Sodhis of Kartarpur which is believed to be the original Granth compiled by Guru Arjan.[2] He criticizes McLeod in this article.

In his *Evolution of the Sikh Community*, McLeod has given the maximum space to the *Ādi Granth*, not because it is controversial but because it is by far the most important of the Sikh scriptures. He refers to the traditional explanation of why Guru Arjan decided to compile the Granth. His enemies, notably the followers of Prithi Chand or the Miṇas, were circulating spurious works bearing the name of Nanak in order to seduce the Sikhs from their loyalty to the legitimate succession and, to combat this threat, Guru Arjan decided to prepare an authorized text bearing his imprimature. His principal source was a collection traditionally attributed to Guru Amar Das. It consisted of two volumes, generally known as the Goindval Pothīs, containing the works of the first three Gurus and several Bhagats. 'The Goindval volumes can thus be regarded as a first recension of the *Ādi Granth* and Guru Arjan's collection as an enlarged second recension'. The works of Guru Ram Das and Guru Arjan himself, with a small number by contemporary Bhagats, were added to the nucleus provided by the Goindval Pothīs. The manuscript was written by Bhai Gurdas.[3]

The history of the manuscript, according to McLeod, is surrounded by a 'considerable mystery'. It is believed to be in the possession of the Sodhis of Kartarpur and there is 'sound reason for accepting this claim'. It is said that the manuscript was stolen by Dhir Mal, the grandson of Guru Hargobind, from the house of his grandfather to buttress his own claim to succession as the Guru. Some thirty years later it was recovered by some followers of Guru Tegh Bahadur who instructed them to return it. They placed it in the river Satlej and Dhir Mal recovered it from there. Guru Gobind Singh asked for it to prepare a new recension but his request was refused and he dictated a copy from memory. After this point, the tradition is silent, carrying the implication that it remained in the possession of the successors of Dhir Mal at Kartarpur. In 1849, the manuscript was found in the custody of the Lahore court. On an application from Sodhi Sadhu Singh of Kartarpur the volume was restored to him in 1850. A copy of the manuscript was presented to Queen Victoria and it is now in the British Library (India Office Library, MSS Panj. E2).[4]

Before the rise of the Singh Sabha Movement in the late nineteenth century, the possession of the original manuscript, though highly prized, was not an issue of prime importance. The *Ādi Granth* was not yet accorded an exclusive authority and the needs of the community were adequately served by the numerous copies which were in circulation. The arrival of the printing press, coupled with the Singh Sabha insistence to give absolute authority to the *Ādi Granth*, changed the situation. Copies of the complete volume, with a standard text and pagination, were made available in print. However, the quest for a definitive authorized version continued. 'The final decision has been continually postponed by minor textual issues and by conflicting claims relating to the authenticity of the *Rag-mala* (the brief work which concluded the collection)'. The Shiromani Gurdwara Prabandhak Committee prepared blocks for printing in 1953, but the completion of the work was postponed due to a dispute 'concerning the correct order of invocation and *rag* title'. A decision was reached in 1962, but the actual printing of the approved version was still pending at the time of McLeod's essay on the Sikh scriptures. The veneration in which the Sikhs hold their scripture explains this cautious hesitation on the part of their highest religious authority.[5]

The affectionate reverence of the Sikhs for the *Ādi Granth* is due to the fact that for them it is the Guru. 'The same spirit which successively inhabited the bodies of ten men is now believed to dwell in this particular Book'. The deep reverence of the Sikhs for the *Guru Granth Sahib* should not be interpreted as worship. The scriptural Guru is not worshipped, just as the human Gurus had not been worshipped by their followers. However, all aspects of Sikh worship relate directly to the *Guru Granth Sahib* and practically 'the entire content of all worship is drawn from it'. The prominence accorded to it in regular *gurdwara* worship is extended to all other Sikh ceremonies.'The centrality of the *Guru Granth Sahib* in Sikh custom, and the manifold uses to which it is put, leave no room for doubt concerning its enormous importance to the Panth'. Its customary usage is of fundamental importance for maintaining the Panth's cohesion.[6]

The language of the *Ādi Granth* is not 'unusally difficult' (as Macauliffe would like us to believe). There is diversity in the language but it is not pronounced. There are words from Sindhi, Marathi, Persian and Arabic, but these provide no more than vocabulary problems. 'They do not affect the essentially homogeneous structure of the *Adi Granth* language'. The basic requirement is a knowledge of Punjabi and Hindi. With this basic requirement a scholar can manage to understand Sadhukari or Sant Bhasha which was employed by religious poets all over northern India during the fifteenth and sixteenth centuries. Guru Nanak's language normally has a strong Punjabi colouring, though in a few cases he drew heavily from the vocabulary of a different language. Guru Angad and Guru Ram Das are also predominantly Punjabi. Guru Amar Das shows more signs of Braj influence which becomes more pronounced in Guru Arjan. The script of the *Ādi Granth* is Gurmukhi which is exceedingly simple, 'even simpler than the Deva-nagri script to which it is closely related'.[7]

An unusually systematic arrangement of its contents is a distinctive feature of the *Ādi Granth*. We find in it a complex and generally consistent pattern of division and sub-division. It opens with the *Japjī* of Guru Nanak which is regarded as the quintessence of the *Ādi Granth* and, together with liturgical selections, serves as the introductory section. The miscellaneous works which could not be accommodated in the main text are looked upon as 'the epilogue'. It consists of collections of *shaloks* or couplets attributed to Kabir and Shaikh Farid, panegyrics in praise of the Gurus, and 'the puzzling' *Rāgmālā* at the end. In the main text, the *rāgs* provide the primary subdivision. Beginning with *Srī Rāg* and concluding with *Jaijavantī*, there are thirty-nine *rāgs*. Each *rāg* is subdivided into several categories. First come the *chaupadās* or four brief stanzas with refrain; then the *ashtpadīs* or eight stanzas with refrain, and then the *chhant*. The longer works of the Gurus in the appropriate metre come next, followed by *vārs* in *pauṛīs* with attached *shaloks*. The *pauṛīs* or stanzas of a particular *vār* are always the work of a single Guru, but the *shaloks* prefixed to the stanzas in small clusters may be by different authors. At the conclusion of each *rāg* are the compositions of various Bhagats, led by Kabir and followed by Namdev and Ravidas. Two Sūfīs are included: Shaikh Farid with four hymns (in addition to 117 *shaloks* in the epilogue) and Bhikhan with two hymns. A single hymn is attributed to Ramanand. Within the *chaupadās, ashtpadīs* and *chhants*, the subdivision corresponds to the succession of Gurus, starting with Guru Nanak. The authorship is indicated by the use of figures with *mahala*, like Mahala 1 for Guru Nanak, Mahala 2 for Guru Angad, and so on. Every *rāg* does not contain all the categories of subdivisions, but all subdivisions have the same order in each *rāg*. Very few exceptions to this rule can be found.[8]

The scripture next in importance to the *Ādi Granth* is the *Dasam Granth*. Its compilation is attributed to Bhai Mani Singh who died in the 1730s. McLeod notes its contents and goes into the theories of its authorship, attributing the whole of the *Dasam Granth* to Guru Gobind Singh as one extreme and only the *Zafarnāma* as the other. McLeod was inclined at one time to accept both the *Bachittar Nātak* and the *Zafarnāma* as authentic, but now he does not feel sure about the former. To the latter, he is inclined to add compositions like the *Jāp*, the *Akāl Ustat*, the *Giān Prabodh*, the

Shabad Hazāre, the *Savaiyye*, and the *Chandī kī Vār*. All these works put together constitute less than a quarter of the entire *Granth*. Its bulk, therefore, was composed by others. McLeod does not rule out the possibility that some of these works reflect the ideas and attitudes of Guru Gobind Singh. What is far more important, during the eighteenth century the *Dasam Granth* was given as much respect as the *Ādi Granth*: 'It too was regarded as the visibly present Guru and thus received the same veneration'.[9]

McLeod looks upon the works of Bhai Gurdas and Bhai Nand Lal as 'supplementary' to the scriptures because they are approved for recitation in Gurdwaras. The *Janamsākhīs* for him are 'semi-canonical', because they are commonly read in the precincts of Gurdwaras. 'The world is poorer', says McLeod, 'for its ignorance of the Sikh scriptures'.[10] That McLeod has shown interest in the whole range of Sikh literature is evident from a book he published in 1984 which is not confined to the *Ādi Granth*, the *Dasam Granth*, the works of Bhai Gurdas, the works of Bhai Nand Lal, and the *Janamsākhīs*. It includes the *Rahitnāmas*, the *Gurbilās* tradition and historical works, the literature produced by the Nirankārīs and the Nāmdhārīs, and the literature produced by Sikh writers in support of and under the influence of the Singh Sabha Movement. From this wide range of literature, he has selected extracts for translation into English, which are arranged in such a manner that they supply information on all aspects of Sikh history and Sikh religion. Here we have Sikh tradition as cherished by the Sikhs themselves, with only brief comments by McLeod to illumine the texts.[11]

McLeod's keenness to take the Sikh tradition to the English reader is reflected also in his English translation of the *B40 Janamsākhī* published in 1981. His sole purpose was to present a well annotated translation without any comment on its value, or lack of value, for the life of Guru Nanak. There is only one comment about its significance. Since the copy was prepared in 1733 for the use of a Sikh *sangat*, McLeod's comment relates to the continued existence of non-Khalsa *sangats* in the eighteenth century. To quote: 'These brief descriptions of the janamsakhis' origins and intentions are of a particular interest in that they so plainly refer to a non-

Khalsa sangat at a point in time when according to tradition Sikh orthodoxy had assumed the form and discipline of the Khalsa, and the Khalsa was itself undergoing a period of intense if intermittent persecution'.[12]

McLeod has published not only the English translation but also the text of a well-known *Rahitnāma*. Selected portions of important *Rahitnāmas* were included by Bhai Kanh Singh in his *Gurmat Sudhākar* in 1901. Piara Singh Padam has discussed this genre briefly in his introduction to his *Rahitnāme* published in 1974. Apart from McLeod's own introductory remarks in the *Textual Sources* and an article published elsewhere, there is no study of this material. There are no annotated texts either. McLeods's is the first one. Based on four manuscripts, it is the earliest *Rahitnāma* known to have come down from the eighteenth century itself. The text of a Nand Lal *Rahitnāma* is also included in this work. McLeod has expressed his views on the significance of its contents in a long introduction and in annotations of the text and its translation. Like the *B40 Janamsākhī*, the *Chaupa Singh Rahit-Nama* is a scholarly work adding much to our understanding of the Sikh community during the eighteenth century.[13]

We may now turn to McLeod's presentation of the problem for which he has been criticized. Though there can be 'few scriptures which possess a structure as consistent as that of the *Adi Granth*', it is by no means free from problems. There is not one single version but rather three different versions plus a number of variants. The variants are disregarded by McLeod but not the three versions. The first is the one known as the Kartarpur version, the Bhai Gurdas version, or the *Ādi Bīṛ*. It was dictated by Guru Arjan and written by Bhai Gurdas, and it was believed to be in the possession of the descendants of Dhir Mal at Kartarpur. One particular feature of this version is that in some places the original text has been obliterated by the application of green ink (*haṛtāl*). The second version is referred to as Banno or Bhai Banno version, the Mangat version, or the *Khāri Bīṛ* (literally, brackish or bitter but by implication 'spurious' or 'apocryphal'). It is believed to be a copy of the original Granth or the *Ādi Bīṛ* prepared by Guru Arjan. The third version is the one dictated by Guru Gobind Singh from memory, in which one couplet of his own and fifty-nine hymns and fifty-six couplets of his father, Guru Tegh Bahadur, were added to the original text. Since this version is believed to have been dictated at Damdama Sahib, it is known as the Damdama version. This version corresponds closely to the Kartarpur version, and the printed *Ādi Granth* follows the Damdama version. In other words, the printed Granth Sahib follows the Kartarpur version in its original text.[14]

The problem appears to arise from a comparison of the Kartarpur and Banno versions. The version which remained in greater currency until well into the eighteenth century was the Banno version and not the Kartarpur version. The Banno version contains some extra material which is absent from the Damdama version and which is believed to be absent from the Kartarpur version too. If the Banno version is a copy of the original, and the Kartarpur version is the original, then this extra material should have been there in the Kartarpur version too. This is where obliterations in the Kartarpur version become relevant.[15]

The most important instances of the extra material cited by McLeod are a hymn by Mira Bai, another by Sur Das, and the third by Guru Arjan. The standard printed edition contains two fragments which correspond to two of the three additional Banno hymns: a single couplet in *Rāg Rāmkalī*, and a single line in *Rāg Sārang*. McLeod draws the inference that the bulk of these two hymns must have been deleted, leaving a small remainder in each case. The *Rāmkalī* hymn by Guru Arjan in the Banno version describes the puberty rites conducted at the initiation of his son Hargobind, involving the shaving of his head. This obviously goes against the later prohibition of hair-cutting. There was a good reason for its deletion. An earlier scholar had suggested that the Kartarpur manuscript was a Banno version, and the original was lost. McLeod too was inclined to conclude that the Banno version was the original text and the Kartarpur manuscript was its shortened version. A few portions were deleted 'because they could not be reconciled with beliefs subsequently accepted by the Panth'. McLeod does not say so but the implication of his argument is clear: the Kartarpur manuscript is not the original Granth prepared by Guru Arjan. The Damdama version could be prepared by omitting the problem passages and by adding the works of Guru Tegh Bahadur. Indeed, the problem passages were 'rather ineptly obliterated' in the Kartarpur manuscript 'to bring the two versions into line'.[16]

That was McLeod's reasoning before Bhai Jodh Singh's *Srī Kartārpurī Bīṛ de Darshan* appeared in 1968. It is not clear, however, why McLeod refers to this reasoning. The Mira Bai hymn, according to Bhai Jodh Singh, is there in the original manuscript. The hymn of Sur Das in *Rāg Sārang*, however, is represented in the original manuscript by a single line, followed by blank space of four lines. Similarly, there is no obliteration in the case of Guru Arjan's *Rāmkalī* hymn: there is only a couplet followed by blank space. This couplet is in the same hand but written with a different pen. In other words, the Damdama version corresponds with the Kartarpur version in two out of the three instances of extra material. McLeod himself says that the hymn of Mira Bai involves an interesting textual problem which is of 'no great importance'. What is important for him is whether or not the *Rāmkalī* hymn was composed by Guru Arjan. If it was, 'the relationship of the later Khalsa discipline to the earlier teachings of the Gurus could be made dramatically clearer'. But a firm conclusion cannot be drawn from the evidence before him.[17]

II

Daljeet Singh refers to 'some oblique but incorrect observations' of McLeod which tend to throw doubt on the authenticity of the Kartarpur manuscript as the original Granth prepared by Guru Arjan. He wonders why without examining the Banno Bīṛ or reading what others have written about it on the basis of personal inspection, and even after reading what Bhai Jodh Singh has written about the Kartarpur manuscript, McLeod has suggested that the Kartarpur manuscript is a copy of the Banno version. This may be due to 'sheer ignorance', or McLeod's anxiety 'to suppress known but awkward facts', or his 'conscious or unconscious bias because of his thirteen years of working and association with a Christian Mission in Punjab'. 'It is now well established that the Banno Bir was prepared not earlier than 1699 (of Bikarmi Sammat) and the

Banno story is a myth. As such, the very basis of the argument about the Kartarpur Bir being a copy of the Banno Bir is knocked out'. Furthermore, Bhai Jodh Singh has observed that the *Rāmkalī* hymn attributed to Guru Arjan was never recorded in the Kartarpur Bīṛ. Therefore the question of its deletion does not arise. Even in the Banno version it is an interpolation in a different shade of ink and in smaller letters. The whole explanation of its deletion after the creation of the Khalsa becomes irrelevant and redundant. Moreover, there are manuscripts of 1675 and 1682, examined by Principal Harbhajan Singh, which do not have the additional hymns of the Banno version.[18]

Daljeet Singh makes some other points in response to McLeod, but without making an explicit reference to him. The primary reason for compiling the Granth was to establish 'the spiritual and ideological identity of the Sikh Religion and Panth'. To obviate the currency of hymns attributed to the Gurus by outsiders was only an additional reason. The Granth compiled by Guru Arjan remained in the custody of Dhir Mal and his descendants at Kartarpur, except when it was kept at the court of Ranjit Singh and his successors as 'a national treasure'. Daljeet Singh does not refer to the sources of Guru Arjan but he mentions the process of compilation. To account for certain incongruities in the Kartarpur Bīṛ he states that 'the work of collection of Bani of the first four Gurus and the Bhagats' was going on at the same time as the *bāṇī* was being recorded in the Granth. Daljeet Singh adds that 'a faultlessly accurate version' of the Guru Granth copied from the Kartarpur Bīṛ was approved and printed by the Punjabi Press, Hall Bazar, Amritsar.[19]

Daljeet Singh's primary purpose in his essay was to establish that the Kartarpur manuscript is the original Granth prepared by Guru Arjan. That is why he thinks it relevant to emphasize that the claim of being the original Granth was never made for any other recension. His main argument, however, is based on internal evidence. This evidence is seen as consisting of two categories: features which are individually conclusive, and features which are conclusive when coupled with other evidence. In the first category, Daljeet Singh presents eight features of the Kartarpur recension as conclusive proofs of its 'originality'. It is the only recension which has the *Japu* recorded from the one in the hand of Guru Ram Das. All other known recensions mention that their *Japu* was a copy of a copy. Or, the words 'Japu Nisan' are recorded. The second important feature of the Kartarpur Bīṛ is the date of the demise of Guru Arjan: it is in the hand of the original scribe but with a pen and shade of ink different from the one used for the dates of demise of the first four Gurus. Moreover, the day is also mentioned in the case of Guru Arjan. In Daljeet Singh's view, this entry was made by Bhai Gurdas later. Equally conclusive are the words '*sudh*' and '*sudh keeche*': these are in the hand of Guru Arjan because the writing resembles that of the *mūlmantar* inscribed by him as his *nishān*. The date of its completion is given as 'Sammat 1661 *miti* Bhadon *vadi ekam* 1 *pothi likh pauhnche*'. It is supported by the date of completion mentioned in historical writings and the Sikh tradition. The unused space of 586 pages out of a total of 1948 pages in the Kartarpur recension could never occur in a copy. Similarly, duplication of *shabads* could occur only in the original compilation. Rectification of inadvertent incongruities, which are pointed out by Daljeet Singh, point in the same direction: no other Bīṛ has a particular set of incongruities in the text and the corresponding portions of the table of contents (*tatkarā*). Finally, a large number of 'corrected mistakes' could also occur only in the original compilation.[20]

Then there are some 'other important factors' which leave no doubt that 'the Kartarpur Bir is the original *Adi Granth* compiled by the Fifth Guru in A.D. 1604'. The *nishān* of Guru Arjan on a profusely decorated page as a mark of adoration and its mention in the *tatkarā*; the words 'the *shabad* is right' in the margin of a page; two additional *shabads* of Guru Arjan and his *Basant kī Vār* included after Bhadon A.D. 1604; the *nishān* of Guru Hargobind who was associated with the collection of the *bāṇī* and the preparation of the scripture, and who presumably added *dhunīs* of some *Vārs* at a later date– all these important factors go to prove that the Kartarpur Bīṛ is not a copy but the Granth compiled by Guru Arjan.[21]

III

Professor Piar Singh does not accept Daljeet Singh's views. His disagreement is fundamental, though rather incidental. Piar Singh did not write his book to refute any hypothesis. If anything he is more critical of McLeod than of Daljeet Singh. In fact he expected his book to serve the interests of the Panth but, ironically, it has given serious offence to its articulate representatives.

We may set aside the formal structure of Piar Singh's book and concentrate on the basic hypothesis that appears to emerge from it. He accepts the tradition that the recension prepared by Guru Arjan and the recension prepared by Guru Gobind Singh were lost. Fortunately, however, copies of both these recensions had come into currency before the loss. Therefore, Piar Singh is in search of the authentic *Ādi Granth.* For this purpose he has analysed a large number of manuscripts coming down from the sixteenth and seventeenth centuries, paying special attention to features like the *mūlmantars*, entries of the dates of death (*chalittar*), the presence or absence of stray numerals (*latakde ank*), whether or not the source of *Japji* is the one written by Guru Ram Das, the presence or absence of additional but genuine compositions (*vādhū shabad*), and the presence or absence of extraneous compositions (*fāltū bāṇiān*).

In Piar Singh's view, there is not one but four or five hands in the Kartarpur recension, and none of these resembles the handwriting in the *gutkā* in the possession of the Sodhis of Kartarpur which is said to be in the hand of Bhai Gurdas. The style of writing and the way in which letters are written appear to have advanced over the known early manuscripts. A large number of blank pages are found in several other manuscripts which are avowedly copies. Therefore, blank pages cannot be regarded as a peculiarity of the Kartarpur recension. Blank space left for a composition of Guru Arjan himself is also very significant.This appears to go against one of Daljeet Singh's arguments in support of the originality of the recension. Piar Singh sees a more intriguing situation in the tables of contents. There are three tables in the recension: *tatkarā rāgān kā*, *tatkarā tatkare kā,* and *tatkarā shabdān kā.* As Bhai

Jodh Singh has noticed, these tables are in a different hand from those of the text. The *shabads* in the text do not correspond to the *tatkarā shabdān kā* in every case. This disjunction is of three kinds: ten *shabads* do not figure in the *tatkarā*; eight lines of *shabads* in the *tatkarā* have a variant reading in the text; and a few *shabads* are shown in the *tatkara* at places different from their actual places in the text. Piar Singh draws the conclusion that the tables of contents were taken from another recension and added to the Kartarpur manuscript. The recension from which these tables were taken contained a smaller number of *shabads* and variant readings. In the *tatkarā shabdān kā*, the entire Bhagat *bāṇī* is indicated with a single entry '*bāṇī bhagtān kī*'. The *shabads* of the Gurus are indicated with their opening lines but the *shabads* of the Bhagats are not. If the tables of contents were taken from a different source, the date of completion given on the *tatkarā* also loses its relevance for dating the Kartarpur recension. This date has been used by Daljeet Singh as an argument in favour of the originality of this recension.[22]

Even more serious is Piar Singh's view of the *nishān* of Guru Arjan which is yet another argument in Daljeet Singh's reasoning. If this *mūlmantar* was an integral part of the manuscript, there was no need to repeat it in the *Japu*. Actually, however, the *Japu* in this recension has its own *mūlmantar*. Piar Singh is inclined to think that the decorated page carrying the *nishān* of Guru Arjan has been pasted on a page of the Kartarpur recension. Furthermore, on folio 540 there is another *nishān*, that of Guru Hargobind, which is believed to be another proof of the recension being the original Granth. Piar Singh finds it rather odd that this *nishān* is mentioned in the 'table of contents' too. If the Granth was completed in 1604, it does not appeal to reason that the *nishān* of Guru Hargobind should be there. Piar Singh suggests that the date of the completion of this recension was later than the time of Guru Arjan.

According to Bhai Kanh Singh Nabha, the *Rāgmālā* was accompanied by several other entries, including the '*ratanmālā*' and the '*rāh mukām*'. It is interesting to note that in the *tatkarā rāgān kā*, the entry is '*rāgmālā tathā singhaldip kī sibnābh rāje kī bidh*' Moreover, the last five words are in a vertical line in continuation of the entry started in a horizontal line. This entry appears to refer to some compositions in addition to the *Rāgmālā*. Bhai Randhir Singh thinks that all the 'extraneous compositions' were there in the manuscript at one time, but they were all removed later except the *Rāgmālā*.[23]

The significance of a large number of deletions in the Kartarpur manuscript is different for Piar Singh than for Daljeet Singh who looks upon deletions as a proof of the originality of this recension. There are deletions because of repetition, but this is not true of all deletions. Kabir's *shalok 'dhar ambar vich velaṛī'* in *Rāg Gauṛī* is deleted. Guru Arjan's *Chaupadā* in *Rāg Āsā*, starting with '*har jan līney prabh chhudāey*', stands deleted. More significantly, it stands deleted in the *tatkarā* too. Piar Singh's inference is that this *Chaupadā* was there in the manuscript from which Kartarpur manuscript was copied. Variant readings worry Piar Singh even more than deletions or additions. Bhai Manna Singh noticed about two hundred variant readings in the Kartarpur recension when compared with the printed Granth Sahib. Sant Gurbachan Singh Khalsa has stated that there are about fifteen hundred variants of this kind. Piar Singh has classified these variants into six categories and looks upon the readings in the Kartarpur recension as incorrect (*ashudh*). He has no hesitation in saying that this recension is not the ideal original with which to correct other recensions. Piar Singh feels convinced that a manuscript written by Bhai Gurdas could not have so many mistakes.[24]

The Kartarpur recension contains stray numerals (*latakde ank*) in *Rāg Gauṛī* and *Rāg Āsā*. These were meant originally to indicate *juz* numbers for the copyist so as to ensure that nothing was left out. In the Kartarpur recension these numbers should actually have been superfluous. If Bhai Gurdas was really the scribe of this manuscript, he could not have left these numbers there. The use of the *mūlmantar* and *mangals* in the Kartarpur manuscript does not conform to what we find in the printed *Granth Sahib*. In some sections of the manuscript there are no *mangals*. In some cases the *sirlekh* or heading precedes the *mangals*. The words '*sudh*' and '*sudh kīchey*' at the end of the *Vārs*, supposed to be the instructions given by Guru Arjan to Bhai Gurdas, are not there in four Rāgs: *Jaitsrī*, *Sūhī*,

Mārū and *Basant*. The survival of several 'old' elements in the Kartarpur recension suggests to Piar Singh that the compiler was making use of some older collections or compilations. This can be seen by disregarding the later changes made in the manuscript. Use of *chhakka* for enumeration at a few places, the presence of undifferentiated *shabads* in some Rāgs, the use of the letter *ūṛā* without the *aunkaṛ*, and the presence of words coming from the oral tradition – all these features point to the manuscript being a copy. Furthermore, some of the errors of the original sources are retained in the manuscript. For instance, the use of '*dakhnī*' with Onkar, of Tall instead of Kall for the Bhatt author, the presence of additional compositions at wrong places, and the presence of unauthentic *bāṇī*.[25]

Piar Singh comes to the conclusion that the Kartarpur recension is a compilation independent of the Granth prepared by Guru Arjan. It was completed in the time of Guru Hargobind at the earliest. Far from being the original Granth prepared by Guru Arjan, it is not even a good copy. However, Guru Arjan did prepare the *Ādi Granth* which was written by Bhai Gurdas. Copies were prepared by some other people in due course. In a recension seen by Bhai Randhir Singh at Patna Sahib it is explicitly stated that it was copied in 1692 from a copy made by Fateh Chand which was a copy of a copy made by Puhkar which had been corrected by comparing it with the one got prepared by Guru Arjan in the hand of Bhai Gurdas. The *Rāgmālā* was not a part of that Granth.[26]

Much before the coming of the British, Guruship was bestowed on the *Ādi Granth* by Guru Gobind Singh. During the rest of the eighteenth century, attempts were made to 'correct' existing manuscripts by comparison. Then, with the establishment of Sikh rule, relics of the Gurus began to be rediscovered and venerated. Revenue-free lands were given to the owners of old recensions in the name of the Granth in their possession. In this situation, an earlier date was sought to be given to the recensions of Bhai Banno and Bhai Būṛa Sandhu. The Kartarpur recension was now proclaimed to be the original Granth inscribed by Bhai Gurdas to receive large grants from the Sikh rulers. This recension had been corrected by a comparison with the original Granth sometime during the seventeenth century, and it could now be used to 'correct' other manuscripts.[27]

Piar Singh is quite categorical that his interest in the compilation and canonization of Gurbāṇī sprang from the controversies about the *Rāgmālā*, the *mangals* and the text variants in Gurbāṇī.[28] He reinforces his earlier arguments with facsimiles in his new book. One of these is meant to show that the *nishān* of Guru Arjan was pasted later. Another is meant to show that all the dates of demise were written 'at one go', enabling Piar Singh to draw the inference that this entry was made after the martyrdom of Guru Arjan. The facsimile of the *sūchī-patrā*, which carries the date, is meant to show that it was 'a lifted document'. Another facsimile is given to show that the *mūlmantar* of the first page of the *Japu* is in the hand of the main scribe and not 'in the hand of the Guru'. There are variations in it from the *nishān*. Therefore, the *nishān* was not there before the scribe when he wrote the *mūlmantar*.

The 'Var Ramkali M3' is not free from mistakes and yet it has the word '*sudha*' at its end. The reference to Guru Hargobind as 'Mahalla 6' in the entry for his *nishān* shows that it was made in the time of Guru Hargobind. A hymn of Kabir, included initially in the compilation but deleted later, is 'so patently out of tune' with Sikh ideology that no Sikh Guru would have countenanced its inclusion in a scripture. Apart from numerous additions, deletions and emendations in the Kartarpuri Bīṛ, there are inaccuracies. All this could never be expected to occur in a Granth written by Bhai Gurdas under the supervision of Guru Arjan. Piar Singh reiterates his earlier conclusion that the Kartarpuri Bīṛ is an independent compilation prepared not much earlier than 1642.[29]

Piar Singh makes some other observations to suggest that a new spirit of repression is gaining ground. No less eminent a scholar than Sardar Kapur Singh, the National Professor of Sikhism, had categorically stated that 'the Bir which the Sodhis of Kartarpur have, is a fake one'. No 'motives' could be attributed to Kapur Singh and no 'ghosts of conspiracy' could be seen in his statement. The suggestion that Guru Arjan gave its present form to the *mūlmantar* had been made by Giani Mahan Singh. Significantly, he expressed this view in the journal of the Shiromani Gurdwara Prabandhak Committee, the *Gurmat Prakash* of January 1968. In those days there was 'no inquisitive body' and 'no people with closed mind' in the Sikh community.[30]

Piar Singh argues at some length that all the constituents of the *mūlmantar* of the Goindval Pothīs are there in *Guru Granth Sahib*. Indeed, the epithet *saibhang* occurs only in the *mūlmantar* and not in the *bāṇī* even of Guru Arjan.[31] Futhermore, the 'doctrine of the same spirit', or the unity of Guruship, gave Guru Arjan the authority 'to make a change in the Holy Word'. They who infringe this doctrine are 'themselves guilty of blasphemy'.[32] What is more to the point, the changes made in the *mūlmantar* do not infringe but elucidate the connotation of the original attributes. These changes are of *sachu* into *sati*, *kartar* into *karta purakhu*, *nirikar* into *nirvair* and *sambhau* into *saibhang*.[33] Piar Singh knows that the whole debate about the *mūlmantar* is intimately linked with the idea of the revelatory character of Gurbāṇī. He subscribes to the idea but he believes that revelation came 'in ideas, concepts or truths' and not as 'linguistic units'. Furthermore, transmission of the *bāṇī*, whether written or oral, involved human agency. Consequently, even the early codices contain colloquial formations, corrupted texts, different sequence of verses, and incomplete hymns. The Kartarpuri Bīṛ too bears the imprint of this situation. It is impossible to think that it was prepared from 'the holographs' of Professor Sahib Singh's hypothesis.[34]

IV

The debate about the Sikh scriptures is no longer confined to the Kartarpuri Bīṛ. Pashaura Singh and Gurinder Singh Mann accept its authenticity. But their work is nonetheless being criticized. They work on the assumption that textual questions can be answered by studying the extant manuscripts – an assumption which they share with Piar Singh. They subscribe to the view that canonization of the Sikh scripture came as the culmination of a historical process in which the compilations made before the Kartarpuri Bīṛ had an important role. Two manuscripts in this context have acquired considerable importance: the Goindval Pothīs and MS 1245.

Piar Singh takes notice of the Goindval Pothīs in his *Gāthā Sri Ādi Granth.* Only two of them are now extant: the Ahiyapur Pothī or the Jalandhar Pothī and the Pinjore Pothī. They contain the *bāṇī* of Guru Nanak and Guru Amar Das in over a dozen *rāgs,* together with the *bāṇī* of a few Bhagats. Each *rāg* begins with a *mūlmantar* that differs from the *mūlmantar* of the Kartarpuri Bīṛ. There are hymns in the name of Ghulam and Sada Sewak in which the pen name 'Nanak' is also used. These hymns stand penned through. At one place '*ghulam*' is identified as 'Jeth Chand' which was the name of Guru Ram Das before he became the Guru. A fly leaf in one of the Pothīs carries the date 1595. There are also a few hymns of Guru Ram Das and Guru Arjan in these Pothīs. Piar Singh concludes that their likely date is 1595. He is equally explicit that Guru Arjan made no use of these Pothīs for the Granth he compiled.[35]

Gurtej Singh looks upon 1595 as an attempt at predating the manuscript. He argues that the Goindval Pothīs were compiled probably much later than 1604, the accepted date of the compilation of the Kartarpuri Bīṛ. Guru Arjan could not have used the Goindval Pothīs. For Gurtej Singh, therefore, the *mūlmantar* of the Goindval Pothīs is irrelevant for discussion. Even if we accept 1595 as their date, the *Japu* in the hand of Guru Ram Das remains older than that of the Pothīs. Therefore, the question of modifying the *mūlmantar* by Guru Arjan does not arise. Furthermore, the note on the fly leaf curses those 'who do not recognize the particular line of succession which the author supports'. Gurtej Singh draws the inference that the Goindval Pothīs were the work of 'a schismatic sect'. It is not surprising, therefore, that they contain 'distorted version of Gurbani'.[36]

In a joint paper, Daljeet Singh and Kharak Singh express the view that the earliest possible date of the Goindval Pothīs can be 1595 but probably it was later. The 'curse' on the fly-leaf points toward a frustrated group like that of Mohan and his descendants. Even if the Pothīs were available to Guru Arjan, 'he kept what he considered to be bani and rejected the rest'. Daljeet Singh and

Kharak Singh believe that any composition that is 'variant in form or content' from the Kartarpuri *Bīṛ* is not true *bāṇī*. 'Therefore, a variant manuscript can neither be used, nor have any claim to authenticity for the purpose of the identity of gurbani'. This definition of 'authenticity' takes care of the variant *mūlmantar* of the Goindval Pothīs. Daljeet Singh and Kharak Singh believe that 'textual analysis' is an 'oblique route' to attack the authenticity of the *Ādi Granth* 'under the guise of western scholarship'.[37]

Gurinder Singh Mann has studied the Goindval Pothīs more thoroughly than any other scholar. His book contains the opening and the concluding verses of all the hymns. He also gives the complete text of the non-canonical compositions, thirty-six in all, which do not figure in the Kartarpuri Bīṛ.

Mann points out that the Goindval Pothīs attracted the attention of Sikh writers because of their connection with the *Ādi Granth*. The earliest reference to this comes from Sarup Das Bhalla's *Mahimā Prakāsh* (1776). This basic account was repeated or amplified in some other Sikh works of the eighteenth and the early nineteenth century. This tradition was accepted by scholars like Bhai Kanh Singh Nabha, Bhai Vir Singh, Bhai Jodh Singh, Teja Singh, Piara Singh Padam, and Giani Gurdit Singh.[38]

The first Sikh writer to marginalize the Goindval Pothīs for the compilation of the *Ādi Granth* was Giani Gian Singh. In his *Tawārīkh Gurū Khalsa* (1891), he put forth the view that Guru Arjan collected his materials from a variety of sources, both written and oral, including the Goindval Pothīs. Even after seeing two Pothīs at Patiala, he did not change his view. The Pothīs were made redundant by Sahib Singh who put forth the view that Guru Nanak had prepared a *pothī* of his hymns and left it for his successor, Guru Angad. This lead was followed by Guru Angad, Guru Amar Das and Guru Ram Das, each of whom added a *pothī* of his own hymns for his successor.

The major flaw in Sahib Singh's hypothesis, according to Mann, is the non-existence of the *pothīs* postulated by him, and the absence of any reference to them in Sikh literature. In fact, the actual handling of manuscripts started only with Gurbakhsh Singh's *Sri Guru Granth Sahib diān Prachīn Bīṛān* (1944). A year later, Bawa Prem Singh examined two Goindval Pothīs and his description remained the primary source for scholars till the publication of Giani Gurdit Singh's *Itihas Sri Guru Granth Sahib* in 1990. The Goindval Pothīs are discussed by him in the last section on the basis of their actual examination.[39]

In Mann's view the Jalandhar and the Pinjore Pothīs are only two of the originally four Pothīs prepared by Guru Amar Das. The two Pothīs seen by Giani Gian Singh at Patiala are described by him. Therefore, it is possible to know that one of them was identical with the Pinjore Pothī and that the other was not the same as the Jalandhar Pothī. It is reasonable, therefore, to conclude that there was a third Pothī. If we take into account the volume of matter in each of these three Pothīs in terms of *rāg* sections and compare it with what we have in the Kartarpur Pothī, or in the *Ādi Granth*, we are left with matter just sufficient to make one more Pothī of Rāgs *Gujrī*, *Tukhārī*, *Mājh* and *Bilāval* – the *rāgs* missing from the three Goindval Pothīs.[40]

Mann gives a facsimile of the statement recorded in the Jalandhar Pothī, bearing the date Māgh vadī 1, Sammat 1652 (A.D. 1595). This statement starts on folio 1 but it is completed on folio 9, the first blank space available after the blank space on folio 1. It is in the hand of the primary scribe who could be alive in 1595. The thrust of the statement is that Guruship stands vested in the family of Guru Amar Das. Indeed, anyone turning away from them 'will surely go to hell'. Mann concludes that this statement was added to the Pothīs in 1595 in the context of the Bhalla-Sodhi competition in order to reinforce the claims of the Bhallas. A hymn attributed to Guru Ram Das in the Kartarpur Pothī and the *Ādi Granth* is attributed to Guru Nanak in the Jalandhar Pothī. Since Sikh scholars have pointed out a few other instances of variation in attribution, this hymn could very well be a hymn of Guru Nanak. A hymn attributed to Guru Arjan in the Kartarpur Pothī and the *Ādi Granth* does not bear any authorship in the Jalandhar Pothī. It is not in the hand of the primary scribe. Mann looks upon it as a later addition to the Pothī. These two hymns do not oblige him to discard the view that the Goindval Pothīs were compiled in the lifetime of Guru Amar Das.[41]

More problematic than these two hymns are the fourteen compositions recorded in the extant Goindval Pothīs under the name of '*gulām sadāsevak*' or simply '*gulām*', who uses the signature 'Nanak' too in the last verse of every composition. On folio 94 of the Pinjore Pothī, the identity of '*gulām*' appears to be revealed by '*gulām mast taidā* Jeth Chand'. Now, Jeth Chand was the original name of Guru Ram Das. Mann suggests that when Guru Amar Das decided to make Jeth Chand his successor he possibly allowed him to use the signature 'Nanak' in his compositions. Sikh scholars like Giani Badan Singh, Teja Singh and Sahib Singh are not averse to the idea that some hymns of the *Ādi Granth* were composed by their authors prior to taking up Guruship.[42]

Mann gives very useful information about the 'internal structure' of the Goindval Pothīs which has a bearing on some arguments used by scholars for or against the authenticity of the Kartarpur Pothī. Almost the entire matter was available to the scribe from the very beginning. Classification into *rāgs* was the basic principle of organization, each *rāg* starting with the hymns of Guru Nanak, followed by the hymns of Guru Angad and Guru Amar Das, followed by the compositions of the non-Sikh saints. The tune (*dhunī*) in which a particular *rāg* was to be sung is also indicated at places. Mann has no doubts that the Goindval Pothīs were used by Guru Arjan for preparing the Kartarpur Pothī. A *rāg*-wise comparison of hymns reveals that the extant Goindval Pothīs contain only three hymns more and five hymns less than the Kartarpur Pothī. The hymns of the non-Sikh saints too are closely reproduced in the Kartarpur Pothī, omitting only three hymns in the hand of the primary scribe of the Goindval Pothīs.The organizational pattern of the Goindwal Pothīs is not discarded in the Kartarpur Pothī. It is elaborated further. The difference in the sequence of hymns is only slight and it was partly due to their transference from one *rāg* section to another. A music-related classification, *ghar* (literally 'home'), is added in the Kartarpur Pothī.[43]

Piar Singh, Pashaura Singh and Gurinder Singh Mann accept MS 1245 as a genuine manuscript completed between the Goindval Pothīs and the Kartarpuri Bīṛ. However, since Piar Singh places the completion of the Kartarpuri Bīṛ around 1640, MS 1245 for him is later than the Granth prepared by Guru Arjan. This manuscript, nevertheless, has its own value as an independent compilation. Both Pashaura Singh and Gurinder Singh Mann place the completion of MS 1245 around 1600 under the supervision of Guru Arjan. However, whereas Pashaura Singh looks upon it as a draft for preparing the canon embodied in the Kartarpuri Bīṛ, Mann suggests that it was meant to be canonical. Later on, however, Guru Arjan decided to replace it by the Kartarpuri Bīṛ. There is much scope for argumentation and informed conjecture because the manuscript has no known history and it bears no date. All arguments for and against its authenticity are based on internal evidence which can be interpreted in widely different ways.

Balwant Singh Dhillon points out the differences between MS 1245 and the Kartarpuri Bīṛ to suggest that the former is an incorrect and incomplete manuscript. Its orthography does not necessarily point to a time earlier than that of the Kartarpuri Bīṛ. A major portion of the apocrypha in this manuscript is ascribed to Guru Arjan, which suggests the hand of his rivals. More crucial are the dates of demise of all the first five Gurus as a single entry, implying a date of its compilation later than the martyrdom of Guru Arjan. The *nishān* of Guru Tegh Bahadur in MS 1245 is a further proof that 'it is a late 17th century product'.[44] Kharak Singh repeats some of these arguments and feels offended that a *shalok* with 'Nanak' as the pen-name is sought to be attributed to Bhai Buddha. He looks upon the *Japu* of MS 1245 as of Miṇa origin and suggests that this manuscript was 'planted' in Guru Nanak Dev University in 1987 'perhaps with ulterior motives'.[45]

Pashaura Singh points out that what is attributed to Bhai Buddha is the scribing of a hymn of Guru Amar Das. He argues that the *nishān* of Guru Tegh Bahadur in MS 1245 was pasted later and, therefore, it cannot be linked with the date of compilation. What it proves is that the owner of this manuscript belonged to 'the mainline Sikh tradition'. An extra-canonical hymn attributed to Guru Arjan in MS 1245 refers to the Miṇas instigating Sulhi Khan against Guru Arjan. This too proves that the Miṇas could not have been the compilers.[46] Piar Singh states that he has compared the *Japu* of MS 1245 with that of Miharban 'very carefully' and asserts that its text conforms more to the *Japu* of *Guru Granth Sahib* than that of Miharban. The *mūlmantar* in MS 1245 ends on *saibhang* while the *mūlmantar* in the Miharban *Janamsākhī* ends on *sambhau*. In Piar Singh's view, repetitions, apocrypha and text-variants are 'but a normal feature of any original compilation'.[47]

Gurinder Singh Mann has paid special attention to the textual relationship of MS 1245 with the Goindwal Pothīs on the one hand and with the Kartarpuri Bīṛ on the other. After a detailed argument he suggests that MS 1245 was compiled before the Kartarpuri Bīṛ. On the basis of his analysis Mann suggests that the manuscript was completed in or around 1600. Furthermore, it seems likely that the Goindval Pothīs were used for this manuscript which in turn was used for the Kartarpuri Bīṛ. This explains why there is no direct agreement between the Goindval Pothīs and the Kartarpuri Bīṛ. The variations which entered MS1245 in copying the Goindval Pothīs appear in the Kartarpuri Bīṛ too. About the absence of Bhagat Bāṇī, Mann suggests that around 1600 Guru Arjan was thinking of excluding it from the Sikh scripture. Eventually, however, he decided to conform to the tradition set by his predecessors. A new *pothī*, the Kartarpuri Bīṛ, was the result of this change.[48]

There is a long distance from J.C. Archer, who advocated textual criticism, to Gurinder Singh Mann, who has pursued textual criticism on a considerable scale. It must be emphasized, however, that this development is not due only to the extension of Western interest to the study of the Sikh scripture. From the beginning of the present century there has been an undercurrent of Sikh interest in the 'authentic' text of *Guru Granth Sahib*. The current debate in which the Kartarpuri Bīṛ, MS1245 and the Goindval Pothīs figure so prominently becomes a kind of confluence of the Western and Sikh streams of interest. Much has been written but the debate is going on.

For a scholar who has not specialized in textual studies, the controversy remains unresolved. However, a few things are clear. Whatever the errors of the critical scholars and the limitations of their approach, their attitude towards the problem is scholarly. It is equally clear that textual criticism does not have the same kind of importance in Sikh studies as in Biblical studies. Furthermore, irrespective of the authenticity of the Kartarpuri Bīṛ, the critical study conducted so far does establish the basic authenticity of *Guru Granth Sahib.*

V

W.H. McLeod has not added much to what he noticed of the *Dasam Granth* in the *Evolution of the Sikh Community.* Nevertheless, the *Dasam Granth* has acquired great importance among the Sikh scholars. Gurtej Singh's article on 'Two Views on Dasam Granth' was one of the specially invited papers to a conference on Sikh studies.[49] He refers to 'disputed' authorship of the *Dasam Granth* ever since its compilation 'in the third decade of the eighteenth century'. In this ongoing controversy Ashta and Jaggi presented two opposing interpretations. Ashta accepts the whole of the *Dasam Granth* as the work of Guru Gobind Singh and tends to treat it as a part of the Sikh canon. Consequently, it appears to him to be 'excellent evidence of influence exercised by Hindu theology, mythology, philosophy and literature in the life and activities of Guru Gobind Singh'. The scope of this influence gets widened in the Foreword contributed by S. Radhakrishnan to Ashta's book. He talks of 'the profound influence' of 'Hindu tradition and mythology' on 'the development of Sikh religion'. Gurtej Singh points out that in his forced interpretation Ashta loses no opportunity to assimilate Sikhism to Hinduism. This appears to be done with 'a definite premeditated design'. He rightly points out that the blanket term 'Hinduism' conceals the 'internal incongruities of the Hindu religious system'. The Shaiva, the Vaishnava and the Shakta systems do not get equated with one another simply by using a common label for them.[50]

Jaggi's study of the *Dasam Granth* is both scientific and objective for Gurtej Singh, though even Jaggi's work is not completely free from mistakes of perception and interpretation. He argues quite convincingly that the letter attributed to Bhai Mani Singh is a later forgery. Furthermore, Jaggi has paid close attention to the extant manuscripts of the *Dasam Granth.* Thus, he bases his conclusions on an analysis of material evidence. The *Dasam Granth* as we have it now was never intended to be a single volume and no compilation was made during the time of Guru Gobind Singh. The compilers of the extant manuscripts did not attach much sanctity to the compositions, not considering them as 'the Guru's Word'. The portions said to be in the hand of Guru Gobind Singh were actually pasted later: they are materially inaccurate. Jaggi is inclined to infer that these portions are later forgeries. Above all, Jaggi demonstrates the glaring difference between the ideology of Guru Gobind Singh in his authentic works and what we find in the remaining bulk of the *Dasam Granth.* The two can never be reconciled.[51]

According to Daljeet Singh, 'the version that Bhai Mani Singh compiled the Dasam Granth, is a distortion that has no historical, ideological or factual basis or possibility'. In the Sikh literature of the eighteenth century there is no reference to anything like the *Dasam Granth.* The only exception is Kesar Singh Chhibber's *Bansāvalīnāma* which was professedly written on the basis of hearsay. Chhibber refers to 'Samundar Sagar' as a Granth got written by Guru Gobind Singh and, later, thrown into a river. Guru Gobind Singh composed other writings which were scattered and lost during the battles of Anandpur. At one place, the Granth referred to is 'Avtar Leela'. There is no reference at all to 'Dasam Granth'. Daljeet Singh infers that Chhibber's story 'adds nothing to our knowledge about the Dasam Granth writings, their compilation or loss'. Till the end of the eighteenth century, thus, nothing was known about any *granth* of the Tenth Guru or any writing now regarded as a part of the *Dasam Granth.*[52]

Daljeet Singh goes on to notice that according to Kesar Singh Chhibber, Bhai Mani Singh compiled a Granth in which the *Ādi Granth* was combined with the writings of the *Dasam Granth.* Elsewhere, however, Chhibber himself says that Guru Gobind Singh had rejected the request of the Sikhs to combine the *Ādi Granth* with his own writings. Furthermore, the evidence provided by Sarup Das Bhalla and Giani Gian Singh contradicts Chhibber's statements about the *Dasam Granth.* Gian Singh indicates that Bhai Mani Singh collected the *bāṇī* of Guru Gobind Singh. Bhalla refers to a Granth called 'Vidya Sagar' which contained translations from

Sanskrit works. The story of the *Dasam Granth* that we find in Bhai Santokh Singh, Giani Gian Singh and Bhai Kanh Singh Nabha, like the letter attributed to Bhai Mani Singh, was a later fabrication. It was meant to give credence to the compilation of the *Dasam Granth*.[53]

Daljeet Singh appears to imply that the *Dasam Granth* was compiled between 1800 and 1840. At this point he turns to the information provided by Ratan Singh Jaggi on the extant manuscripts of the *Dasam Granth*. The so-called Bhai Mani Singh Bīṛ, purchased by Raja Gulab Singh of Delhi in 1944-45, was clearly sought to be pre-dated to 1713. Its scribe had good knowledge of neither Gurmukhi nor Punjabi, nor of the Sikh tradition. Daljeet Singh suggests that this compilation was not the work of a Sikh. Alternatively, the person or persons who were responsible for its compilation were out 'to confuse the Sikh ideology'. The manuscript has 'no historical or academic value as an authentic *bir*'. The Moti Bagh Bīṛ has no verifiable history. It could not be an eighteenth century work. The Sangrur Bīṛ, like the so-called Bhai Mani Singh Bīṛ, combines Gurbāṇī with chapters from the *Dasam Granth*. The inclusion of Charitropakhyan in this manuscript enables Daljeet Singh to conclude that this manuscript 'could never be a compilation of Sikh quarters, much less could it be by the Tenth Guru'. It has no historical or academic value. The Patna Bīṛ is similar to the Sangrur Bīṛ and cannot be an eighteenth century compilation. There is no uniformity between any two *bīṛs*, but all of them present a 'mix-up' of Sikh literature with Puranic and Avtar literature 'so as to show both of them as parts of a single tradition'.[54]

Daljeet Singh gives several reasons as to why the *Dasam Granth* cannot be regarded as an authentic Sikh compilation. In the first place if Bhai Mani Singh had compiled the *Dasam Granth* and copies were prepared from it, the character of the extant manuscripts would not be so heterogeneous as it actually is. Secondly, the ideological contradictions between Gurbāṇī and the bulk of the *Dasam Granth* are so glaring and fundamental that it is impossible to reconcile the two. The theory of incarnation stands rejected in the authentic compositions of Guru Gobind Singh as much as in *Guru Granth Sahib*. It is no less significant that the writings included in the *Dasam Granth* were 'originally all separate and unconnected *pothis*'. The early title used for the compilation was *Dasam Pātshāh kā Granth*, which does not suggest authorship by Guru Gobind Singh but only associates the compilation with him. Most of its parts were called *Bachittar Nātak Granth*, a name which occurs 151 times in the Puranic parts of the compilation. The writings embodying the idea of incarnation were scribed or compiled by non-Sikhs. The present-day insinuation that Guru Gobind Singh drew inspiration from Puranic literature, or brought the Panth into Hindu fold, is a logical extension of the original attempt at assimilating the Sikh to the Hindu tradition by mixing up Puranic literature with authentic compositions of Guru Gobind Singh. Incarnation literature could never come from a Sikh source, and much less from the Tenth Master.[55]

Jagjit Singh reinforces Daljeet Singh's position on the *Dasam Granth*. Underlining the need of establishing the authenticity of a document, he turns to Jaggi's analysis of the four *bīṛs* of the *Dasam Granth* and comes to the conclusion that these manuscripts do not come from the eighteenth century. Chhibber does not provide any reliable evidence on the *Dasam Granth*. The eighteenth century literature gives no clue to it. The nineteenth century story of the *Dasam Granth* is not even near contemporary. Jagjit Singh concludes that there is no historical evidence to link the *Dasam Granth* 'either with the Tenth Master, or with the literature thrown or lost, or with the name of Bhai Mani Singh, or with any known or tangible material existing for over a century before it'. Jagjit Singh's argument is less detailed but more emphatic: the extant *Dasam Granth* is a nineteenth-century production coming from non-Sikh interests.[56]

The view of the *Dasam Granth* taken by Daljeet Singh and Jagjit Singh is radically different from the traditional view. On the question of the authenticity of its contents, however, their view is not radically different from that of W.H. McLeod. They are all agreed on the authenticity of the *Jāp*, *Akāl Ustat* (minus the stanzas in praise of Durga), *Sawaiyas* and the *Zafarnāma*. They are also agreed that the bulk of the *Dasam Granth* cannot be attributed to Guru Gobind Singh. Their differences are confined mainly to

Bachittar Nātak and *Chandī dī Vār*. Qualitatively, this is a serious difference. Furthermore, the issue raised by Daljeet Singh, presumably in response to McLeod, still remains: to what extent were the compositions now included in the *Dasam Granth* influential among the Sikhs during the late eighteenth and the early nineteenth century? According to Daljeet Singh, the *Dasam Granth* was compiled in the early nineteenth century. But his hypothesis postulates the existence of separate *pothīs* before they were put together in a single compilation.

Kesar Singh Chhibber goes into the detail of how Guru Gobind Singh invoked the Goddess for instituting the Khalsa. Chhibber was familiar with writings on Chandi, the *Bachittar Nātak*, the *Sawaiyas* and the *Zafarnāma*. His reference to the *Dasam Pātshāh kā Granth* has to be seen in this context. By 1769, the idea had become current that Bhai Mani Singh collected the writings which had formed parts of a *Granth* compiled by Guru Gobind Singh, and put them together. Was there any single compilation of such writings? Chhibber refers to the Granth of the Tenth Master and talks of two Granths: one compiled by Guru Arjan and the other by Guru Gobind Singh. The older Granth was chosen for vesting Guruship. But the younger one too commanded veneration. For Chhibber, both had the status of the Guru.[57] This indicates that a *granth* associated with Guru Gobind Singh was already in existence. Who compiled it, why and for what purpose – these are important questions. And the question of its influence among the Sikhs during the late eighteenth century does remain to be answered.

The *Dasam Granth* can never be bracketed with the *Ādi Granth* in terms of their status. The bulk of the *Dasam Granth* cannot be attributed to Guru Gobind Singh. However, the status of the authentic compositions of Guru Gobind Singh does carry a question mark. In any case, a thorough study of these compositions can afford a better understanding of Guru Gobind Singh and his Khalsa. Then there is the question of 'influence'. Even if the authenticity of *Chandī dī Vār* and *Bachittar Nātak* is rejected, we have to reckon with their relative popularity among the Sikhs during the late eighteenth and the early nineteenth century. The possible influence of other writings of the *Dasam Granth* can be examined, even if the answer turns out to be negative. The *Dasam Granth*, thus, remains important, both historically and academically.

NOTES

1. *Perspectives on the Sikh Tradition*, p. 10.
2. *Advanced Studies in Sikhism*, pp. 138-60.
3. McLeod (1975), pp. 59-61.
4. Ibid., pp. 61-62.
5. Ibid., pp. 62-63.
6. Ibid., pp. 63-69.
7. Ibid., pp. 69-70.
8. Ibid., pp. 70-73.
9. Ibid., pp. 69-89.
10. Ibid., pp. 81-82.
11. McLeod (1984).
12. McLeod (1981), p. 20.
13. McLeod (1987).
14. McLeod (1975), pp. 73-75.
15. Ibid., pp. 75-76.
16. Ibid., pp. 76-78.
17. Ibid., pp. 78-79.
18. *Advanced Studies in Sikhism*, pp. 138 and 152-59.
19. Ibid., pp. 138-41.
20. Ibid., pp. 139 and 141-50.
21. Ibid., pp. 150-52.
22. Piar Singh (1992), pp. 175-78 and 181-86.
23. Ibid., pp. 187-89.
24. Ibid., pp. 190-200.
25. Ibid., pp. 178-90 and 450-54.
26. Ibid., pp. 454-56.
27. Ibid., pp. 472-74.
28. Piar Singh (1996), pp. 1-2.
29. Ibid., pp. 81-111.
30. Ibid., pp. 115 and 135-36.
31. Ibid., pp. 137-44.
32. Ibid., pp. 153-56.
33. Ibid., pp. 148-51 and 157-58.
34. Ibid., p. 152.
35. Piar Singh (1992), pp. 71-112; (1996), pp. 18-20.
36. *Abstracts of Sikh Studies* (July 1994), pp. 99-101.
37. *Planned Attack*, pp. 115-21.

38. Mann (1996), pp. 2-3 and 8-9.
39. Ibid., pp. 4, 7-8, 9-10, 12 and 13-14.
40. Ibid., pp. 25-29.
41. Ibid., pp. 16-22 and 25.
42. Ibid., pp. 22-24.
43. Ibid., pp. 29-45.
44. *Planned Attack*, pp. 85-107.
45. Ibid., pp. 112-14.
46. Pashaura Singh (1994), pp. 197-222.
47. Piar Singh (1996), pp. 116-27.
48. 'The Making of Sikh Scripture'. Gurinder Singh Mann's doctoral thesis, seen through his courtesy in typescript.
49. *Fundamental Issues in Sikh Studies,* p. xii.
50. Ibid., pp. 179-83.
51. Ibid., pp. 183-84.
52. *Abstracts of Sikh Studies* (July 1994), pp. 81, 82 and 84.
53. Ibid., pp. 83, 84 and 85.
54. Ibid., pp. 85-88.
55. Ibid., pp. 88-94.
56. Ibid., pp. 95-99.
57. Chhibber (1972), pp. 5, 50-51, 109, 126, 135-37, 143, 144, 153, 161, 163-64, 197, 198, 215, 221 and 222.

12. Historical Methodology and Religious Studies

Modern historical writing began by discarding the supranatural and the divine for rational understanding of the past and for explaining historical change. This assumption is found reflected in the earliest European writings on the Sikhs. This historical approach did not, as it cannot, ignore the operation of ideas in history, including of course Sikh history. In fact, J.D. Cunningham attached a great deal of importance to the role of Sikh ideology in Sikh history without in any way compromising the historical method. Nevertheless, it is possible to criticize historical methodology *per se*. It is more easily possible to criticize the work of any historian from the viewpoint of methodology. The critics of W.H. McLeod and Harjot Oberoi try to do both, to criticize their work from the viewpoint of historical methodology and to criticize historical methodology itself in its application to the field of religious studies. The debate on research methodology can be appreciated in this twin context.

I

Noel Q. King's essay in the *Perspectives on the Sikh Tradition* was 'hurriedly written during intensive travelling on field research in India', but it is based on his considered views about the present state of religious studies in the West. He outlines significant developments in the study of Judaism and Christianity, both from within and outside the Church, and comes to the conclusion that critical study and Christianity 'have come to a *modus vivendi*'. It is also clear that 'critical scholarship is a native growth in Judaism and Christianity'. King holds the view that 'weapons' developed in the study of one religion can be dangerous when turned to the study of another religion. Furthermore, the scholar's own status in terms of belief or non-belief affects his attitude towards other people's religion. In other words, it is not simply a question of a Christian denouncing Islam or Hinduism; one who is critical of Christianity, or cherishes anti-religious ideas and feelings, would be critical of other religions too.[1]

King goes briefly into the work of the Orientalists on religion in Asia and Africa and comes to the conclusion that the personality and circumstances of the scholar are extremely important. King has been frequently quoted on this point. Therefore, we may reproduce his comment:

> In a Natural Science like Chemistry it may not be necessary to know anything about the human being who is writing. In any subject which entails human subjects, the work must be put into a personal context. Accordingly, one feels every work of critical scholarship should have a government statutory warning that its consumption may be deleterious to the soul's health. If it is to do with religion it should also have a statement of ingredients, including the religious standing of the writer. If he or she is a believer it is necessary to know this, so that the critical reader can allow for bias. If he or she is not a believer, we should have some indication of that too, lest the disillusionment or enlightenment of a post-Christian, a post-Jew or a post-whatever should give the critic rosy-coloured spectacles or a jaundiced outlook.[2]

In academic circles it is assumed that a scholar's motives come from 'rational intellectuality'. But this is not always true. To go into 'personal context', therefore, should not be regarded as hitting below the belt.[3]

Having made these general observations, King turns to Sikh studies to notice first of all that 'not many Western critically trained scholars' have turned their attention to Sikhism. This relative neglect of its study should be a concern of the Sikhs too, 'especially if they desire to have their religion interpreted to a wider world'. Among the fully equipped foreign scholars of Sikhism, King mentions Ernest Trumpp whose 'general bitterness and disappointment is expressed in his vicious remarks about Sikhism in his Preface'. He also apparently suffered from 'some racist views', despised his local informants, and offended them by smoking a cigar while reading the Sikh scriptures. M.A. Macauliffe did much to 'set right the balance' by the felicity of his work and by showing respect for Sikhism. Foreigners still enter the study of Sikhism through Macauliffe. The third scholar mentioned by King is C.H. Loehlin who had deep respect for the Sikh people. A loyal Christian, he revealed to the world the importance of Sikh religion. He refused to discuss anything which might be interpreted as derogatory to the Sikhs in any way.[4]

In his pursuit of Sikh studies, King has been assisted 'beyond measure' by W.H. McLeod who is 'easily in the lead among foreign scholars, past or present'. It is unlikely that his linguistic competence 'will be surpassed'. His 'meticulously carried out' work is based on a careful use of 'text-critical, form-critical and other-critical methods' developed in the West during the last two centuries. The issues raised by McLeod may be answered by highly qualified local scholars. King's concern is with 'relating them to a wider world and human context'.[5]

An educated person in the English-speaking world wanting to learn about Sikhism turns to the books of McLeod which have been published by the Oxford University Press, commanding a world market and world publicity. To an uninitiated reader, however, his books seem to reiterate the notion that 'a great amount of Sikh belief ' is based on 'uncritical religiosity'. Furthermore, McLeod's books disappoint the reader by not tapping 'the well-springs' of Sikhism, something which made Guru Nanak 'tick', 'the heart of Sikhism'. Instead, what we find in McLeod's publications is 'meticulously and exhaustively carried out drills in certain methods of western criticism'. For example, his search for the historical Nanak, which brings in the issue of the nature of the *Janamsākhīs*, when seen in the background of the quest for the historical Jesus, enunciates a basic tenet of critical scholarship. McLeod's readers, who want to know something different, get 'the wrong answers'. Thus, his purpose and their interests differ widely.

King reiterates the known principle of historical or critical methodology that if you get a non-sense reply from your source then you must re-think your question. For King, a *Janamsākhī* is neither biography nor hagiology, but a genre *sui generis*, a unique literary form. On the point of what was said and done by Guru Gobind Singh according to the Sikh tradition, King thinks that McLeod has ignored oral evidence. 'There is a living unbroken reliable tradition of the sayings and doings of 1699 quite apart from writing, still alive in the Punjab'.[6]

McLeod is outstanding for his exhaustive field-work but he does not seem to have tried to collect oral evidence on Panja Sahib which is available with Sikhs, and he has not tried to visit Panja Sahib to see things for himself. His critical scholarship has performed less than its best in dealing with 'one of the sacred things for which Sikhs are willing to lay down their lives'. McLeod's evidence on Guru Nanak's visit to this place comes from European writers of the nineteenth century. McLeod treats it as 'aetiological legend', that is a story which tries to account for a thing in existence. It is treated by McLeod as a tradition by 'invention'. King is inclined to dismiss the evidence of European officers as a 'Sirdarji joke'. This is discussed by King as a specimen, with the implication that there are other examples of wrong inferences drawn by McLeod from the evidence adduced.[7]

King comes to the conclusion that McLeod's critical attitude is not confined to Sikhs or any feature of Sikhism but embraces 'religion and religious phenomena as a whole'. He has absolute faith in 'the intellectual critical method' as he understands it, and he does not treat 'religious criteria' on any wider basis. Reason is not necessarily opposed to religion. In fact they 'go hand in hand'. In the final analysis, however, it has to be realized that 'the intellect and its methods', as they are known at present, are not perfect or absolute; they are not infallible; and they do not comprehend the whole to see things in 'focus'. Nevertheless, King does not call for 'a moratorium on critical scholarship'. He wishes to underline 'the need to be humble, considerate and courteous'. He favours the idea that 'due place be given to the *deshi* homegrown production of critical scholarship'. Sikhism, like other great religions, needs critical scholarship 'if it is to meet the intellectual need of its increasingly highly educated followers'. If anything, there is not enough of indigenous critical scholarship at present. Sikh scholars, writing in English in the Punjab, wish to remain 'in the good books of the Establishment' and they studiously avoid 'sticking their necks out'. They are as much responsible for the present situation as W.H. McLeod. He stands out precisely because there are no critical scholars among the Sikhs, at least not critical enough for King.[8]

In the *Advanced Studies in Sikhism,* King goes into some important aspects of the development of critical methodologies in the West in the context of major historical and intellectual movements and in relation to the emergence of a number of new disciplines. It is almost impossible to deal with such a vast subject adequately in a few pages, but the conclusion drawn by King is clear enough. He refers to Tacitus's observation on the Emperor Galba that by the consensus of all he had the capacity to rule 'as long as he was not Emperor'. This is true of the critical method. If it is allowed to become absolute, it fails to deliver the promised goods. In its 'proper place', however, it can be a wonderful goad to greater effort. Its proper place is that of a 'slave-tutor' who could be very stern and demanding but only as 'a servant'. The fire of critical method can burn away whatever is gross in a religious tradition, and enable the believers to retrieve the pure metal.[9]

King holds the view that if sympathetically understood and fairly presented, 'Sikh scripture and tradition has nothing to fear from any true criticism properly used'. Sikhism is a world religion, different from all others. Its study should be of interest to all those scholars who are interested in the study of religion. Publications in the English language are necessary for those who do not possess linguistic equipment to study the original sources. This *instrumenta studiorium* would consist of concordances, dictionaries, glossaries, commentaries, encyclopaedias, annotated translations, and the like. Though Sikhs have nothing to fear, they should not 'sit around and be overtaken by the outside world and by misunderstanding'. They have to establish the truth and be prepared to 'argue it out'. They have to keep their own people and their well-wishers well informed.

The ignorant are not necessarily 'enemies' but the Sikhs must tell others 'the truth about their religion'.[10]

Professor James R. Lewis can be seen partly as illustrating King's ideas about the possible biases of social scientists. Lewis talks of 'misrepresentation' of the Sikh tradition in the textbooks on world religions written in the West. He refers to the colonial framework in which Europeans held a position of dominance. They carried on a kind of monologue among themselves on the basis of their pre-suppositions in a conscious or unconscious effort to justify their attitudes and to legitimize their dominance. Lewis points out many errors of fact in the work of those who have used the works produced by the colonial writers. Because of their superficial acquaintance with the subject and their sloppy scholarship they compound errors of fact with errors of judgement. This is true even of some recent publications. This is true also of publications which contain extended treatment of the Sikh tradition. Nevertheless, there are some exceptions, made possible either by an author's reliance on good secondary work or by his own familiarity with original sources. Incidentally, Lewis mentions W.H. McLeod among the exceptions.[11]

Lewis states that every emergent religion relies on prior religious traditions as points of reference for a new vision of spiritual reality. This is true of Sikhism too. However, many a European writer has looked upon Sikhism as a syncretism, a mixture of Islamic and Hindu features. The Hindu and Muslim influences are assumed to be so dominant that there appears to be little new in Sikhism as a religion. Lewis thinks that the notion of syncretism originated with Christian missionaries, or some other group of colonial officials. Their idea carried the implication that Sikhism was something 'spurious'. This view was meant to demonstrate the superiority of Christianity. Lewis rightly points out that McLeod has deliberately and consciously discarded the concept of syncretism and he has emphasized the 'originality' of Guru Nanak. Another problem of the Western writers on Sikhism relates to the contrast which they see in Guru Nanak's 'pacifism' and Guru Gobind Singh's 'militancy'. Lewis points out that Christianity has its own history of militancy. But the Christian writers who criticize Sikhism remain silent about Christianity. Their view of the Sikh tradition is a projection 'of their own (un-expressed or repressed) condemnation of the Christian tradition'.[12]

II

Daljeet Singh welcomes the growing interest in India and abroad in the study of Sikh religion, its institutions and its history. It is a healthy development. However, partly because of the differences in the cultural background of the scholars drawn to Sikh studies and partly because of the methodologies they follow, there are a few problems which have to be faced and solved. Daljeet Singh identifies three such problems, of which one is 'methodology'. But the other two also get related to it in Daljeet Singh's presentation. Therefore, we may take note of all the points made in his essay.

The problem of methodology for Daljeet Singh is 'ontological' in nature. By 'ontology' he does not mean 'metaphysics concerned with the essence of things or being in the abstract'(as a dictionary may define it), but 'the spiritual base of a religion' (as explained by Daljeet Singh). It is basic to almost every religion that there is a Spiritual Reality which is different from and more real or true than the sensually perceived empirical reality. Its description and definition becomes the basis of the study of a religion. The structure of a religion is determined by answers to the question whether or not that Reality is creative and attributive, and they serve as clues to its character and therefore to its study. No student of Guru Granth Sahib can fail to see that 'for the Gurus, God is not only Creative and Attributive but He is also immanent, reveals Himself to man, and operates in history with His Will'. Similarly in other religions there are certain conceptions of Reality, or God, which are essential to their proper understanding.[13]

This raises a basic problem. Since the advent of modern science, materialistic philosophies have gained great importance, and materialistic interpretations are accepted by and large as valid in the fields of sociology, economics, political science, psychology and history. All these studies relate to the phenomena of the empirical world, and they take little or no account of the transcendent world. From the viewpoint of religion, the world-views of these disciplines are partial and lop-sided. Their methods and assumptions can be regarded as valid within their own domains. But the problem arises when they are regarded as valid for the study of religion as well. Religion relates primarily to the transcendent world which is of little concern to the social scientist. Consequently, the methods of social sciences are of little use for the study of religion. Therefore, religion has developed its own methodology and principles of study leading to a world-view which is holistic and comprehensive instead of being limited and narrow. The *raison d'etre* of the study of religion is 'the spiritual element'. Deny it, and there is no need of religious studies. Ontology is too central to be ignored.[14]

According to Daljeet Singh, the highest level in human progress is God-consciousness resulting in truthful living. Thus, 'real knowledge' comes from the area of the transcendent. It is noetic, or supersensual. It was not his social milieu but his noetic knowledge of Spiritual Reality that gave Guru Nanak his world-view and his ideology. But in social sciences, the mystic world and its experience are 'just unexplored areas of darkness'. Furthermore, there is no trace of the ethical in the reflective thought of man. That is why for social sciences morality is 'just a defence mechanism' or reaction formation 'in response to environmental impacts'. Religion is treated as a 'behavioural phenomenon'.

Daljeet Singh goes on to state that from the viewpoint of the man of religion the study of religion by an anthropologist is limited, partial and inadequate because of his methodology (and the assumptions on which it is based). Furthermore, as pointed out by Neol Q. King, it is important to know the personal context of an author, his or her personality and circumstance, including the religious standing of the writer if his work relates to religion. 'If he or she is a believer, it is necessary to know this, so that the critical reader can allow for bias'. If the author is not a believer, that should also be indicated, because disillusionment with a religion or 'enlightenment' can also give 'rosy-coloured spectacles or a jaundiced outlook'. Daljeet Singh reinforces the point with reference to Freud, who in one situation placed personal authority above truth, and with reference to Mahatma Gandhi, who referred to inter-dining and inter-marrying as 'a superstition borrowed from the West'. These examples show that even great men are not free from personal or cultural prejudices. Therefore, it is essential to know 'the background, beliefs and predilections' of an author. The reader can then assess and appreciate 'the value of his views and the slant of his vision'. Like the methodology of an author, it is necessary to know 'who the writer is and what is his own faith or training'.[15]

There is one peculiar problem related to Sikh studies. In Indian religions there is dichotomy between the spiritual life and the empirical life of man. Guru Nanak was the first man to break this dichotomy, leading logically to the doctrine of Mīrī and Pīrī. This doctrine looks odd to 'the votaries of pacifist religions'. The militancy of Guru Gobind Singh is not appreciated by Indians like Mahatma Gandhi and Rabindra Nath Tagore, just as the socio-political activities of Prophet Muhammad are not appreciated by Arnold Toynbee. Muhammad Iqbal can admire the great stature of Guru Nanak, but McLeod cannot. Indeed, whereas Muslim writers in general see no ideological difference between Guru Nanak and Guru Gobind Singh, the Indian and Christian writers see in them two different phenomena due to their cultural conditioning.[16]

Another related problem arises from the increasing secularization of life, so much so that the modern state has also been secularized. In the Indian context, this development has a peculiar bearing on Sikhism with its doctrine of Mīrī and Pīrī, or the integral combination of the spiritual and the empirical life of man. To some this has appeared to be the cause of the recent crisis in the Punjab. Others look at distinct Sikh identity as 'downright unpatriotic'. There are still others who believe that Sikhism in its social aspect has become redundant because the programmes of social reform have been taken over by the state. According to Daljeet Singh, the men of religion feel that 'in view of the growing secularization of modern life', and its tendency 'to encroach on the religious field', it is necessary to study religion with the tools of its own discipline. It is also necessary that the funding and functioning of religious studies 'should be kept free from the influences of modern state and its secular life'.[17]

Gobind Singh Mansukhani has written briefly on the 'origin and development' of Sikh studies. But he talks neither of origin nor of development. He says nothing about the first century of modern Sikh studies. For him, Trumpp's *Ādi Granth* 'dates the origin of Sikh studies'. For the past century he merely catalogues the works produced and that too rather at random. His information is woefully incomplete. There is nothing new in the elementary information he provides and there is no coherence in his presentation. Mansukhani is totally unaware that a number of scholars have already written about historical writing on the Sikhs, and on the development of Sikh studies. He has little to say about the personal or social biases of authors, their presuppositions, purposes, motives or methodology. With this kind of simple approach he could hardly be expected to make any meaningful contribution to 'research methodology'.[18]

According to Gobind Singh Mansukhani, Sikhism has now been accepted as one of the major religions of the world, and constitutes a new area for religious studies. Western scholars in the area of Sikh studies have been using techniques and criteria of disciplines like history, sociology, anthropology, philosophy and linguistics. Their methodologies, though valid in their own disciplines, are not useful for in-depth study of Sikhism as a 'revelatory' and 'sovereign' religion. Mansukhani pleads for 'a balanced, homogeneous and impartial examination of the sources' to pursue 'integrated methodology'.[19]

Mansukhani looks upon the Guru Granth Sahib, the accepted *gurbāṇī* in the *Dasam Granth*, and the approved compositions of Bhai Gurdas and Bhai Nand Lal as 'primary' sources for Sikh studies. The *Janamsākhīs*, the *Gurbilās* literature, *Hukamnāmas*, Gurmatās, *Rahitnāmas* and other books from the eighteenth century to the present day are 'secondary' sources. The works specifically placed in this category are *Gurbilās Pātshāhī Chhevīn*, which in his view was written by Sohan Kavi in 1718, Ratan Singh Bhangu's *Prāchīn Panth Prakāsh*, Giani Gian Singh's *Tawārīkh Gurū Khalsa* and Kavi Santokh Singh's *Gurpartāp Sūraj*. Muslim writers have generally supplied biased or wrong information in their chronicles, which misled European writers, with the exception of J.D. Cunningham. To these is added later in the essay another source: *Bhatt-Vahīs*, which can supply 'missing links' in our present knowledge of Sikh history. All these primary and secondary sources can be used in the 'new methodology' proposed by Mansukhani.[20]

Mansukhani points out that the Western scholars of Sikhism suffer from three main handicaps. One of these is their notion that Sikhism is a part of Hinduism. Second, they are preconditioned by their acquaintance with Semitic religions. They call Sikhism 'a tradition' as if it is something less than a religion. They use the word syncretism for Sikhism to imply that it is not a 'revealed' religion. They give 'differential treatment' to Sikhism by using different sets of criteria for Sikhism and their own faith.Their third handicap is their analytical methodology. Mansukhani believes that rational standards and scientific techniques applied to revelation are useless, in fact counter-productive. 'Intellectual knowledge' is not enough in dealing with matters religious.[21]

Mansukhani goes on to mention the 'drawbacks' of analytical methodology. It it not suited to comprehend spiritual phenomenon. The laws of logical proof cannot be applied to the experiential aspects of man and his feelings of love, beauty, truth, peace and happiness. The vision of God cannot be analysed, and revelation cannot be dissected. Secondly, the 'external' approach in itself excludes sympathy with the religion under study. Thirdly, the analytical critic of religion tends to neglect the spiritual nature of man, who is not merely the body but also the mind and the soul. Spiritual experience cannot be quantified. 'Religion is an inner experience, beyond the prism-pendulum-chronograph methods of the scientist'. Familiar examples are given from the works of W.H. McLeod with their familiar criticism. Mansukhani draws the conclusion that scholars, whether Western or Eastern, would go on making mistakes so long as they do not understand 'the Gurbani, the Sikh thesis and its doctrines'.[22]

Mansukhani's 'new methodology' consists of two main parts: one, 'a consideration of Sikh traditions' and the other, 'its relevance in *Gurmat*'. 'Sikh traditions' are a part of the oral history. The 'secondary' sources belong to this category. Whatever in the secondary sources is not in conformity with *gurmat* has to be rejected. If the author of a *gurbilās* says that Guru Gobind Singh invoked the Goddess, it has to be rejected because it infringes *Gurmat*. Some controversies also can be settled with reference to *Gurmat*, like the one about whether or not 'outcaste' Sikhs were to be allowed to enter the Golden Temple and offer *kaṛāh parshād*.

Mansukhani comes to the conclusion that in the study of religion, there are two distinct areas. One of these relates to the 'historical authenticity of the record' and the other, to the 'internal consistency of the religious doctrines and practices'. Separate techniques are required for each of these two areas. The lack of evidence for an event cannot be taken as a proof of its non-occurrence. So far as the Sikh way of life is concerned, what is enuciated in 'primary' sources does not become invalid in the absence of corroborative evidence in 'secondary' sources. Mansukhani assures us that his 'integrated methodology' will be useful and 'richly improve the quality of Sikh studies'. It is a project for the future.[23]

III

As Noel Q.King points out, 'critical' methodology was developed in the West for the study of Judaism and Christianity. It was assumed that it possessed universal validity, and it was applied by many scholars to the study of religions other than Judaism and Christianity. Both the assumption and the application can be questioned. King also points out that the critical method has its limitations. It should not be allowed to hold undisputed sway in the study of religion. Furthermore, the critical scholar is not free from biases arising out of his or her personal context. In fact this is equally true of the believer. It is not always safe to assume that a scholar's motives arise strictly from 'rational intellectuality'. King's general observations are applicable to all scholars. In his well considered view, critical scholarship is not dispensable. It has its uses.

King observes that McLeod's intentions differ widely from the expectations of his readers. They want to know something positive to account for the charisma of Guru Nanak and the achievement of his followers. But what they get is discussion of issues raised in Western scholarship. King seems to imply that issues which are important in one society are not necessarily important in another. McLeod has a complete faith in the critical method, and his attiude towards religion in general is completely rational in the sense that he treats it as a social phenomenon. McLeod is mistaken in regarding *Janamsākhīs* as hagiology. But so are they who regard them as biographies. *Janamsākhīs* constitute a unique literary form. We may agree with King. But what he does not tell us is their relevance for a biography of Guru Nanak, or the actual incidents of his life. King would treat European evidence on Panja Sahib as a 'Sirdarji joke', but he does not tell us which other evidence is there to support his view. Sikh evidence is merely referred to. What we are left with is the rather late evidence of the *Janamsākhīs* with which McLeod started. In other words, King has not really grasped the basic argument put forth by McLeod. It is not surprising that he has not met McLeod's argument. About the sayings and doings of Guru Gobind Singh, King mentions unbroken oral evidence but he does not tell us where it is. On the whole, thus, King's criticism of McLeod relates to his methodology in general and his rational, as opposed to religious, attitude in general. What King offers is a criticism, essentially, not of this or that historian but of the historian's assumptions and his methods. Otherwise, he has a lot of praise for McLeod's work. What is more, he subscribes to the view that critical scholarship is much needed in Sikh studies. It may, therefore, be added that Justice Gurdev Singh and some other critics of McLeod quote King rather inappropriately and for wrong reasons.

Daljeet Singh underlines the importance of ontology in religion, with the implication that the foremost question which may be asked about a religion is its conception of the supersensual spiritual reality, or God. Since this spiritual reality is marginal to the social scientists, their methods remain inadequate for the study of religion. Logically, therefore, the principles and methods followed in religious studies are different. However, Daljeet Singh does not tell us what those principles and methods are. He does not refer to any other writer in this connection. If these methods and principles are something different from what he has said about the general approach to religion, it is difficult to know what they are. The only alternative is to look at the methods and techniques used by those scholars who are supposed to have studied religion without the methods and techniques of the social sciences.

Mostly what we have from the critics is the assertion that the methodology of social sciences is not adequate for studying religion. It may be pointed out that the methods of social sciences have not remained fixed and static, and they are still evolving. The social scientists themselves do not subscribe to the idea that their methods are perfect. All that they insist upon is empirical evidence and its explanation in rational and natural terms. They also prefer multi-causal explanations to mono-causal explanations. What they share is 'methodological atheism', and the techniques which are related to this method. It is not clear what is being objected to as distinct from the rational assumptions and empirical attitudes of the social scientists.

As Daljeet Singh himself underlines, the study of religion does not leave the empirical world out. On the contrary, the relationship of religious ideologies with the empirical world is so important that he can look upon history as an expression of ideology. He finds it amply demonstrated in Sikhism. Even in general terms he insists that historical development should not be studied in isolation from ideas. It becomes difficult to understand the real nature of Daljeet Singh's objection to the historical approach. Ideas are not ignored by the historians. There are differences of degree in the importance attached to ideas by different historians. Only the poor or an indifferent kind of historian would leave ideas out. Indeed, in a certain sense the historian subscribes even to the idea that God enters history: in the sense that faith in God can be a motivating force. The conception of God itself is the greatest idea known to mankind. But whereas Daljeet Singh would look upon the ideas and attitudes springing from religious faith as all important, the historian would look for other factors too in his explanation. We noticed earlier that McLeod objects to Jagjit Singh's explanation precisely because he attaches too much importance to ideology. Nevertheless, it would be reasonable to look upon their difference as a difference of degree rather than kind. What is objected to in McLeod is the role he is prepared to assign to ideology in Sikh history. To suggest that only the Sikhs can appreciate Sikh ideology is to imply that non-Sikhs cannot understand Guru Nanak's conception of God, which is not really convincing. Nearly all the critics of McLeod admire J.D. Cunningham who was a believing Christian and who attached great importance to ideology in Sikh history. In theory, therefore, any historian can assign important or crucial role to ideas in a given historical situation.

Mansukhani has talked of 'integrated' or 'new' methodology as a project for the future. Whatever the merit of his proposal there is no suggestion that it is based on the practice of any scholar or historian of religion. Like Daljeet Singh, he states that critical approach and critical methodology are unsuitable or inapplicable to the study of religion. He points out that Western scholars have generally treated Sikhism as a part of Hinduism or as a syncretic formation. Their critical methodology is also a handicap. There can be no logical proofs in the realm of ethics and aesthetics; the inner experience cannot be dissected or quantified. Critical approach is said to make a scholar unsympathetic to the subject of his study. Mansukhani can be seen as reinforcing King and Daljeet Singh on critical methodology but not going beyond them.

Mansukhani divides evidence on Sikhism and Sikh history into primary and secondary sources. The former consist of scriptures and the work of Bhai Gurdas and Bhai Nand Lal. The rest of the evidence is secondary. Sikh secondary evidence is placed by Mansukhani in the category of oral. Why is it called 'oral'? Presumably, the assumption is that the *Janamsākhī* and *Gurbilās* literature was written on the basis of oral evidence, or on the basis of written works originally based on oral evidence. The primary significance of this distinction for Mansukhani is that primary evidence gets precedence over secondary evidence for the study of Sikh history as well as the study of Sikhism. Consequently, the secondary sources can only be corroborative or supplementary. They have no intrinsic value. Mansukhani is interested in 'who has said what' and not in the question 'what does it mean?'. This question introduces a crucial change in the historian's attitude towards his sources. Mansukhani's idea that lack of evidence does not mean that a certain event did not occur is even more revealing. He appears to believe that 'historical facts' exist without being established on the basis of empirical evidence. If they do, we can accept them on faith, and that is not historical knowledge. His suggestion that the authenticity of a source should be established is not new. It has been the standing practice in historical studies. Similarly, there is nothing new in his suggestion regarding internal consistency. In fact, Mansukhani leaves the impression that he has not seen any literature on the philosophy and methods or techniques of history. By now there is a wide range of literature on this subject, and historians often base their understanding of 'what is history' on this kind of literature. The 'second-order history', or the history of historical thought and writing, goes into the question of unconscious assumptions, attitudes, personal biases and social prejudices of historians. There is hardly any doubt that the historians themselves are much more conscious of what is involved in being a historian than what we find in Mansukhani's new methodology. His suggest-ions appear to be addressed not to historians but to believers writing for believers. The scope of Sikh history in his new methodology gets extremely restricted.

IV

We may now turn to the two historians who have been criticized the most for their methodology: W.H. McLeod and Harjot Oberoi. Our concern with them is limited to illustrating their approach and method with a few concrete instances. To see McLeod at work we may turn to his treatment of the *Rahitnāmas* which has been regarded as controversial. The idea belatedly enunciated by Mansukhani with regard to the 'historical authenticity' of a source and its 'internal consistency' was not unknown to McLeod. In fact, it is his working priniciple. According to McLeod, part of our problem with the *Rahitnāmas* arises from lack of 'early manu-scripts'. To search for the earliest possible manuscripts is a well known principle of historical research. It is equally important to identify manuscripts 'in terms of author, place and time'. In the absence of early manuscripts we have to fall back on 'analysis of language and content', and we are obliged to examine putative authorship rather carefully. Furthermore, we have to make a clear distinction between 'tradition' and 'history'. The former is virtually what is believed about the past and the latter is a form of knowledge based on verifiable evidence. Applied to the *Rahitnāmas*, this would mean that what is generally believed or said about them should find support from the *Rahitnāmas* as we know them.[24]

McLeod has seen nine *Rahitnāmas* dating from before the middle of the nineteenth century. Some of these are very brief, concentrating on particular features of the *rahit*. Relatively comprehensive *Rahitnāmas* cover all aspects of the *rahit*: fundamental doctrines, personal behaviour, the Khalsa ceremonies, and offences against the *rahit*. It is generally assumed that the substance of the *rahit* was determined by Guru Gobind Singh, a large portion on the occasion of the founding of the Khalsa in 1699 and the remainder shortly before his death. During his lifetime thus, Guru Gobind Singh is believed to have effectively promulgated a definitive version. This traditional scheme does not find support in the *Rahitnāmas* themselves. The traditional account demands consistency and a regular unambiguous form. This is not the pattern which we find in the *Rahitnāmas*. The claim that the authors of the *Rahitnāmas* were associated with Guru Gobind Singh cannot be accepted on its face value. One *Rahitnāma* states that its author had heard Guru Gobind Singh speaking at Avchalnagar (Nander), but the date given is 1699 (when Guru Gobind Singh was actually at Anandpur). In all cases, the language indicates a significant remove from the time of Guru Gobind Singh and his environment. To detach the *Rahitnāmas* from the time of Guru Gobind Singh does not oblige us to advance their date far into the eighteenth or to the early nineteenth century: there are features which indicate a relatively early date. The *Chaupa Singh Rahit-Nama*, edited and translated by McLeod, can be safely placed between 1740 and 1765. Till today, this is the 'earliest of the datable *rahit-namas*'. Furthermore, the composite character of this *Rahit-Nama* points clearly to earlier sources, and it is conceivable that 'portions of it may indeed go back to Chaupa Singh Chhibbar of the tenth Guru's entourage'. But these portions are extremely difficult to identify. Then there are other elements which can certainly be identified as later. Therefore, McLeod is inclined to look upon the *rahit* as evolving in time. In any case, the principle on which McLeod is working is rather simple: the evidence of a literary work gains importance and value if we know the date of its composition or compilation. At present, therefore, the *Chaupa Singh Rahit-Nama* provides the most valuable evidence on the *rahit* of the Khalsa in the middle decades of the eighteenth century.[25]

McLeod gives the essential features of the Khalsa *rahit* as it emerges from the *Chaupa Singh Rahit-Nama* and then draws the conclusion that a 'version of the Rahit was certainly current during the lifetime of Guru Gobind Singh but that version must be regarded as a nucleus, and not as the full-fledged twentieth-century Rahit'. A process of growth took place during the middle decades of the eighteenth century which produced the essential lineaments of the modern *rahit* by the end of the eighteenth century. The developed *rahit* may thus be ascribed to an extended period 'rather than limited to explicit pronouncements' by Guru Gobind Singh. This does not mean that Guru Gobind Singh made no pronouncement at all. Indeed, the first important source of the *Rahitnāmas* was the 'intention of the Guru' during the formative years of the Panth's growth, and it was 'codified by Guru Gobind Singh as a nucleus of the later Rahit'.[26]

McLeod has been criticized for suggesting that the 5Ks were not introduced by Guru Gobind Singh on the Baisakhi day of 1699 when the Khalsa was instituted. The evidence he has examined does not mention 5Ks till we come to the nineteenth century. Therefore McLeod's suggestion is not baseless, and it is not irresponsible. But, of course, he may be wrong. The only way to correct his mistake would be to argue on the basis of known evidence, following the accepted principles of source-criticism in historical studies, or to produce fresh evidence which may clearly establish that Guru Gobind Singh introduced the 5Ks in 1699. A distinction can be made between the present formulation of the

5Ks and their earlier prototypes. The probability of the prototypes of the 5Ks having been introduced in 1699 can indeed be visualized. The other sources of Khalsa *rahit* suggested by McLeod are related to his inference that this *rahit* was not enunciated or promulgated in its entirety during the lifetime of Guru Gobind Singh. In his methodology, obviously, McLeod attaches a great deal of importance to empirical evidence and tries hard to interpret it through the known techniques of historical interpretation. He has not invented any new method or new technique in his approach to the *Rahitnāmas*. The criticism directed against him is virtually directed against historical methodology.[27]

Harjot Oberoi's approach is explicitly stated in the Introduction to his *Construction of Religious Boundaries*. The first point he makes is about the scope of the study of religion. In his view, religious traditions are rarely placed at the centre of social analysis in histories of modern India. In the historical treatment of the socio-religious movements of the nineteenth century – such as the Arya Samaj, the Singh Sabha and the Aligarh Movement – the religious factor is brought in to explain other social developments, parti-cularly as 'a handy smokescreen for power-hungry elites'. Consequently, too many questions concerning religion are left unanswered. People appear to play no role in the making of their own history: they are seen as 'betrayed' or 'hoodwinked' by the religious elites. Attention remains concentrated on the urban sections of the population, leaving the rural people virtually out. It is of paramount importance to separate the practice of religion from its manipulation: the two may be related but they are not the same. Furthermore, religious movements generate division as well as solidarity. Even religious texts like the *Ādi Granth* can be interpreted in favour of divergent identities. Also there is always a significant difference between the religion of the elite and popular religion. Finally, we have to look at religion 'as a social and cultural process; not something given but an activity embedded in everyday life, a part of human agency'. Therefore, a historian of religion has to examine 'the range of people's relations with the sacred and the supernatural'; he or she has to consider how these relations order the world of individuals and groups; 'what feelings, moods and motives they encourage or try to repress'; and he or she has to see 'what means are offered to move people through the stages of their lives, to prepare for their future, and to cope with suffering and catastrophe'. Equally if not more important for the historian is 'the context of popular religious life' and 'religious change'.[28] The scope of the study of religion for Oberoi, thus, is very wide, embracing ideas in their relationship with the day to day practices in the lives of all the people, and embracing changes in ideas and their relationships.

That Oberoi takes the problem of historical change seriously is evident from his understanding and use of the concepts of episteme and praxis. The concept of episteme is taken by Oberoi from Michel Foucault who defines it as 'the total set of relations'. It is not a form of knowledge or type of rationality. It is 'the totality of relations that can be discovered for a given period' to be analysed 'at the level of discursive regularities'. Furthermore, in any given culture and at any given moment, only one episteme 'defines the conditions of possibility of all knowledge, whether expressed in a theory or silently invested in a practice'. Foucault explores and defines the epistemes of the Renaissance, 'the classical age', and 'the modern age' in Europe. However, he deploys his concept 'to document the intellectual production of a given historical period', and he does not go into the problem of change from one episteme to another. Human societies are not merely episteme governed; they are also subject to 'an unceasing intervention of human practices'. It is on account of such practices that 'much historical change occurs'.[29]

At this stage of the argument, Sherry Ortner's concept of praxis becomes relevant and helpful for Oberoi. Praxis is one of the three modes of action postulated by Ortner, the other two being routine activity and intentional action. Routine activity is the stuff of everyday life and it prevents our personal and social life from collapsing. Through intentional action people enact their interests, desires, and intentions, pursuing their goals, plans and projects. What is important here is to determine what kinds of cultural, political or economic forces shape intentional action. Praxis is radically different from intentional action as well as routine activity.

It has the potential of transforming existing social and cultural relationships. Oberoi does not say what praxis is though we can read between the lines. What is more important for his purpose, the concepts of episteme and praxis can be synthesized. There is a dialectical relationship between an episteme and human practice, whether routine or intentional: 'one cannot exist without the other'. Therefore, changed social, cultural and economic contexts 'can lead to a situation of praxis, potentially carrying the possibility of a historical rupture'. This can account for the dissolution of one episteme and the eventual rise of another. Oberoi's aim is to understand 'the entire process underlying the rise and dissolution of an episteme' with the help of materials from the Sikh past.[30]

Having clarified his conception of the scope of the study of religion and his approach to the study of change, Oberoi discusses the state of Sikh studies. In his view two principles have been at work in historical writing on the Sikhs, as in other areas of historiography. One of these is the principle of silence, silence about diversity within the Sikh Panth and the prevalence of popular religion among the Sikhs. The second principle is that of negation. According to this principle, when diversity or popular religion is brought in, it is treated as relapse into Hinduism or deviation or superstition. This approach ultimately goes on to establish that Sikhs were 'delivered from the bondage of un-Sikh beliefs' by the intervention of the late nineteenth-century Singh Sabha Movement. The scholars who favour this view look upon the Singh Sabha reformers as the upholders and propagators of traditional Sikh doctrines. Oberoi's explanation of the general acceptance of the principles of silence and negation is that European observers of the Sikhs were far more concerned with what Sikhism ought to be like rather than what it was; they had far greater interest in recording the ideals of the faith rather than the actual behaviour of its practitioners. Their preoccupation with texts led to 'essentialist formulations' of Sikh tradition. The practices which did not conform to such formulations were treated with disdain and regarded as corrupt accretions, explicable in terms of 'the moral lassitude of the Khalsa, the decline in the political fortunes of the Sikhs, and the boa-like advances of Hinduism'. European assumptions and attitudes were picked up by the Sikh literati which emerged under the shadow of the Raj to reinforce the European discourse. So powerful is this discourse that 'contemporary scholarship either tends to ignore vast terrains of Sikh life in the nineteenth century or views it as superfluous addition which has to be negated'.[31]

Oberoi makes one more point with a bearing on the problem of interpretation. There is a basic difference between the ideology of a period and its explanation. Instead of accepting and repeating the value judgements and categories of the Singh Sabha reformers, a historian of the Singh Sabha Movement should try to explain why at a particular juncture certain forms of behaviour came to be viewed with suspicion and invited censure. 'A firm distinction ought to be made between the way certain beliefs and rituals came to be represented in the rhetoric of socio-religious movements like the Singh Sabha, and their actual place and function in the everyday life of people'. Many a scholar of Sikhism has failed to make this distinction. Oberoi cites the example of G.S. Dhillon who had written a doctoral thesis on the Singh Sabha Movement, largely based on contemporary sources and simultaneously covering the intellectual, educational, religious and reformative facets of the movement. Dhillon accepts the Singh Sabha records at their face value. Consequently, the ideology of the movement is distinctly imprinted on his work. No clear line is drawn between the 'first-order interpretation' or the statements of the leaders of the movement and the 'second-order interpretation' or the conclusions drawn by Dhillon. His work, from Oberoi's standpoint, remains rooted in the principle of negation. 'A norm is constructed, and the world outside this norm is viewed as deviant, marginal, threatening or unimportant'. The implication of this interpretation is 'to negate differences and applaud unities'. It becomes a 'political effort' to generate homogeneity and to represent the Sikhs as 'a collectivity which shared the same values and movements'. Instead of recognizing ambiguity, interpretation, and reinterpretation in the process of Sikh history, the historians like Dhillon postulate an 'unproblematic corporate identity'. Such historical literature prevents us from seeing the Sikhs 'in a world constantly constructed and reconstructed by them'. Sikh studies can become respectable only if they 'fully open up to the gaze of history'. In other words, no area of Sikh life should be regarded as too sacrosanct or too contemptible to be the subject of rational investigation.[32]

Oberoi raises three issues pertaining to historiography: the scope of historical studies, the concern of the historian with change, and the problem of interpretation involving the historian's attitude towards sources. All these are basic issues of historical thought and method. Oberoi's rationale is intimately linked with a whole range of reflection on these issues by a number of philosophers and historians. To import or adapt concepts from other disciplines, including social anthropology, is not a new thing.

However, a clear distinction can be made between Oberoi's conception of the scope and methods of historical studies and the application of his theory to his actual interpretation of the Sikh tradition. Even if we accept his rationale we may differ with its application and, therefore, with his findings. In fact it is possible to argue that the concepts of episteme and praxis, which induce him to look for ruptures, make him prone to over-emphasize change and to under-estimate the strength of continuities. Like W.H. McLeod, Harjot Oberoi is well aware of what is involved in historical methodology. It is possible to refute McLeod and Oberoi in detail by using the techniques of historical methodology itself, and to reject or modify their findings by interpreting the same evidence or by invoking evidence which they have not used. To perform this function, one has to have a firm hold on historical methodology, and not to discard it.

V

Harjot Oberoi's work, which has provoked many to criticize him, is highly praised by N. Gerald Barrier.[33] Whereas Gurtej Singh sees nothing good in *Studying the Sikhs*,[34] Bruce La Brack admires its scholarly quality and usefulness.[35] More interesting perhaps is Mark Juergensmeyer's review of Daljeet Singh's *Sikhism: A Comparative Study of its Theology and Mysticism*. Juergensmeyer appreciates the main thrust of this work: it 'might have forced Weber to amend his conclusions' on Indian religions 'at least with regard to the Punjab'. Juergensmeyer agrees with Daljeet Singh that the

Sikh perspective is quite 'dissimilar to the Brahmanical and Vedantic point of view'. The kind of 'worldly asceticism' that Weber sees in protestantism is discernible in Sikhism too. However, Daljeet Singh's work is not without limitations. In the first place, the sources he uses for the religious traditions other than Sikhism are not only secondary but also hopelessly inadequate. Secondly, his conception of mysticism is too simplistic to account for the great variety in the phenomenon of mysticism in the history of religion. Daljeet Singh is at his best when he deals with Sikhism, but even here his sampling of Sikhism is restrictive: 'Both the teachings of the Gurus and the heritage of the tradition are richer than that'. Nevertheless, for Juergensmeyer, Daljeet Singh raises important questions for comparative study of religion. This in itself is a valuable contribution.[36]

In the assessment of another reviewer, Daljeet Singh's approach to the study of comparative religion does not do justice to religious traditions other than Sikhism. Daljeet Singh assumes that different religions of the world can be studied through the uniform standard he has evolved for the study of Sikhism. He ignores the fact that every religious tradition has to be viewed as 'a complete, closed and unique world in itself'. Therefore, no uniform theological framework can be used for studying different religions 'without a danger of misunderstanding them and having a distorted representation of those religions'. A framework based on Sikh theological categories of thought can hardly be said 'to do justice to those dimensions of other religions which are different from Sikhism'.[37] In other words, Sikh-centrism would be as much open to objection as Euro-centrism for a comparative study of religion.

We may now turn to a reviewer who professes to be neutral between the contestants. He notices an increasing divergence in scholarship on Sikhism between 'Indian' and 'Western' academics. This divergence is clearly reflected in 'polemic' over Harjot Oberoi's *Construction of Religious Boundaries*. However, when Barrier admires Oberoi's book, he does not realize the limitations of the Western academia and omits to mention the relationship between the Western academy today and similar institutions during the colonial eras in their role as the arbiter of 'cultural representation'. Barrier tends to dismiss 'the harsh, and often overtly personal onslaught' against Oberoi as 'communal rhetoric or internal partisan politics'. This dismissal reflects 'a fundamental failure' to acknowledge the existence of a problem concerning the nature of South Asian studies generally, and Sikh studies in particular. Oberoi's own methodology appears to the reviewer to be an 'up dated successor of the earlier colonialist epistemology'. Thus, both the Singh Sabha tradition and the academic tradition within which Oberoi writes 'are historically linked'. Oberoi talks of 'repressive hypothesis' in the historiography of the Singh Sabha. This hypothesis is equally operative 'within his own adopted methodology'. Nevertheless, the kind of debate that his work has generated may lead to 'a new agenda in Sikh studies'.[38]

This new agenda, obviously, is not the one pursued by Oberoi's critics. The reviewer sees in the *Recent Researches in Sikh Studies* 'a continuing polemic against recent Western interpretation of Sikhism'. Many of the papers in this volume are intended to be rebuttals of 'the more contentious issues' raised by the work of McLeod and Oberoi. Several other papers merely 'fill up space' rather than tackle 'any specific issues'. The main protest is rather poorly articulated. Nevertheless, the book does raise a very important question concerning Western methodology as applied to Eastern religions. Ironically, however, the procedural methods of the authors of these papers are based upon the same 'episteme' as that of their opponents. Therefore, the problem degenerates into a question of the subjective status of the contestants: 'insider versus outsider' or 'believer versus non-believer'. The critics of McLeod and Oberoi have not yet managed to develop 'a rigorous hermeneutic that properly confronts reductionist methodology'. Nevertheless, the students of religion, history and anthropology should read books like the *Recent Researches* to have 'a more balanced picture of the current state of Sikh studies'.[39]

The basic difference between the critical scholars and their critics does not arise from any differences in their methodology. But their conception of historiography differs widely and gets related to their world-views and their political imagination. Their attitude towards the Sikh tradition is intimately linked to their conception of history. For the critical historian, the entire Sikh tradition can be subjected to critical analysis for discovering past truths. For their critics, certain aspects of the Sikh tradition are sacrosanct and cannot be the subject of rational analysis. This difference in their attitudes becomes essentially a difference between 'beliefs' about the past and its rational cognition. The two need not always be in opposition to each other but the difference is nonetheless fundamental. A matter of belief is not debatable. A rational cognition based on empirical evidence is open to modification all the time. Whenever rational cognition appears to impinge upon a matter of belief, there is the possibility of controversy.

The critical historian often ventures out in search of truth. The believer goes out sometimes in search of proof of the truth already in his possession. They have to meet on the common ground of evidence. They see different kinds of significance in the evidence before them. Not that the critical scholars agree among themselves, or their critics agree among themselves. However, the grounds of disagreement are different in each situation. Debate and dialogue is thus inevitable and can be accepted by contestants with reasonable grace. This acceptance may eventually narrow the gap between the committed discoverers of truths and the committed defenders of the truth.

In historical studies, a crucial role is played by the 'question'. This should be equally true of Sikh studies. Whereas the method is not rooted in culture the question is. The Western scholars may appear to be distinguished by their methodology but actually they are not. They are interested in asking and answering those questions in which their own society is interested. The cultural roots of questions and their social relevance determine the difference between 'the west' and 'the east'. We may be optimistic, therefore, that awareness of this basic difference may lead to a better mutual understanding.

NOTES

1. *Perspectives on the Sikh Traditon*, pp. 41-44.
2. Ibid., pp. 46-47.
3. Ibid., p. 47.

4. Ibid., pp. 47-48.
5. Ibid., pp. 48-49.
6. Ibid., pp. 49-50.
7. Ibid., pp. 50-51.
8. Ibid., pp. 51-52.
9. *Advanced Studies in Sikhism*, pp. 1-11 and 13.
10. Ibid., pp. 11-13.
11. Ibid., pp. 165-69.
12. Ibid., pp. 271-74.
13. Ibid., pp. 16-17.
14. Ibid., pp. 17-18.
15. Ibid., pp. 18-23.
16. Ibid., pp. 24-26.
17. Ibid., pp. 27-28.
18. *Fundamental Issues in Sikh Studies*, pp. 127-35.
19. *Recent Researches in Sikhism*, p. 109.
20. Ibid., pp. 109-10 and 117.
21. Ibid., pp. 110-21.
22. Ibid., pp. 112-16.
23. Ibid., pp. 110 and 117-20
24. McLeod (1989a), pp. 28, 36 and 37.
25. Ibid., pp. 30-34.
26. Ibid., pp. 34-35.
27. Ibid., pp. 39-41.
28. Oberoi (1994), pp. 19-23.
29. Ibid., pp. 26-28.
30. Ibid., pp. 28-30.
31. Ibid., pp. 30-32.
32. Ibid., pp. 32-35.
33. *International Journal of Punjab Studies*, Vol II, No.1, pp. 103-12.
34. *Abstracts of Sikh Studies* (January 1994), pp. 110-15.
35. *International Journal of Punjab Studies*, Vol I, No. 1, pp. 144-46.
36. *Journal of Sikh Studies*, Vol VII, No.2 (August 1979), pp. 139-41.
37. Ibid., pp. 141-45.
38. *International Journal of Punjab Studies*, Vol II, No. 1, pp. 217-36.
39. Ibid., Vol I, No. 1, pp. 140-43.

Conclusion

Sikh studies may be said to have begun in the late eighteenth century as study of the Sikh past launched by amateur scholars associated with the East India Company to serve its diplomatic and political purposes. They valued rational knowledge as a source of power. Their interest in the Sikh past increased in proportion to their interest in the kingdom of Ranjit Singh. They rejected all supernatural and mythical elements to formulate rational interpretation of the evidence at their disposal. This historical approach was later to be called 'methodological atheism'. It was their cardinal assumption that rational cognition of the past was possible only in terms of the human and the natural as opposed to the divine and the supranatural. Paradoxically, the Christian belief in Divine Providence reinforced their 'methodological atheism' in relation to non-Christian peoples.

Nevertheless, the early European writers differed widely in their understanding of the Sikh tradition. For some of them, Guru Nanak was a Hindu reformer and Sikhism was a part of the *bhakti* movement. Most of them looked upon the Sikh faith as syncretism of Islam and Hinduism, especially Sūfism and Bhakti. A few of them saw Sikhism as a new religion. For nearly all of them, Guru Nanak and the Nanak-Panthīs were 'pacifist' and Guru Gobind Singh and his Khalsa were 'militant'. There was a great difference between the two. *Inter alia*, whereas the Nanak-Panthīs were no different from the Hindus, the Khalsa had a distinct identity of their own. Thus, the early European writers raised three important issues for Sikh studies: the status of Sikhism in the history of religion, the nature of the developments from Guru Nanak to Guru Gobind Singh, and the issue of Sikh identity.

J.D. Cunningham was rather exceptional in postulating correlations between Sikh ideology, Sikh polity, Sikh social order and Sikh identity. This was the time when the kingdom of Lahore was being finally liquidated by the British. After the annexation, Cunningham's interpretation of the Sikh past could not suit the purposes of the new rulers. The Sikhs had become one of the subject peoples. There was no point in glorifying their past. The British administrators of the Punjab wrote largely in self-justification to legitimize colonial rule, turning to fresh evidence only for writing on the Sikh chiefs and the Sikh 'aristocracy', both of which were seen as 'allies' of the colonial rulers. The only area in which research could be undertaken more or less seriously was that of religion in which the Christian missionaries too were interested because of their evangelical concerns. It is not surprising that the two outstanding writers of the colonial period, Ernest Trumpp and M.A. Macauliffe, turned to the early Sikh tradition for seeking answers to the old questions on the basis mainly of Sikh sources, especially the *Ādi Granth* and the *Janamsākhīs*.

It is significant to note that Trumpp and Macauliffe came up with opposing interpretations of the Sikh tradition. Trumpp reinforced the earlier view that Sikhism was little more than a form of Hinduism; it was an extension of the reform movement started by the *bhaktas* like Kabir. If anything, Guru Gobind Singh relapsed into Hinduism, believing in the incarnations of its gods and goddesses. The Khalsa represented a secular militarized arm of the Sikh Panth. This was ironical. Trumpp's work was published on the eve of Sikh resurgence in which Sikh ideology, Sikh polity, Sikh social order, and Sikh identity were seen and projected as correlated. This view was represented by Macauliffe. No religion of the world was so 'original' as Sikhism. Sikh identity was not only distinct from that of the Hindus, it was also more valuable – for the British, for the Sikhs, and for the world at large. Both Trumpp and Macauliffe gave great importance to the *Janamsākhīs*. In theory, they were both critical of the supernatural and mythical elements in the *Janamsākhīs*. In practice, however, only Trumpp raised the question of discovering the historical Guru Nanak. The *Janamsākhīs* did not contain enough material for a historical biography. Almost unconsciously, Trumpp added the fourth major item to the agenda of Sikh studies.

The early Sikh writers undertook study of the early Sikh tradition to rectify 'misrepresentations'. They do not say so, but we know that they had in mind mainly the 'misrepresentations' made by Trumpp. They rejected his interpretation of the Sikh tradition and tended to agree with Cunningham and Macauliffe. A good understanding of the Sikh sources was a strong point of their scholarship. And their treatment of the Sikh sources was critical, in fact more critical than that of Macauliffe. Bhagat Lakshman Singh virtually accepted 'methodological atheism', interpreting his evidence completely in natural and human terms. Sewa Ram Singh, who believed in the 'divinity' of Guru Nanak, nevertheless tried to invoke the supranatural only rarely in his biographical account of Guru Nanak. Khazan Singh too was more or less critical in his attitude towards the Sikh sources.

The early Sikh writers emphasized the uniqueness and the universality of the message of Guru Nanak and Guru Gobind Singh, which in their assessment was the same. They minimized the supposed gulf between the Nanak-Panthīs and the Khalsa in social as well as doctrinal terms. They underlined the distinctive identity of the Khalsa but looked upon the Sahajdhārīs, and even the Udāsīs, as a part of the Sikh Panth. They emphasized the importance of the doctrine of Guru-Granth and the Khalsa *rahit*, showing due regard at the same time for the genuine compositions of Guru Gobind Singh. They highlighted the ideal of equality and minimized the differences of caste and gender in the Sikh Panth. There is no doubt that these Sikh writers, inspired by their faith, made a decisive advance towards a sympathetic yet rational interpretation of the Sikh tradition. They transformed an 'orientalist' dialogue in Sikh studies into a European-Sikh dialogue.

Study of the early Sikh tradition was enriched further by Bhai Kanh Singh who added the *Mahān Kosh* to his earlier works, including his classic statement on Sikh identity in *Hām Hindū Nahīn*. Professor Teja Singh, Bhai Jodh Singh and Professor Sahib Singh published annotated texts and exegeses. Bhai Jodh Singh and Professor Sahib Singh published textual studies related to the Kartarpuri Bīṛ and the *Ādi Granth*. C.H. Loehlin's interpretation of Sikhism, though ambiguous in terms of its status, was not unsympathetic. J.C. Archer emphasized the essential originality of Guru Nanak's message. At the same time he emphasized the need of a historical biography of Guru Nanak, posing the problem deliberately in terms of 'the Nanak of faith' and 'the Nanak of history', carrying the implication of a thorough analysis of the *Janamsākhīs*. Both Archer and Loehlin made pleas for textual criticism in relation to the *Ādi Granth* in general and the Kartarpuri Bīṛ in particular. Loehlin published a critical study of the *Dasam Granth*.

Historical studies were published by a number of historians, with a critical attitude towards their Persian, Punjabi and English sources. Teja Singh and Ganda Singh highlighted the unique identity of Sikhism and the Sikhs. Sardar Kapur Singh published a philosophic interpretation of the Khalsa, bringing out in the process the unique character of Sikhism in the larger context of the Indian religious tradition. The political achievement of the Sikhs began to be appreciated, especially after Independence. The Sikhs under colonial rule were included in the scope of historical studies. Critical studies began to appear from the universities of the Punjab in the areas of history, religion and literature, to be disseminated through journals too. The celebration of centenaries produced a large volume of literature related to Sikh studies.

Seen in this historiographical context, the work of W.H. McLeod does not appear to introduce any new themes for discussion. His first work, *Gurū Nānak and the Sikh Religion*, published in 1968, related to the life and teachings of Guru Nanak. Besides giving a systematic exposition of his teachings, McLeod tried to examine his ideas in the religious context of his times, coming to the conclusion that some of these ideas were already there in what some scholars refer to as the Sant Tradition. For the life of Guru Nanak, McLeod analysed each *sākhī* on the basis of a set of criteria in order to determine its relevance and value. He came to the conclusion that only a bare outline of the life of Guru Nanak was provided by the *Janamsākhīs*. A more valuable source for the historical personality of Guru Nanak was his compositions.

McLeod's interest in the *Janamsākhīs* was not confined to their value for a biography of Guru Nanak. They had their own intrinsic value as a source of our knowledge of the early Sikh tradition. This part of his interest in the *Janamsākhīs* was published in an essay in the *Evolution of the Sikh Community* in 1975, and in a far more comprehensive study, the *Early Sikh Tradition*, in 1980. The newness of McLeod's work consisted not in the choice of themes but in their rigorous and comprehensive treatment. The other essays in the *Evolution of the Sikh Community* related to the Sikh scriptures, caste in the Sikh Panth, the evolution of the Sikh community, and 'cohesive ideals and institutions' in the history of the Sikh Panth. Only the last of these brought in a relatively new theme. The treatment of all these themes was marked by two assumptions: one, that later evidence cannot be taken at its face value; two, that pulls and pressures of the environment are as important as ideas, if not more.

McLeod's work proved to be controversial from the very beginning. However, the academic community, by and large, was either appreciative of his work or critical only of its limitations. Sardar Daljeet Singh was the severest critic of the *Evolution of the Sikh Community*. It was not a coincidence that the points he raised in his review of McLeod's book were repeated by Justice Gurdev Singh in his Introduction to the *Perspectives on the Sikh Tradition* which was the first frankly polemical work directed against W.H. McLeod. The art of this publication lay in concealing the art. Three of the 'contributors' to this volume had nothing to say against McLeod: H.R.Gupta, Ganda Singh and Harbans Singh. An impression was nevertheless created that they were critical of McLeod. Even Jagjit Singh was only partially and mildly critical. Noel Q. King was made to appear as a critic of McLeod and not mainly of critical methodology. Only Daljeet Singh's criticism of McLeod was brusque and trenchant, leaving the impression that McLeod was not a serious scholar. Justice Gurdev Singh tried to make a fool-proof case against McLeod by representing his position partially and somewhat unfairly. On the mere assumption that Christian missionaries were out to undermine non-Christian traditions, Justice Gurdev Singh categorically attributed extra-academic, or infra-academic, motives to McLeod. The *Perspectives on the Sikh Tradition*, echoing the title of the Berkeley volume, not only set the tone for the later controversy but also provided its basic agenda.

Polemics may not be the best mode of protest but polemics do represent a form of protest. The present controversy does appear in some ways to represent a new phase in the history of Sikh studies. Though the themes which are being debated are not altogether new themes, and the methods of research that are being used are not new methods, a persistent criticism of the on-going research obliges us to ask whether or not this on-going research has some limitations and some implications which are sought to be articulated through this protest. It also obliges us to ask whether or not the critics themselves have made some positive contribution to our understanding of the Sikh tradition.

II

Justice Gurdev Singh's charge that McLeod presents Sikhism as 'only a rehash of an effete Hindu creed' is not justified. It ignores McLeod's positive exposition of Guru Nanak's teachings which in 1968 was perhaps the most thorough exposition of the theme in English. It also ignores McLeod's appreciation of Sikhism as 'a religion of refined and noble quality'. It was not a 'rehash' of any creed. The Sant synthesis as presented by McLeod could not be equated with either Vaishnava *bhakti*, or Yoga, or Sūfism. It transcended each one of them. Furthermore, the system of Guru Nanak was not exactly bracketed with the system of Kabir by McLeod. And the latter by no means was 'effete'. We also know that the system of Kabir was neither Hindu nor Muslim. To regard it as Hindu is anachronistic. Daljeet Singh has no hesitation in stating that the concepts of the Guru and the Shabad were common to Kabir and Guru Nanak. Essentially, McLeod does not insist upon anything more than the commonality of ideas in the system of Guru Nanak and the so-called Sant Tradition. But his insistence that Guru Nanak can be squarely placed in the Sant Tradition or that he can be called a Sant confuses the issue. It emphasizes the importance of similarities in ideas at the cost of the differences in the systems of Guru Nanak and Kabir. It becomes a case of a part being confused with the whole.

Daljeet Singh underlines that in Sikhism there is no renunciation, no asceticism, and no *ahimsa*. The woman is accepted as an equal part of humanity. Liberation-in-life is for life, a motivation for altruistic action. The Sikh conception of the path and the goal eliminates the distinction between the temporal and the spiritual. This conception of spirituality underlines the great originality of Guru Nanak's faith and its uniqueness. It was the outcome of Guru Nanak's experience in which the Truth was revealed to him. What makes Sikhism unique and its message universal is, thus, a new ideology for social reconstruction on the basis of justice and equality. We can see that, whereas McLeod gives primacy to 'interiority', Daljeet Singh gives primacy to social action. For him, the process of social reconstruction started in the lifetime of Guru Nanak. Ideas and institutions went hand in hand. This view of the starting point in Sikh history gives Daljeet Singh a decisive edge over McLeod.

Justice Gurdev Singh caricatures McLeod's position by saying that he looks upon the *Janamsākhīs* as the 'brainchild' of Guru Nanak's followers. McLeod appears to be more critical of the *Janamsākhīs* than all of his predecessors mainly because he analyses each *sākhī* to determine what kind of evidence it offers in terms of the concrete incidents of Guru Nanak's life. That he may be mistaken in the application of his well formulated criteria can be readily conceded. But it is difficult to see how a historical biography of Guru Nanak can be written on the basis of the *Janamsākhīs* alone. Justice Gurdev Singh is wrong in saying that McLeod does not take the compositions of Guru Nanak into account. He does, but in subordination to his primary concern with *sākhīs*. The question 'what do the *sākhīs* tell us about the concrete incidents of Guru Nanak's life'? is not the same as the question 'what can we know about Guru Nanak's life'? McLeod's approach tends to become negative not in the sense in which Justice Gurdev Singh says it is but in the sense that McLeod forgets the second question, with which a biographer of Guru Nanak should remain occupied all the time. It is true that a historical biography of Guru Nanak has not yet been written. This does not mean that such a biography cannot be written. McLeod's critics appear to evade this challenge precisely because they refuse to see it. But the challenge is not for them alone. It is for all historians.

Justice Gurdev Singh attributes to McLeod the idea that the successors of Guru Nanak deviated from his position. McLeod does talk of 'innovations' but in relation to institutions and not in relation to doctrines. Therefore, the basic question is how to conceptualize Sikh institutions. McLeod takes the position that Guru Nanak was opposed to institutionalization of any kind. This is a wrong reading of Guru Nanak's position. As McLeod himself states in his *Gurū Nānak and the Sikh Religion*, congregational worship, the use of Guru Nanak's own compositions for this purpose, community meal, and the choice of a successor marked his stay at Kartarpur where, according to McLeod himself, Guru Nanak gave tangible shape to his ideals. In other words, institutions based on the ideas of Guru Nanak began to take shape in his lifetime. His successors extended the process and expanded the scope of this institutionalization. To say that Guru Amar Das reverted to a Hindu practice when he built the *bāolī* at Goindval to create a new centre of pilgrimage is a misconception of the situation. A broad similarity between institutions cannot be interpreted as 'reversion'. McLeod himself recognizes that Goindval was not a 'Hindu' centre. His confusion arises from the assumption that his own understanding of Guru Nanak's position is an established fact.

McLeod's statement that the traditional presentation of the development of the Sikh Panth starts too late and ends too soon is meant to suggest that some of the ideas of Guru Nanak's system were already current and that some of the developments associated with the institution of the Khalsa actually took place in the eighteenth century. He suggests that the whole process was rather complex and factors other than individual decisions were involved in the process. The objective conditions of the Sikh Panth were as important as the ideas of the Sikh Gurus in shaping the course of Sikh history. In this broad context he tries to deal with the issues of militarization, the Khalsa *rahit*, the doctrines of Guruship, and in a sense the question of caste in the Sikh Panth. He presents hypotheses, speculation and informed conjectures, presumably to promote further research.

On the question of militarization due to Jat influx, there is no credible evidence for the crucial first decade of seventeenth century. The available evidence fails to establish whether the egg came first or the chicken. For the economic depression of the peasantry, Professor Irfan Habib, who has propounded the hypothesis, himself maintains that Sikh ideology served as the cohesive force for the revolt of the Sikh peasantry. For the Shakti cult, it is uncertain when Puranic literature began to exercise influence over the Khalsa and to what extent. McLeod and Jagjit Singh hold fundamentally different views on causation in history and this gets reflected in their debate which itself is conducted on the basis of limited and partial evidence on both sides.

About the Khalsa *rahit*, especially the 5Ks, McLeod is right that explicit references to 5Ks are rather late. But to assume that the 5Ks were introduced in the eighteenth century is wrong. It is necessary to make a distinction between the formulation and its substantive prototypes. The formulation came later but the substantive symbols were there from the time of instituting the Khalsa. The contemporary evidence on *kesh* and arms leaves hardly any doubt about this. McLeod's suggestion that the 5Ks came from the Jat culture is not substantiated by credible evidence. It is not even an 'informed' conjecture. However, McLeod's general idea that new items were added to the *rahit* with the passage of time is supported by the evidence he cites.

There is contemporary evidence also for the vesting of Guruship in the Bāṇī and the Panth. The *bāṇī* certainly included the *Ādi Granth*. What is not clear is the status of the genuine compositions of Guru Gobind Singh. The *Dasam Granth* was compiled much later and there is no evidence that it was compiled on the authority of Guru Gobind Singh. It is true, however, that some Sikhs gave it the status of the Guru. But it was never exactly bracketed with the

Ādi Granth. McLeod does not appear to be right in suggesting that the doctrine of Guru-Panth became current first and then the doctrine of *Guru-Granth*. These two doctrines appear to be the two sides of the same coin of authority. Both had their immediate basis in the injunction of Guru Gobind Singh, and both crystallized in the eighteenth century.

On caste in the Sikh Panth, McLeod and Jagjit Singh underline the enunciation of an ideal carrying the implication of social equality. Both of them see the idea of equality embodied in the institutions of the *sangat* and the *langar*. Both of them see the idea of equality reinforced by the institution of the Khalsa. Both of them see commensality and connubium as central to the discussion of caste and equality. Both agree that the old patterns of connubium did not change. They do not notice any exceptions but there is the evidence of Kesar Singh Chhibber that the Khalsa set aside the distinctions of caste for matrimony at least for some time or in some cases. Neither McLeod nor Jagjit Singh says so, but the continuation of the old patterns of matrimony would also imply the continuation of patriarchal values and structure. On the question of commensality, Jagjit Singh argues that no distinction whatever was made on the basis of caste, and even the outcastes could eat with others. McLeod argues that the practice was extended to only the *shudras*. McLeod appears to be right. Both McLeod and Jagjit Singh emphasize that the Sikh social order was much more egalitarian than the social order in contemporary India. We may agree with Jagjit Singh that the idea of inequality as the basis of social relations was completely discarded by the Gurus. In fact, no inequality of any kind was explicitly upheld.

Textual criticism has emerged in Sikh studies largely in the 1990s. Given McLeod's views on this issue, he could be expected to encourage research in this area. His critics look upon it as a further proof of his design to undermine the Sikh tradition. They tend to accept Professor Sahib Singh's hypothesis about the compilation of the *Ādi Granth*, feel convinced that the Kartarpuri Bīṛ is the original Granth compiled by Guru Arjan, and they are extremely suspicious of historical approach to the compilation and canonization of the Sikh scripture. Nevertheless, Daljeet Singh and

Jagjit Singh are far more critical of the *Dasam Granth* than McLeod. Significantly their approach involves acceptance of the canons of historical and textual criticism. The debate is still going on. The critics are right in asserting that textual criticism does not have the same kind of importance in Sikh studies as in Biblical studies. It must be added, however, that textual criticism is not a wholly imported item. Sikh scholars of the twentieth century have shown concern for an authentic text of the Sikh scripture. It is also clear from the research done so far that the authenticity of the Sikh scripture is beyond any doubt. Textual criticism is not likely to affect the Sikh doctrines. It has significance only for textual history. It may be a fascinating dimension of Sikh history, but it is not really a dimension of any crucial importance. We may add that all textual problems cannot be solved only by proving the authenticity of the Kartarpuri Bīṛ. We are inclined to agree with Professor King that the Sikhs have nothing to fear from genuine textual criticism.

The critics of critical scholarship may be shocked to hear that they subscribe to 'methodological atheism'. Their methods are no different from the methods of those whom they criticize. Differences arise in their application of methods and techniques. Harjot Oberoi, despite his sophisticated conception of historical methodology, can come up with highly inadequate interpretation of the known empirical evidence. His critics, with no great awareness of historical methodology, can point out flaws in Oberoi's interpretation. Daljeet Singh has not evolved a new methodology but a different approach to the study of Sikhism. Even if we accept his proposition that ideology is all important in Sikh history, it has to be demonstrated event by event, epoch by epoch, on the basis of empirical evidence.

The critics of critical scholarship have some reservations. They believe in the sanctity of certain aspects of the Sikh tradition on the basis of their belief in the received truth. They do not venture out in search of historical truths. They move out only to look for proofs of what essentially belongs to the realm of belief. This is the real source of tension. The critical scholars and their critics differ in their evaluation of rational knowledge. The historical method, like the scientific method, no longer belongs to the West. To equate the historical method itself with Euro-centrism is a conceptual error. The difference between 'the west' and 'the east' arises from the culturally rooted questions and not from 'methodological atheism'. Enlightened self-interest dictates appreciation for all forms of rational knowledge. It is an issue of grave importance not only for the future of Sikh studies but also for the future of the Sikh community.

Works Cited

Abstracts of Sikh Studies. Ed. Kharak Singh. Chandigarh: Institute of Sikh Studies.

Advanced Studies in Sikhism. Ed. Jasbir Singh Mann and Harbans Singh Saraon. Irvine: Sikh Community of North America, 1989.

Archer, J.C. (1946). *The Sikhs in relation to Hindus, Moslems, Christians, and Ahmadiyyas: A Study in Comparative Religion*. Princeton: Princeton University Press.

Ashta, Dharam Pal (1959). *The Poetry of the Dasam Granth*. New Delhi: Arun Prakashan.

Avtar Singh (1983). *Ethics of the Sikhs*. Patiala: Punjabi University.

Barrier, N. Gerald (1970). *The Sikhs and Their Literature*. Delhi: Manohar Publications.

Bhangu, Ratan Singh (1962). *Prachīn Panth Prakāsh*. Ed. Bhai Vir Singh. Amritsar (4th ed).

Chhibber, Kesar Singh (1972). *Bansāvalīnāma Dasān Pātshāhiān Kā*. Ed. Ratan Singh Jaggi. *Research Bulletin of Punjabi Language and Literature*. (Ed. S. S. Kohli). Chandigarh: Panjab University, Vol II.

Cunningham, J.D. (1955). *A History of the Sikhs*. Delhi: S. Chand & Co (reprint).

Current Thoughts on Sikhism. Ed. Kharak Singh. Chandigarh: Institute of Sikh Studies, 1996.

Daljeet Singh (1984). *The Sikh Ideology*. New Delhi: Guru Nanak Foundation.

__________(1987). *Essays on the Authenticity of Kartarpuri Bir and the Integrated Logic and Unity of Sikhism*. Patiala: Punjabi University.

_________(1990). *The Sikh Ideology*. Amritsar: Singh Brothers.

_________(1994a). *Essentials of Sikhism*. Amritsar: Singh Brothers.

_________(1994b). *Sikhism: A Comparative Study of its Theology and Mysticism*. Amritsar: Singh Brothers (first published by Sterling, New Delhi, 1979).

Dhillon, G.S. (1989). *Researches in Sikh Religion and History*. Chandigarh: Sumeet.

_________(1991). *Insights into Sikh Religion and History*. Chandigarh: Singh and Singh Publishers.

_________(1992). *India Commits Suicide*. Chandigarh: Singh and Singh Publishers.

Dictionary of Islam. Lahore: Premier Book House, 1984 (first published in 1885).

Field, Dorothy (1914). *The Religion of the Sikhs*. London.

Forster, George (1970). *A Journey from Bengal to England*. Patiala: Languages Department Punjab (reprint).

Fox, Richard G. (1985). *Lions of the Punjab: Culture in the Making*. Berkeley: University of California.

Fundamental Issues of Sikh Studies. Ed. Kharak Singh, Gobind Singh Mansukhani and Jasbir Singh. Chandigarh: Institute of Sikh Studies, 1992.

Ganda Singh (1962). *Early European Accounts of the Sikhs*. Calcutta: Firma K. L. Mukhopadhyaya.

_________(1967). *Hukamnāmey*. Patiala: Punjabi University.

_________(October 1970). 'Editorial'. *The Panjab Past and Present*. Vol IV, part 2.

Grewal, J. S. (1969). *Guru Nanak in History*. Chandigarh: Panjab University (reprinted in 1979).

_________(1972). *From Guru Nanak to Maharaja Ranjit Singh*. Amritsar: Guru Nanak Dev University (reprinted in 1982).

_________(1975). *Medieval India: History and Historians*. Amritsar: Guru Nanak Dev University.

_________(1989). 'Social History in Sikh Literature'. *Studies in Sikhism and Comparative Religion*. New Delhi: Guru Nanak Foundation, Vol VIII, No. 1.

_________(1990). *The Sikhs of the Punjab*. Cambridge: Cambridge University Press. Vol II.3. *The New Cambridge History of India*.

_________(1992). *Guru Nanak in Western Scholarship*. Shimla: Indian Institute of Advanced Study.

_________(1993). *Guru Nanak and Patriarchy*. Shimla: Indian Institute of Advanced Study.

_________(1995). 'Ernest Trumpp's Interpretation of the Japuji'. *Journal of Sikh Studies*, Vol XIX.

_________(1997). *Historical Perspectives on Sikh Identity*. Patiala: Punjabi University.

Griffin, Lepel (1957). *Ranjit Singh*. Delhi: S. Chand & Co (reprint).

Gurnam Kaur (1990). *Reason and Revelation in Sikhism*. New Delhi: Cosmo.

Gurtej Singh (1996). *Tandav of the Centaur*. Chandigarh: Institute of Sikh Studies.

Harbans Singh (1984). *The Heritage of the Sikhs*. New Delhi: Manohar.

International Journal of Punjab Studies. Ed. Gurharpal Singh & others. New Delhi: Sage Publications.

Invasion of Religious Boundaries. Ed. Jasbir Singh Mann, Surinder Singh Sodhi and Gurbakhsh Singh Gill. Vancouver: Canadian Sikh Study and Teaching Society, 1995.

Jagjit Singh (1981). *Sikh Revolution: A Perspective*. New Delhi: Kendri Singh Sabha.

_________(1985). *Perspectives on Sikh Studies*. New Delhi: Guru Nanak Foundation.

Jodh Singh, Bhai (1966). 'Note on Kartarpur Granth'. *Proceedings Punjab History Conference*. Patiala: Punjabi University.

_________(1968). *Srī Kartārpurī Bīṛ de Darshan*. Patiala: Punjabi University.

_________(1993). *Bāṇī Bhagat Kabir Jī Steek*. Patiala: Punjabi University (third time).

Journal of Sikh Studies. Amritsar: Guru Nanak Dev University.

Kapur Singh (1989). *Parasharprashan: An Enquiry into the Genesis and Unique Character of the Order of the Khalsa with an Exposition of the Sikh Tenets*. Amritsar: Guru Nanak Dev University.

_________(1993). *Sikhism: An Oecumenical Religion*. Ed. Gurtej Singh. Chandigarh: Institute of Sikh Studies.

Khazan Singh (1970a). *History of the Sikhs*. Patiala: Languages Department Punjab (reprint).

_________(1970b). *Philosophy of the Sikh Religion*. Patiala: Language Department Punjab (reprint).

Lakshman Singh, Bhagat (1963). *A Short Sketch of the Life and Work of Guru Gobind Singh, the 10th and Last Guru of the Sikhs*. Ludhiana: Lahore Book Shop (reprint).

Loehlin, C.H. (1958). *The Sikhs and Their Scriptures*. Lucknow: Lucknow Publishing House.

_________(1966). 'A Westerner Looks at the Kartarpur Granth'. *Proceedings Punjab History Conference*. Patiala: Punjabi University.

_________(1971). *The Granth of Guru Gobind Singh and the Khalsa Brotherhood*. Lucknow: Lucknow Publishing House.

Macauliffe, Max Arthur (1995). *The Sikh Religion: Its Gurus, Sacred Writings and Authors*. 3 Vols. Delhi: Low Price Publication (first published in six volumes by Clarendon Press, Oxford, 1909).

Malcolm, John (1812). *A Sketch of the Sikhs*. London.

Mann, Gurinder Singh (1996). *The Goindval Pothis: The Earliest Extant Source of the Sikh Canon*. Cambridge (Massachusetts): Harvard University Press.

McLeod, W.H. (1968). *Gurū Nānak and the Sikh Religion*. Oxford: Clarendon Press.

_________(1975). *The Evolution of the Sikh Community*. Oxford: Clarendon Press.

_________(1980). *Early Sikh Tradition: A Study of the Janam-sākhīs*. Oxford: Clarendon Press.

_________(1981). *The B-40 Janamsakhi*. Amritsar: Guru Nanak Dev University.

_________(1984). *Textual Sources for the Study of Sikhism*. Manchester: Manchester University Press.

_________(1987). *The Chaupa Singh Rahit-Nama*. Dunedin: University of Otago.

_________(1989a). *Who is a Sikh? The Problem of Sikh Identity*. Oxford: Clarendon Press.

_________(1989b). *The Sikhs: History, Religion and Society*. New York: Columbia University Press.

Oberoi, Harjot (1994). *The Construction of Religious Boundaries: Culture, Identity and Diversity in the Sikh Tradition*. New Delhi: Oxford University Press.

Perspectives on the Sikh Tradition. Ed. Gurdev Singh. Patiala: Siddharth Publications, 1986.

Pettigrew, Joyce (1975). *Robber Noble Men: A Study of the Political System of the Sikh Jats*. Boston: Routledge and Kegan Paul.

Piar Singh (1992). *Gāthā Sri Ādi Granth* (Pbi). Amritsar: Guru Nanak Dev University.

_________(1996). *Gatha Sri Adi Granth and the Controversy*. Michigan: Anant Education and Rural Development Foundation.

Planned Attack on Aad Sri Guru Granth Sahib: Academics or Blasphemy. Ed. Bachittar Singh Giani. Chandigarh: International Centre of Sikh Studies,1994.

Pritam Singh (1989). *Bhai Kanh Singh Nabha: Pichhokar, Rachnā te Mulankan* (Pbi). Amritsar: Guru Nanak Dev University.

Recent Researches in Sikhism. Ed. Jasbir Singh Mann and Kharak Singh. Patiala: Punjabi University, 1992.

Religious Change and Cultural Domination. Ed. David N. Lorenzen. Mexico: El Colegio de Mexico, 1989.

Sahib Singh. *Gurbāṇī Viākaran* (Pbi). Amritsar: Singh Brothers, 1994 (tenth time).

_________*Ād Bīṛ Bāre* (Pbi). Amritsar: Singh Brothers,1996 (sixth time).

Sewa Ram Singh (1988). *The Divine Master: Life and Teachings of Guru Nanak*. Ed. Prithipal Singh Kapur. Jalandhar: ABS Publications (reprint).

Sher Singh (1986). *Philosophy of Sikhism*. Amritsar: SGPC (reprint).

Sikh History and Religion in the Twentieth Century. Ed. Joseph T.O'Connell, Milton Israel, Willard G. Oxtoby, W.H. McLeod and J.S. Grewal. Toronto: Centre for South Asian Studies, University of Toronto, 1988.

Sikh Studies: Comparative Perspectives on a Changing Tradition.

Ed. Mark Juergensmeyer and N. Gerald Barrier. Berkeley: Graduate Theological Union, 1979.

Studying the Sikhs: Issues for North America. Ed. John Stratton Hawley and Gurinder Singh Mann. Albany: State University of New York Press, 1993.

Teja Singh and Ganda Singh (1989). *A Short History of the Sikhs*. Patiala: Punjabi University (reprint).

The Sikh Religion: A Symposium. Calcutta: Susil Gupta Private Ltd. 1958.

Trilochan Singh (1994). *Ernest Trumpp and W.H. McLeod as Scholars of Sikh History, Religion and Culture*. Chandigarh: International Centre of Sikh Studies.

Trumpp, Ernest (1989). *The Adi Granth*. New Delhi: Munshiram Manoharlal (reprint).

Wilson, H.H. (1958). 'Civil and Religious Institutions of the Sikhs'. *The Sikh Religion: A Symposium*. Calcutta: Susil Gupta Private Ltd. (reprint).

Index